FAITH, FREEDOM, AND HIGHER EDUCATION

# Faith, Freedom, and Higher Education

Historical Analysis and Contemporary Reflections

Edited by
**P. C. KEMENY**

PICKWICK *Publications* · Eugene, Oregon

FAITH, FREEDOM, AND HIGHER EDUCATION
Historical Analysis and Contemporary Reflections

Pickwick Publications
An Imprint of Wipf and Stock Publishers
199 W. 8th Ave., Suite 3
Eugene, OR 97401

www.wipfandstock.com

ISBN 13: 978-1-61097-993-1

*Cataloguing-in-Publication data:*

Faith, freedom, and higher education : historical analysis and contemporary reflections / edited by P. C. Kemeny.

x + 200 p. ; 23 cm—Includes Bibliographical references.

ISBN 13: 978-1-61097-993-1

1. Church and college. 2. Church and college—United States. 3. Education—Aims and objectives. I. Title.

LC383 F35 2013

Manufactured in the USA

Chapter 5, "*God and Man at Yale* Revisited," by George H. Nash, was previously published in *Reappraising the Right: The Past and Future of American Conservatism* (Wilmington, DE: ISI Books, 2009), 133–47. Used by permission of ISI Books.

# Introduction

## P. C. Kemeny

IN THE PAST TWENTY years, the role of religion—Christianity in particular—in American higher education has been the subject of popular debate and scholarly investigation. Some have nostalgically lamented the decline of religion's role in higher education. Others have warmly welcomed it. A number of studies have attempted to explain the secularization of higher education. George M. Marsden's 1994 work, *The Soul of the American University: From Protestant Establishment to Established Nonbelief,* stands out as one of the most important. The work surely disappointed conspiracy theorists who thrive on making Christianity the victim of the malevolent secularists. Eschewing nostalgia, Marsden's richly textured study contends that the leaders in American higher education—Harvard, Yale, Princeton, Duke, and other prestigious schools—aspired to create a national nonsectarian Protestant culture in the late nineteenth and early twentieth centuries. During this period, these flagship schools gradually jettisoned beliefs and practices deemed incompatible with modernity or too exclusive for the kind of nonsectarian liberalism they viewed as essential to maintaining their role as America's cultural custodians. During the social turmoil of the 1960s, the leading schools gradually dropped the vestiges of liberal Protestantism because it, too, had come to be seen as contrary to the inclusive character of national culture. Secularization, Marsden contends, was ultimately an inside job. Mainline Protestants, in other words, encouraged the secularization of higher education. Consequently, Christianity plays little role today in the real workings of the American university—its classroom, its research, and its educational philosophy. To be sure, Christianity continues to thrive at many secular universities, but primarily as an extracurricular activity. In his book's "Concluding Unscientific Postscript," Marsden makes a case for the inclusion of religiously informed perspectives inside American universities within institutional pluralism. *The Soul of the American University* precipitated not only a great deal of debate but also further historical studies. In *The Outrageous Idea of Christian Scholarship*, published in 1997, Marsden responds to criticisms of his argument for the place of religiously informed perspectives inside the academy.[1]

Since the publication of *The Soul of the American University* and *The Outrageous Idea of Christian Scholarship*, scholars from a variety of different religious traditions or no tradition have weighed in on the conversation.[2] Some scholars have revisited the history of their own religious tradition's colleges.[3] Others have attempted to express how their faith community has offered constructive perspectives on educational issues that avoid the pitfalls of militant sectarianism.[4] *Faith, Freedom, and Higher*

1. George M. Marsden, *The Soul of the American University: From Protestant Establishment to Established Nonbelief* (New York: Oxford University Press, 1994); Marsden, *The Outrageous Idea of Christian Scholarship* (New York: Oxford University Press, 1997). See also George M. Marsden and Bradley J. Longfield, eds., *The Secularization of the Academy* (New York: Oxford University Press, 1992).

2. For constructive critiques of Marsden's work, see Leo P. Ribuffo, "God and Man at Harvard, Yale, Princeton, Berkeley, etc.," *Reviews in American History* 32 (1995) 170–75; Thomas Bender, "Putting Religion in Its Place," *Culturefront* 3 (1994) 77–79; Bruce Kuklick, review of "The Soul of the American University," *Method & Theory in the Study of Religion* 8 (1996) 79–84. On the history of religion in American higher education and the question of secularization, see, for example, D. G. Hart, *The University Gets Religion: Religious Studies in American Higher Education* (Baltimore: Johns Hopkins University Press, 2002); Jon H. Roberts and James Turner, *The Sacred and the Secular University* (Princeton: Princeton University Press, 2000). For cultural conservative critiques of American higher education, see, for example, Dinesh D'Souza, *Illiberal Education: The Politics of Race and Sex on Campus* (New York: Free Press, 1991); Roger Kimball, *Tenured Radicals: How Politics Has Corrupted Higher Education* (New York: Harper & Row, 1990).

3. See, for example, Douglas Sloan, *Faith and Knowledge: Mainline Protestantism and Twentieth-Century American Higher Education* (Philadelphia: Westminster, 1994); Philip Gleason, *Contending with Modernity: Catholic Higher Education in the Twentieth Century* (New York: Oxford University Press, 1995); Kathleen A. Mahoney, *Catholic Higher Education in Protestant America: The Jesuits and Harvard in the Age of the University* (Baltimore: Johns Hopkins University Press, 2003).

4. See, for example, Theodore M. Hesburgh, ed., *The Challenge and Promise of a Catholic University* (Notre Dame: University of Notre Dame Press, 1994); Robert Benne, *Quality with Soul: How Six Premier Colleges and Universities Keep Faith with Their Religious Traditions* (Grand Rapids: Eerdmans, 2001); Stephen R. Haynes, ed., *Professing in the Postmodern Academy: Faculty and the Future of Church-Related Colleges* (Waco: Baylor University Press, 2002); Douglas V. Henry and Michael D. Beaty, eds., *Christianity and the Soul of the University: Faith as a Foundation for Intellectual*

*Education: Historical Analysis and Contemporary Reflections* extends this conversation further.

The collection of essays offers historical analyses as well as contemporary reflections upon the role of Christianity in contemporary higher education.[5] In the opening essay, George M. Marsden discusses the impact of *The Soul of the American University* on the debate over the secularization of American higher education and the place for religiously informed perspectives within the academy. Marsden also reflects upon the role that the "culture wars," which were at their height in 1994, played upon the reception of *The Soul of the American University.* The other essays in this section examine the history of religion in higher education. Mark Graham's essay provides deep background to the contemporary discussion over the history of religion in the modern university by exploring the emergence of the university in medieval Europe. My essay provides further nuance to Marsden's thesis by demonstrating how the leaders of Princeton University, Woodrow Wilson in particular, adapted liberal Protestantism to the realities of modern higher education, thus easing the transition from the "old time" Christian college to the modern research university. D. G. Hart's essay offers a provocative challenge to conservative Christian complaints about the secularization of higher education. Contrary to Marsden, Hart contends that the secularization of the academy is a good development because exclusion allows Christians to insulate themselves from the corrosive effects of modernity. George H. Nash reflects upon the legacy of William F. Buckley's provocative 1951 *God and Man at Yale: The Superstitions of "Academic Freedom"* and its impact upon the post–World War II conservative movement in America. These essays also further enrich our understanding of the history of Christianity in higher education and the debate over its place. Finally, they demonstrate that Christian scholars are not in complete agreement over the consequences of the secularization of American higher education.

---

*Community* (Grand Rapids: Baker Academic, 2006); Douglass Jacobson and Rhoda Jacobson, *The American University in a Postsecular Age* (New York: Oxford University Press, 2008); Mark R. Schwehn, *Exiles from Eden: Religion and the Academic Vocation in America* (New York: Oxford University Press, 2005); Andrea Sterk, ed., *Religion, Scholarship, and Higher Education: Perspectives, Models, and Future Prospects; Essays from the Lilly Seminar on Religion and Higher Education* (Notre Dame: University of Notre Dame Press, 2002); Ralph C. Wood, *Contending for the Faith: The Church's Engagement with Culture* (Waco: Baylor University Press, 2003).

5. The essays were originally presented at Grove City College's 2009 Center for Vision and Values Conference, "Faith, Freedom and Higher Education."

The second half of the volume presents four contemporary reflections upon the role of Christianity in collegiate education. Janice B. Brown explores the thought of Dorothy L. Sayers on education. James G. Dixon considers the significance of C. S. Lewis's work for contemporary Christian higher education. Andrew J. Harvey meditates upon the work of Wendell Berry and its significance for discussions of college curricula and attitudes toward contemporary culture. Michael Coulter offers an extended critical review of Allan Bloom's *The Closing of the American Mind* (1987). The second half of the collection is bookended by two substantive essays on the place of Christianity in higher education. Gary Scott Smith articulates a conservative Christian vision of the mission of self-identifying Christian colleges in America's post-Christian culture, and William P. Anderson Jr. outlines a roadmap for how to keep a Christian college genuinely Christian. Together, the essays provide a rich and constructive vision of the place that Christianity can have in modern higher education. Written by scholars representing a broad range of Christian traditions—including Anglican, Eastern Orthodox, Episcopalian, Presbyterian Church USA, Orthodox Presbyterian Church, and Roman Catholic—the essays embody the kind of Christian scholarship that Marsden advocates. They also embody a broad cross section of views that continue to thrive within Christian higher education today.

I would like to thank the Center for Vision and Values, especially Richard Jewell, Paul Kengor, Lee Wishing, and Brenda Vinton for their support and help with this publication project. I also want to thank my student assistants, Sean G. Morris and Ethan Kreimeyer, for their help. I am also grateful for Renada Arens's editorial expertise in getting the manuscript ready for publication. Finally, I want to thank the authors, who have not only contributed their work but also demonstrated their patience with me throughout the project.

# 1

# *The Soul of the American University*
## Revisited

## George M. Marsden

IN THIS ESSAY I want to reflect on how things may have changed with respect to the role of Christianity in American higher education in the years since the publication of *The Soul of the American University: From Protestant Establishment to Established Nonbelief* in 1994. I also want to consider how, in the light of such changes, the case for augmenting those prospects may be made more effectively today than it was in that book.

I should say that 95 percent of *The Soul of the American University* is a pretty straightforward history of the role of religion in mainstream American higher education from the founding of Harvard into the latter half of the twentieth century. Most of this historical narrative is descriptive and analytic, driven by the quest to understand the dynamics that led to the marginalization of most religion in higher education. The last 5 percent of the book, however, is prescriptive. In what I called "Concluding Unscientific Postscript" I argued that even while we can understand that there were some good reasons why our pluralistic public culture—of which mainstream universities are a part—is no longer dominated by a Protestant establishment, have we not perhaps overcompensated for the

1

earlier Protestant dominance by removing *all* religion to the margins? And so might we find ways to create room for a variety of substantive religious perspectives in such a pluralistic setting? That postscript became, as one reviewer put it, the tail that wagged the dog. So most reviewers responded more to the postscript than to the merits of what I hoped was a nicely crafted historical narrative.

I still stand by the narrative, but I think that today I would write a different postscript. It is not that I have changed my mind on the prescription, but I think I might alter the tone, since I think that led to some misunderstandings of what the whole book was about. More important, I think the situation with regard to religion in mainstream academia has changed considerably since I was writing in the early 1990s, and I want to reflect here on those changes.

A good place to begin talking about where American higher education is headed today is Harvard, both because that is where the history of American higher education began almost four centuries ago and because Harvard continues to be, if not a typical, a sort of flagship school.

In 2006 Harry Lewis, the former academic dean of Harvard College, published a book with the revealing title *Excellence without a Soul: How a Great University Forgot Education*. In it Dean Lewis reflects on what he sees as a sad decline in Harvard undergraduate education. A Harvard grad himself, he laments the loss of a sense of coherence in the curriculum since the time when he was an undergraduate in the early 1960s. At that time American higher education was still in the "consensus" era, and Harvard education was still under the influence of the "Best in the West" ideal developed in a famous curricular report of 1945 called "Free Education in a Democratic Society." (Almost sounds like Grove City.) In the twenty-first century, says Lewis, the college does very little toward contributing to what used to be a major goal of undergraduate education, that is, to "transform teenagers . . . into adults with the learning and wisdom to take responsibility for their own lives."[1]

Having been an academic dean, Lewis has much frontline experience in analyzing why Harvard and other similar universities have lost what he considers should be the "soul" of higher education—that is, providing wisdom for students that will help them mature into wise and responsible adults. As a dean, one is constantly battered by conflicting and contradictory demands that make principled and coherent reform impossible. Basically, Lewis says, these are the demands of people shaped by the demands

---

1. Harry R. Lewis, *Excellence without a Soul* (New York: PublicAffairs, 2006), xiv.

of a consumerist society in which everyone is used to choosing their own lifestyle packages. Parents, students, faculty, alumni, other donors, and funding agencies all have their agendas. Parents and most students see higher education as a step toward economic or professional success. Faculty in the meantime are hired on a basis of publishing success in a narrow specialty, and the tenure system offers little encouragement for spending a lot of time thinking about how one's teaching might contribute to the general welfare of students. As a result, faculties offer a bewildering number of courses in their various specialties. Although students are required to take courses in broad subject areas—such as some natural science, some social science, and so forth, almost no common knowledge is required. Lewis sees this as resulting in a hollow education. Meanwhile, he says, the constant pressures of consumer competition mean that colleges have to expend ever-increasing resources on providing comforts and diversions that will keep the students happy. If this is the situation at Harvard, one can imagine what happens at the universities that the vast majority of Americans attend, which often do not even attempt to provide any more than technical education.

This is not new. In the early 1980s, when I was teaching at Calvin College, I headed a small graduate program that offered a Master of Arts in Christian Studies. For the applications to the program we asked students to send us a writing sample. One very bright applicant from a state university responded that he had never written a paper in college. He had been a marketing major and the best writing sample he had to offer was a blue-book exam that had to do with the importance of good packaging when shipping goods. He was a fine student with an inquiring mind and just the sort of person that our MA program was suited for, but he simply had not received a college education in the traditional sense. In fact, in university education as a whole, the vast majority of what goes on is dedicated to technical research and teaching technical skills. University education has become mass education and overwhelmingly vocational education, so that the percentage of students majoring in the humanities nationally has sunk somewhere well into the single digits.

The shape of contemporary universities is dictated primarily by the fact that they are designed to serve the economic interests of our consumerist society. That is why technical study and vocational preparation dominate most of higher education. A related feature is that universities serve a consumer and global economy by teaching, above all, the values of tolerance and lifestyle choice these are traits that fit well with a consumer society. The highest value becomes the freedom to design your own life, most often signaled by where you live and what you own. In these respects, universities do not differ substantially from the mainstream media and entertainment industries.

If one asks the question, then, as to where traditional religious belief might fit in modern universities shaped by technical and vocational concerns for most things and relativistic pluralism for the rest, it becomes obvious that there is no simple solution to the problem. There is no way, for instance, that it would make any sense to talk about reclaiming American mainstream universities and making them once again Christian institutions. Harvard, Yale, and Princeton were once not just Christian but Reformed Christian institutions. But if you study the history of how they lost their Christianity, it will become clear that going back to anything approaching that would be absurd. There is no way in our contemporary cultural setting to turn back the clock on these large-scale historical trends. Briefly put, these universities, as much as the giant state universities, have become de facto public institutions. Huge economic forces as well as concerns for equity dictate that they serve the entire society as pluralistic institutions in which all sorts of unbelievers as well as believers in other religions, such as Judaism, Islam, Buddhism, and the like all have equal standing, and there is no way we can change that. We simply have to work with it.

I make this point so strongly because the most puzzling response to *The Soul of the American University* has been that some scholars have misread me to say that I am, in fact, suggesting such a revolution or Christian takeovers of universities that once were Christian. In my books I explicitly and repeatedly said that is *not* what I thought or believed. But a number of scholars who should know better have insisted that this is really what I am saying—even when I deny it. They see me as having written a narrative of simple decline in which I describe the loss of a golden age when American higher education was Christian. Such readers then jump to the conclusion that I must be advocating a stock narrative of a return to that lost golden age—despite the fact that I do not advocate anything like that in my postscript, and in fact my historical account shows why that could not happen in a society like ours.

So why the puzzling misunderstandings? I don't raise this point just to vindicate myself against misreadings, but rather because puzzles like this are sometimes important clues to understanding a historical moment.

I think these misreadings are related to the fact that the book came out in 1994 at the height of the culture wars. That was the time, you may recall, of the ascendancy of Newt Gingrich and the Contract with America. And since I talked about "Christian scholarship" and the like, it was assumed that I was, despite my disclaimers, promoting essentially the agenda of the Christian right—since they are the most prominent group to use *Christian* as an adjective. I think it has become a general rule since the culture-war era that when one says "Christian" (as in the Reformed community people long have talked about "Christian scholarship"), many people automatically translate it as "fundamentalist."

Whatever the merits of the Christian right—which are considerable—one of their demerits is that in their understandable zeal to challenge the secularism of our age they have invoked a sort of Constantinian rhetoric in response. The way they tell the story is that in earlier America, Christians—that is Protestants—dominated the public culture, including leading universities, and so they have talked about "taking back" American culture as though we might win mainstream universities back to traditional Protestantism. I am calling such rhetoric Constantinian, not because it literally involves Christianity established by the state, but rather because it looks back to an informal Protestant establishment that had a dominant role in earlier American culture.

One of the basic arguments of *The Soul of the American University* is suggested in its subtitle: *From Protestant Establishment to Established Nonbelief.* Basically I wanted to concede that in the interest of equity in the public sphere, it was unfair to Jews and Catholics or unbelievers to have a virtual establishment of Protestantism in nineteenth-century America's de facto public institutions, such as leading universities and even state universities. So if the virtual establishment of one type of Christianity was wrong in the nineteenth century, then by analogy we can see that the virtual establishment of nonbelief as the privileged view in universities today was equally inequitable. Our society has overcorrected for a virtual Protestant establishment by building a virtual secular establishment.

The point that I was trying to make is that, from a Christian perspective, if we really believe in religious freedom, then we should be opposed to all Constantinianism, including the informal Constantinianism of the Protestant virtual establishment in early America. The problem, however, with that rendering of the story is that it does not fit the usual story told by traditionalist American Protestants. They still speak as though the answer to a secularist establishment is to restore an essentially Christian establishment. So some critics assumed that despite what I *said* I wanted, what I really wanted was to reclaim mainstream universities for traditional Christianity.

So one thing I think necessary for us all to clarify at this point is our stance regarding pluralism and cultural diversity. Essentially what we should be saying, it seems to me, is that in our pluralistic public culture we want to maximize freedom for all religious expressions. We must be clear, then, that we are *not* proposing to reestablish privilege in public institutions for our own position. Pluralism should, of course, include pluralism of institutions—so it is good to have private institutions like Grove City College that strongly represent a particular religious heritage—and such institutions need to continue to be protected so that they can define themselves according to their religious convictions. But if we are talking about mainstream universities such as Harvard or Penn State, we should acknowledge that these are essentially pluralistic institutions that should serve the whole public, and hence we should be advocating freedom for religious expression within a pluralistic setting.

In my own case I have found it helpful in making this point to prove that I am not working from the viewpoint of the old nineteenth-century American evangelical heritage of informal Constantinianism but rather from that of the Dutch heritage in the tradition of Abraham Kuyper. Kuyper, as most readers will know, was a theologian, university founder, and also prime minister of the Netherlands about a century ago. Kuyper's outlook is valuable particularly because while it is not Constantinian in suggesting that there should be a state religion, it is also not sectarian in the sense of saying that Christians should withdraw from society or mainstream culture—as early twentieth-century American fundamentalists did. Rather it is, I think, most essentially an elaboration of the position of being in the world but not of the world. It emphasizes, as Reformed Christians long have, that while maintaining a strong sense of our distinctiveness, we should engage the culture and be leaders in education. The whole ideal of the "integration of faith and learning," which has become so widespread in evangelical colleges and universities, grows out of this ideal that Christians while not compromising the distinctiveness of their outlook as informed by faith and God's revelation, should at the same time engage the best of higher learning.

With respect to the question of the relation of church to state, the Kuyperian heritage is very helpful in making clear that church and state each have a degree of sovereignty in their own spheres. The church should not dictate to the state and neither should the state dictate to the church in matters that are properly theological or ecclesiastical. The United States, of course, has also long had separation of church and state, but for a long time American Protestants ran almost everything so that most American Protestant groups did not develop a very good theory as to how that separation should work. Kuyperianism, drawing from the Dutch heritage and Continental European thought, provides such a theory based on the premise that civil societies should be genuinely pluralistic with respect to religions.

Specifically the Kuyperian heritage affirms, first (over against establishments), that no religion or other comparable quasireligious comprehensive ideology (such as secularism) should be established or have a de facto monopoly supported by the state. But second, one cannot have truly equitable pluralism if all religions are driven from the public arena and relegated to a private sphere of individual choice. And third, that the state and other public regulatory powers (such as public university administrations) should develop policies that address the issue of how justly to maximize free expression for religious as well as for secular individuals and groups in the public arena. Their basic question should be, how can we put all these outlooks on more or less equal ground without violating the legitimate demands for keeping good public order? Some religious practices, like some nonreligious practices, do have to be limited in the public domain, but the goal should be to keep those limits to the necessary minimum. Hence their goals should be to provide equal treatment for as wide a range of religious and secular ideologies as is compatible with maintaining civil order so that representatives of all those viewpoints may have voices in the public domain as well as in private lives.

By way of contrast, in the mainstream American academy since the later decades of the twentieth century, religious beliefs have been treated as essentially private matters, and therefore the prevailing view has been that the influence of such beliefs in the classroom should be minimized. The unwritten if not universally enforced rule has been that one should check substantive religious views at the door of the university classroom. As attractive and as seemingly equitable as that solution may sound to some, it is discriminatory against people who have strongly religious views that bear on their thinking. It has also proven to be a rule that cannot be reasonably enforced on a comprehensive basis. Religiously based views often *do* make a difference in scholarship, and there is no reason why religious scholars should not be encouraged to reflect on those differences, so long as they work within the bounds that make pluralistic academic discourse possible.

My first major point, then, is that Kuyperian principles can be useful in explaining how Christians and people of other faiths may participate in the mainstream academy, but in the latter part of my reflections I want to say that I think that these principles are especially useful today. That is because in the past fifteen years I think the attitude in the mainstream academy has been changing for the better with respect to the place of religion. The situation is not the same as when I began working on this topic twenty years ago.

In the spring of 2009 I taught a course on "Faith and Learning in America" at Harvard Divinity School, and that inspired me to think that it might be useful at some time to write a much briefer sequel to *The Soul of the American University*. It might be called something like *The End of the Secularist Era in American Academia* to indicate that was an era that reached its peak in the twentieth century but that is now receding. Or another thought for a title, which perhaps is more accurate, though less engaging, is *Naturalism in American Academia: Its Rise and Its Limits*. As these indicate, I am using *secularist* as a close equivalent of "exclusively naturalist," or the view that the highest intellectual standards should exclude supernatural reference.[2]

The argument I would make in that sequel begins by elaborating some of the key points I make in *The Soul of the American University* concerning twentieth-century American academia. One of its focal points would be on the very important relationship between secularism or, more accurately, naturalism, as a *methodology* and secularism or exclusive naturalism as an *ideology*. Let me elaborate briefly on that distinction, which I think is central to thinking about the situation today.

A naturalistic *methodology* refers to practices people engage in without substantive religious reference, like fixing a car or hitting a baseball—or perhaps swinging and missing a baseball. Though some may supplement these activities with spiritual practices such as prayer, they engage in the activities themselves by dealing with purely natural causes and effects. But

2. As I revise this in 2010, I am inclined to make this argument part of a larger study of American culture in the 1950s and the early 1960s, which I am provisionally titling "The Twilight of the American Enlightenment." It is in that era that secular, exclusive naturalism became the norm in American academia as well as in most mainstream American intellectual life, whether as scientific naturalism or in emphasis on individual autonomy. But while there were practical reasons for that triumph, the intellectual rationales for these outlooks had become internally incoherent and contradictory.

naturalism as an *ideology* that involves metaphysical naturalism goes further in that it is the belief that natural forces are all there is, or all we can know about, and hence one's view of reality should exclude supernatural religious reference.

Of these two, methodological naturalism is by far the most widely accepted. Most people since the modern era in the West have accepted that one might greatly limit or exclude religious reference for methodological or practical reasons but not necessarily as part of an overall view of reality. The United States Constitution, for instance, prescribes a largely secular civil polity but presumes and to some degree protects what most of its authors considered higher religious concerns. Almost all natural scientists are "methodological naturalists" in that they exclude divine or spiritual explanations of technical matters they are studying, but they may or may not believe that there is a higher spiritual realm. The same is true of technicians. And in today's world we all have to be amateur technicians who rely on nonreligious understandings of most of our activities. Praying may help me, but it does not help me to figure out how to find the list of missed calls on my cell phone. And in our diverse culture it is helpful and desirable in many activities for co-workers to limit their references to their particular religious beliefs just to help everyone to get along. So we all live in a highly secularized world, but only some of us are secularists who would extend the secular outlook to be definitive of all of reality or at least of the highest truths that we can know.

This distinction between metaphysical naturalism and the ubiquitous practical naturalistic character of so much that shapes the modern world suggests an especially important dimension of this history and of why it seldom has been clearly understood. Throughout the twentieth century, nonreligious secularists advocated ever widening extension of exclusively secular understandings of all manner of human activities, including academic thought. But at the same time many religious people, including most mainline Protestants, who controlled mainstream academia through the first two-thirds of the century, advocated very similar secular approaches to most of the same matters. Such religious people advocated such secularizing both for methodological reasons and sometimes as a matter of equity in a diverse society. Such broadly religious people who were responding to broad social forces and practical (including economic) concerns had more to do with removing substantive religious concern from most of the mainstream academy than did the efforts of metaphysical naturalists. Nonetheless, the convergence of the interests of the religious secularizers and of the metaphysical naturalists in so many areas meant that, in academia at least, metaphysical naturalists had relatively easy sailing in promoting most dimensions of their cause and could easily present their outlook as an essentially nonsectarian stance rather than as a sectarian ideology. A particularly attractive reason for expanding and maintaining essentially secular rules in most of academia was that equity demanded that Protestant sectarianism be thoroughly removed from the advantageous position it had recently held in mainstream academia. Secularists could offer their various forms of exclusive naturalism as "nonsectarian" rationales for that laudable cause.

Metaphysical naturalists, as might be expected, have been among the chief promoters of making methodological naturalism into an academic orthodoxy. To the extent possible, they have insisted, substantive religious concerns should be kept out of mainstream academia. Such a rule was never universally accepted—mainstream academia has always been too diverse for that—but sometime in the second half of the twentieth century that rule reached a peak of influence.

Broadly speaking, the twentieth-century metaphysical naturalism came in two versions—or two *kinds* of versions, with many varieties of each. One version of this outlook, especially prominent during the first two-thirds of the century, was the belief that the positivistic or natural scientific method produced the most reliable truths and therefore should be regarded as the highest standard for understanding human behavior, meaning, and standards for morality. The other type of version, also found throughout the century but more prominent during its last third, was that the human mind, individually or collectively, is all that we have access to and that "truths" are constructions of our minds. These two versions of metaphysical naturalism have been found in various combinations, but they agree that there is no higher source of truth beyond our own investigations or constructions.

In the last third of the twentieth century, the second version of this naturalism that I have described undermined the authority of the first. The old positivistic arguments—as in "logical positivism" for limiting "truth" to what could be demonstrated logically or through empirical investigation—were greatly weakened. The natural scientific method came to be seen as socially located and to some extent a point of view. So metaphysical naturalists, who appeal to the reliability of natural science as a reason for making a naturalistic outlook the highest standard for all intellectual inquiry, no longer have anything approaching a consensus for their most basic argument.

In fact, all they have left is an appeal to the virtues of *methodological* secularism. But if *that* is the standard, then we are just talking about pragmatic rules for the academy, and there is little argument for insisting that these might not be adjusted to maximize a plurality of religiously informed voices, rather than to minimize those voices.

I need to make clear here, in order to counter one misreading of my argument in *The Soul of the American University,* that I am not arguing for the inclusion of religious perspectives on the basis of a postmodernist subjectivist philosophy that would say, in effect, "anything goes" so why not religion? Rather, I'm arguing for inclusion of religious perspectives on *pluralistic* grounds. (I'm just pointing out that in the present academic climate that includes postmodern views, the old positivist arguments for marginalizing strong religious perspectives can now be seen, even by many secular people, as just one point of view among many.)

At the same time that the intellectual defenses for metaphysical naturalism have been greatly weakened, two other developments have contributed to changes in viewing the role of religion in the American academy. I'll just mention these briefly.

First are the worldwide political and cultural changes of the past decades. Especially important is the aftermath of the fall of the Soviet Union that revealed that what remained shaping much of international politics were religious ideologies that had not disappeared as predicted; 9/11 brought this point home dramatically. Since then it has been far easier to gain recognition that religion is and is going to remain an important dimension of the outlooks of many people in the twenty-first-century world. The rapid growth of all sorts of religion throughout the contemporary world has made clear that the Western European story of secularization is far from the typical story. Even secularists recognize that religions of all sorts and their points of view have to be taken seriously. And in such an atmosphere it is more difficult to exclude traditional religiously based points of view.

In making this point, however, I must take note that the same set of developments that is encouraging with respect to recognizing the importance of religious perspectives in the modern world has a downside in the culture-wars atmosphere that reinforces ongoing prejudices against traditional Christian perspectives. The culture-wars factor is not new, but as long as it remains intense, many mainstream academics are going to continue to equate Christian perspectives with fundamentalist perspectives. No matter how good the case for including high-quality traditional Christian scholarship in the mainstream academy, they are going to resist on the grounds of its perceived political associations. Nonetheless, the recognition of religious resurgence around the world is new and creates conditions favorable to the reception of faith-informed scholarship that can transcend the culture-wars mentality.

Finally, the second and probably the most significant factor contributing to hope for a positive change in the atmosphere is the emergence of a strong cohort of largely younger evangelical scholars in the mainstream academy. Michael Lindsay has documented this change in *Faith in the Halls of Power: How Evangelicals Joined the American Elite.*[3] I have been noticing this development for the past couple decades. If one attends, for instance, an InterVarsity Graduate Fellowship group at most any of the top universities, one is likely to find outstanding young scholars, including in the humanities. Some of these people are taking their positions at top universities. Others, just as significantly, are shaping the faculties of Christian colleges such as this one. Because so many outstanding evangelicals are going into academia today, schools such as the hundred or so in the Council of Christian Colleges and Universities are genuinely competitive academically with the best secular schools, and they have outstanding caring community settings to offer as well. It is no wonder that these schools have been growing at disproportional rates compared with other sorts in recent years. From 1990 to 2004, all public four-year campuses grew by about 13 percent, all independent four-year campuses (including many schools with broad religious or denominational connections) grew by about 28 percent. But schools associated with the CCCU grew by nearly 71 percent.[4] One reason they are growing is that although I cannot claim that they are little Harvards, they can offer something that Harvard cannot offer: that is excellence *with* soul.

So, on the whole, in the years since the publication of *The Soul of the American University* I have become more optimistic about the future of substantive Christian scholarship becoming well accepted in the mainstream of American academic culture and in the culture at large. One reason is that at the schools of the Council of Christian Colleges and Universities are some very talented undergraduates who are being inspired by

3. Michael Lindsay, *Faith in the Halls of Power: How Evangelicals Joined the American Elite* (New York: Oxford University Press, 2008).

4. Associated Press, "How College Has Changed in the Past 20 Years," *Daily Herald,* September 5, 2006,

very talented faculties to view service in academia as a Christian calling. I do not think that academic work is the most important of Christian callings. The body of Christ has many parts, and some work contributes more directly to the kingdom than others. But at the same time, as the Apostle Paul emphasizes, *all* the parts are essential. One of the essential parts is to have scholars who can serve others by helping us to better understand God's creation, our cultures, and ourselves. That calling is especially important for serving the larger American evangelical community, which has tended to be anti-intellectual. We need scholars of real faith who can bridge the gap between the church at the popular level and the academy. So I urge any of you who may have the talents and the interest to consider whether that is the Christian calling for you. It is a calling in which the future looks bright, but also one in which we need to continue the momentum that has been building in recent decades.

# 2

# The Opening of the Western Mind

## The Emergence of Higher Education in the "Dark Ages"

Mark W. Graham

MOST HISTORIANS AND ALL thinking conservatives take it as axiomatic that one cannot truly understand an institution without knowing at least something of its origins. A look at the birth of an institution with one eye fixed on the present can reveal how that institution has progressed or, depending on one's stance, lost its roots. Such a comparative glance might even, on occasion, impart valuable wisdom to the current age. The Western university[1] remains one of the world's most critical and venerable

1. I use the qualifier "Western" here to distinguish what I am exploring from the Islamic university, which actually predates it yet differs in fundamental ways. While some have argued that the Western university in fact developed from the Islamic university, this is far from conclusive, and represents a small minority of scholars of medieval Europe. See Mehdi Nakosteen, *History of Islamic Origins of Western Education, A.D. 800–1350* (Boulder: University of Colorado Press, 1964); Olaf Pederson, *The First Universities: "Studium generale" and the Origins of University Education in Europe,* trans. Richard North (Cambridge: Cambridge University Press, 1997); and Walter Rüegg, "The University as a European Institution," in *A History of the University in Europe,* vol. 1, *Universities in the Middle Ages,* ed. Hilde De Ridder-Symoens

institutions; an account of its origins is, among other things, a dynamic story of struggles over faith and freedom.

Most historians also posit that understanding the early history of any institution means considering its original context. The problem here is that the Western university emerged in what is today the most misunderstood epoch in Western history. It might seem an odd proposition to seek wisdom from the medieval period, the so-called Dark Ages of European history.[2] We are deluded by two common and equally misleading modern images of this period. On the one hand are romantic dreams of the Middle Ages as an era of lords, ladies, castles, knights, courtship (with all that loaded term entails), and ideal Christendom (whatever that means). The other picture is clear in the jarring *Oxford English Dictionary* quotation from Quentin Tarantino's *Pulp Fiction*—"I ain't through with you by a [bleep] sight; I'm gonna git *Medieval* on your [bleep]"; or, less colorfully, by the epithet for the medieval period as "a thousand years without a bath." Thus, the modern Western mind usually sees in the Dark Ages either a fantastic bedtime story or a savage nightmare. I suppose that fire-breathing dragons might fit either one.

Yet somewhere between the images of Disneyland castles and hairy unwashed brutes lie some very valuable lessons for higher education today. Shedding some much-needed light on the Dark Ages might just help us understand the university a bit better. We could profit, in fact, from returning to some of its roots; we might also do well to stop repeating some of its foundational mistakes. To understand the emergence of Western higher education, we must begin with the structures of education—lower and higher—which the medieval world inherited from the classical. With the collapse of the Roman Empire in the West in the late fifth century, classical structures of learning limped on into the medieval world, and did not suddenly collapse. Even at the height of the Roman Empire, it must be noted, classical education had never really soared, by any modern standard. Classical learning could be, as one famous classicist dryly put it, remarkably "barren" and "meager," little more than a "crushing load on the memory" and driven by an aim that "had remained unchanged for some 800 years."[3] The body of authoritative texts at its center were actually

(Cambridge: Cambridge University Press, 1992), 19–27.

2. Anyone who remains incredulous about the vital importance of the medieval intellectual program to Western culture should consult Marcia L. Colish, *Medieval Foundations of the Western Intellectual Tradition, 400–1400*, Yale Intellectual History of the West (New Haven: Yale University Press, 1997), for starters.

3. Peter Brown, *Augustine of Hippo: A Biography* (Berkeley: University of California

very few in number and excessively well worn—Cicero, Sallust, Terence, Virgil. Its highest goal was simply to produce orators who could imitate the greats of the past. Creativity and originality, so prized in our modern setting, were the enemy, to be driven far from the battlefield that was the young person's mind.

Right at the time when the imperial structures of the later western Roman Empire were beginning to sag, classical education was infused with a new vigor thanks to the Christianization of the Roman Empire. When incorporated into the educational system of the later Roman Empire and the early Middle Ages, Christianity provided the first real innovation in centuries to hit this weary, shallow, and repetitive educational world. Christians had already been struggling for some time with how to incorporate their central text—the Scriptures—into an educational system that resisted intrusions of texts not within the tiny and exclusive canon of the classical greats. At a basic level, Christians had long wrestled with how to teach grammar to children, for example, when the only "worthy" exemplars were pagan authors.[4] At higher and more theoretical levels, Christians pondered how to read Virgil or Cicero; or whether they even should. In the end, the infusion of Christianity into the educational system transformed classical structures beyond anything a Virgil or even a young Augustine of Hippo (354–430), thoroughly trained in the classical tradition, would have recognized. In his older years, bishop Augustine would articulate a vision for education, which would in time animate medieval education at all levels; his most focused expression is *De Doctrina Christiana—Concerning Christian Teaching* (a work which still deserves a far wider readership than it gets).

On balance, and by any feasible measure, classical educational structures in fact did go into precipitous decline in the early Middle Ages, despite the sincere efforts of even most of the "barbarian invaders" who inherited them from the classical world. This decline was, as most scholars now agree, not a simple tale of stinky barbarians ransacking Roman schools, sending schoolmaster and children running and screaming in terror. The truth is actually far more complex and interesting (as usual); nearly all of the so-called barbarian kingdoms that carved up the western Roman Empire at least attempted to preserve much that was Roman education in its Christianized form.

---

Press, 1967), 36.

4. See M. L. W. Laistner, *Thought and Letters in Western Europe, A.D. 500–900* (Ithaca, NY: Cornell University Press, 1966).

The central educational figure throughout the later Empire and into the early medieval period was the bishop, who, like his late Roman political and administrative predecessor, was a highly educated community leader. The office of early medieval bishop, though, began to take on more and more exclusively political roles (for reasons far beyond the scope of this study), and the emphasis on classical/Christian learning, or learning by any name, declined drastically. At one time the most highly educated man among educated elites, the bishop became cut off from late Roman cultural and intellectual traditions—he no longer *needed* an education to preserve his position. Within a few centuries of the collapse of the western Roman Empire, the bishop was being judged almost solely on the basis of how effectively he could control the material resources of his diocese, not by how well he could read and interpret texts (if, in fact, he could now read texts at all).[5] The educated elite, no longer valued or needed as such, rather quickly disappeared from the West or retreated to the monastery. Now the bishop was no longer a member of an intellectual elite so much as an effective administrator of a region of a Germanic kingdom. Two of the last classically educated men of the West, Cassiodorus (490–585) and Pope Gregory the Great (r. 590–604) well recognized their positions as essentially the last of a dying breed.[6]

If any period of western Europe may be termed Dark Ages, the ensuing era just might be it—about two centuries with literacy rates falling to about 1 percent in many areas. But this night was not to last for long, as historians reckon time. In the late eighth century, the Frankish king Charlemagne began to reverse these trends, aiming, above all else, to restore a world that had been lost. The efforts he kickstarted, a collective movement known as the Carolingian Renaissance, was one of the most remarkable educational (if not cultural, social, and intellectual) reforms in history.[7] In his own words, he was trying to produce full and worthy mem-

5. See Patrick Geary, *Before France and Germany: The Creation and Transformation of the Merovingian World* (New York: Oxford University Press, 1988), for an in-depth look at the transformation of the office of bishop. J. M. Wallace-Hadrill, *The Frankish Church* (Oxford: Oxford University Press, 1984), provides a broader overview of the Frankish church from the Merovingians to the Carolingians. Yitzhak Hen, *Culture and Religion in Merovingian Gaul, A.D. 481–751* (Leiden: Brill, 1995) traces Christianity as a cultural force among the early Franks.

6. For a detailed study of the decline of literacy in a specific geographic setting, see Armando Petrucci, *Writers and Readers in Medieval Italy: Studies in the History of Written Culture*, trans. Charles Radding (New Haven: Yale University Press, 1995).

7. The Carolingian Renaissance has been well chronicled in multiple works by Rosamond McKitterick, the most important of which appear below. Her most recent

bers of a *communitas fidelium*, a community of the faithful. He knew that his Christian empire would never succeed without a strong educational infrastructure. Reviving learning at all levels, from the youngest children all the way up to the bishops, took some intense effort, but the movement was a stunning success. It is said, for example, that it quickly became fairly common for four- and five-year-olds to memorize the entire Psalter in preparation for learning to read. The early medieval cultural and intellectual slide was effectively halted.

A vision of the Christian Roman imperial past was the touchstone of Charlemagne's efforts to restore the Roman Empire (*renovatio Romani imperii*). Alcuin of York, Paul the Deacon, Peter of Pisa, Einhard, and other luminaries helped him shape an educational agenda for the large and expanding Carolingian realm. Educational reform and religious reform went hand in hand in Charlemagne's decrees, and he pushed for a training through which Europeans could "praise God and pray in the proper manner." The bishops were instructed to teach "in the Roman tradition," that is, using the form and substance of the late classical/Christian tradition.[8]

To help them fulfill this task correctly, Charlemagne mandated that the priests and bishops themselves be carefully trained and educated. Like his Merovingian Frankish predecessors, he retained control of the appointment of bishops—if his system was going to work, reversing centuries of intellectual and cultural decline, it would take strong political enforcement from the top down. The bishops remained the key political functionaries of Europe at this time; Charlemagne did nothing to challenge this trend. In fact, he probably took firmer control of the office of bishop even while insisting that bishops could no longer function simply as political figures; they now had to learn the Scriptures and the best of the classical tradition. Higher educational schools would have to be founded to carry out this ambitious mission.

The problem was, though, that his appointment of bishops—a practice known as lay investiture—was in direct violation of church tradition and law. The laity were not supposed to appoint bishops. If, as is maintained by most who understand the Carolingian Renaissance, Western Europe was rescued at this point intellectually and culturally, it is well to

installment is *Charlemagne: The Formation of a European Identity* (Cambridge: Cambridge University Press, 2008).

8. See Rosamond McKitterick, *The Frankish Church and the Carolingian Reforms, 789–895*, Studies in History (London: Royal Historical Society, 1977). See also her *Frankish Kingdoms under the Carolingians, 751–987* (London: Longman, 1983) for a presentation that focuses more specifically on the political makeup of the Carolingians.

remember the whole story: this was made possible only through heavy-handed government enforcement that itself violated church traditions. The results, although laudable from many perspectives, were far from unproblematic. We free-market folks would probably not want to reflect overly long on the simple fact that government interference, in effect, saved Western civilization.

Ancient texts were central to Charlemagne's educational program. Alcuin and company strove to recover the ancient classics as a way of restoring a lost world. To do so, textual production had to be revived. Book making, which had all but disappeared since the earliest medieval centuries, was restored over the course of several decades, with great effort. The results were astounding; for the ninth century alone we have seven times more surviving texts than the total number of texts that survive from all of human history up to the year 800. Every bishop was commanded to set up a local school for teaching these classic texts and Scripture. Teachers now had access to texts in a way not seen since the glory days of the Roman Empire. A lower-educational program, upon which higher education would be built, trained children in what is known as the *trivium* (grammar, dialectic, rhetoric) and *quadrivium* (geometry, music, arithmetic, astronomy). As an aside, although the term *trivium* is often associated with classical education, the word itself, in fact, is no older than Charlemagne.

As the movers and shakers of the Carolingian Renaissance fully appreciated, scholarship and "practicality" are not two separate spheres. The learning they envisioned was never *simply* learning for its own sake, but for the application of knowledge in the service of the Christian faith and in a Christian imperial polity. The influence was felt broadly and deeply. A specialized training was instituted for bishops and priests so that they could serve effectively as the intellectual and spiritual conduits of the imperial reform agenda. As usual throughout history, so-called ivory-tower developments are never really separated from what goes on in the culture at large (for better or for worse)—they both reflect and produce societal change (often, simultaneously). The weekly sermon was envisioned as a means not only for imparting the essentials of the Christian faith to Europeans but for social mores to be developed, imagination and aesthetic sensibilities awakened; indeed, the social conscience of the people to be carefully cultivated.[9] Ancient texts like St. Augustine's *De Doctrina Christiana* were very useful in instructing clergy how to communicate deep and powerful truths to common people.

9. See McKitterick, *Frankish Church*, 81.

The training necessary for this type of program demanded a new birth of higher education in the West; what emerged, in fact, has no classical precedent. Carolingian cathedral schools, the first postclassical institutions of higher education, arose to meet the needs of a more specialized training for church and state functionaries. The highly trained bishops were, of course, both. These schools were founded in the cathedrals of major European towns, with some of the major ones in the western Frankish realm—Paris, Chartres, Notre Dame, etc. The pupils were largely clerics-in-the-making, generally drawn from the immediate environs. The schools were, in effect, the training ground for political figures—a cathedral school education now was necessary if one would hold the powerful and important office of bishop. The Masters of these schools were, then, not beating the bushes for tuition-paying students.

It was in these cathedral schools that Western higher education as we understand it began. Although unprecedented as an institution, the cathedral schools' educational emphasis would be immediately recognized by any late Roman—the study of letters and *mores*. Classical texts—i.e., Cicero, Seneca, Ovid—and the Scriptures were its core curriculum. The schools aimed to teach *humanitas*—the social quality of amiable graciousness, charm, wit, grace, humor, respect, and learning that characterized the classical gentleman of old and, once again, would come to characterize the bishops. The bishop should be as comfortable in the king's court as in the bishop's chair. Many of our words that begin with the root *court—courtesy, courtly, courtship*, etc.—have their origin in the ideals set forth for these bishops, courtier bishops, as they are called. As medievalist C. Stephen Jaeger puts it, "learning for its own sake had no legitimate role in this period. Studies had to be subordinated to a higher goal. For secular studies this goal was virtue and composed manners."[10] It would be hard to find a more visible manifestation of Charlemagne's educational program than the highly educated courtier bishop who moved naturally and gracefully through the king's court and cathedral school during the week and delivered eloquent educational sermons on Sunday. He was a dynamic and suave amalgam of church and state.

The cathedral master—the teacher—was the very foundation and font of this type of learning. His personal authority and charisma stood at its educational epicenter. His students looked to him as a source of

---

10. C. Stephen Jaeger, *The Envy of Angels: Cathedral Schools and Social Ideals in Medieval Europe*, Middle Ages Series (Philadelphia: University of Pennsylvania Press, 1995), 118.

learning; he embodied learning for them, both through his words and his actions, which were meant to be imitated, to be put into practice by courtier bishops. As one recent scholar puts it, he was himself a central text to be studied.[11] His authority, like that of a classical teacher, was generally unquestioned; originality, reason, and critical thought were not to the fore in this setting. A short list of the more famous cathedral school Masters would include Anselm of Laon, St. Anselm of Bec/Canterbury, Ivo of Chartres, and William of Champeaux. A regional chancellor generally oversaw the masters.

By the middle to end of the twelfth century, though, the foundation of the cathedral school was beginning to crumble, although few could have known it at the time. Two major challenges unwittingly helped undermined this initial, if false, start to Western higher education. The first was monastic reform, vigorous and ongoing throughout the Middle Ages, which refused to accept that bishops were legitimately put in place by lay rulers; no matter how noble the ends, they did not justify the means, these reformers maintained. The cathedral school system heavily depended upon lay investiture, as kings would appoint bishops from the ranks of those with a higher education per Carolingian law. Without the political carrot of high church office and the stick of a higher education, the cathedral schools would never have come into being in the first place. The second challenge was a much broader movement inspired in part by the first challenge—the famous Investiture Controversy (Conflict, Contest) of the late eleventh and early twelfth centuries, one of the most important moments in Western political and ecclesiastical history. Monastic and papal reform together took on the Carolingian practice of lay ordination, and won. By 1122 with the Concordat of Worms, medieval kings had lost their coveted right to appoint bishops after about a half century of bitter struggle with reforming popes, most notably Pope Gregory VII.[12]

11. Ibid.

12. Three excellent books provide diverse overviews of the Investiture Controversy. I. S. Robinson, *The Papacy, 1073–1198: Continuity and Innovation*, Cambridge Medieval Textbooks (Cambridge: Cambridge University Press, 1990), explores the popes' relationship with the churches and kingdoms of western Europe; Gerd Tellenbach, *The Church in Western Europe from the Tenth to the Early Twelfth Century*, Cambridge Medieval Textbooks (Cambridge: Cambridge University Press, 1993), provides a detailed study of church and "state" for the specific period of the Investiture Controversy; and Colin Morris, *The Papal Monarchy: The Western Church, 1050–1250* (Oxford: Oxford University Press, 1991), gives the best explanations of the far-reaching changes in the office of the pope at his most powerful point in history.

An unforeseen consequence of this loss was that the peculiar relationship between the court and the bishop (exemplified by the courtier bishop) dissolved rather quickly by the middle of the twelfth century. Ironically, some of the very voices of reform unwittingly ended up undermining their own positions. St. Anselm of Bec/Canterbury, for example, one of the major opponents of lay investiture, weakened his own position as a master when the system supporting the courtier bishops (i.e., his livelihood) came under fire. In short, with the direct papal challenge to the lay filling of court/church positions, the raison d'etre of the cathedral school system of higher education rather suddenly disappeared. If a rigorous education in the cathedral schools would not necessarily get you a high-paying or high-status church/state job, then what was the point of sacrificing all that time and money? Of course, there will always be a tiny handful of people who pursue learning for learning's sake, but never enough to actually support an institution of higher learning. The cathedral school more or less died in the generation after the Concordat of Worms, which officially put a nail in the coffin of lay investiture.[13]

At the very period the cathedral school master was unknowingly losing his future, a new type of teacher was emerging who would fill the coming void and meet the changing needs of uncertain times—the professor. He would, in fact, be the seed for the whole system of the university, which would far surpass the cathedral school in the history of Western higher education. Often a disputatious, controversial, and original thinker, the professor came to challenge the recognized master of the cathedral school. Although none of the players at the time could have had any clue of it, the sometimes vitriolic and personality-driven debates between the new professor and the old cathedral schoolmaster were signs of changing times, a deep shift in Western higher education.

The most famous (notorious?) early professor was Peter Abelard (of "Abelard and Heloise" fame), who chronicled his famous disputes with cathedral masters in his *Historia Calamitatum* (*The Story of My Misfortunes*). While in Abelard's telling, his disputes with his cathedral masters were often rather personal, his own account reveals the tensions between new and old, between one mode of higher education challenging another.

> I came at length to Paris . . . and there did I meet William of Champeaux, my teacher [cathedral schoolmaster], a man most distinguished in his science both by his renown and by his true

13. See Jaeger, *Envy of Angels*, for an excellent description of the impact of the Investiture Controversy on the cathedral schools.

merit. With him I remained for some time, at first indeed well liked of him; but later I brought him great grief, because I undertook to refute certain of his opinions, not infrequently attacking him in disputation, and now and then in these debates I was adjudged victor . . . Out of this sprang the beginning of my misfortunes, which have followed me even to the present day.[14]

It would certainly be a mistake and a drastic overstatement to give Abelard sole credit for undermining the existing system. Yet, his mode of thought was, in fact, the star rising on the horizon while the cathedral was losing its way. The cathedral master was dealt a serious double blow—decreased demand for his particular knowledge and training and a perfectly viable alternative.

Behind Abelard's arguments with cathedral schoolmasters was a fundamental difference in educational philosophy.[15] For the cathedral school master, acceptance of authority was everything—both the inherent authority of ancient authors and, by implication, the unchallengeable authority of the master dispensing the knowledge and wisdom of the ages. Disputation, dialectic, and disagreement—the tools of the professor— were neither welcome nor, generally, thinkable in the cathedral school setting. But Abelard did not play by the rules, and he questioned the masters' authority and thus the system at its very core. He intentionally provoked, challenged, and debated with his cathedral masters, proposing reason as a key arbiter of truth, not simply authority.[16] Early in his education, after some disappointments with his initial Master, he set out to sit under the most renowned Master of his day, Anselm of Laon, himself a student of St. Anselm (then of Bec, later of Canterbury):

> I sought out, therefore, this same venerable man, whose fame, in
> truth, was more the result of long-established custom than of the
> potency of his own talents or intellect. If any one came to him
> impelled by doubt on any subject, he went away more doubtful
> still. He was wonderful, indeed, in the eyes of these who only

14. *Historia Calamitatum*, trans. Henry A. Bellows (Mineola, NY: Dover, 2005), II.

15. I will leave aside the famous debates between Nominalists and Realists here; although this dispute was indeed a part of Abelard's conflict, the key point relevant to this essay is his confidence in challenging cathedral masters via Scholastic reason.

16. See Charles Radding and William Clark, *Medieval Architecture, Medieval Learning: Builders and Masters in the Age of Romanesque and Gothic* (New Haven: Yale University Press, 1992), for a nuanced and broader presentation of the developments behind Abelard's thought. Radding and Clark trace his thought as a wider process in discipline formation. They present Abelard as well as contemporary architects as producers—as opposed to reflectors—of cultural change.

listened to him, but those who asked him questions perforce held him as nought. He had a miraculous flow of words, but they were contemptible in meaning and quite void of reason.[17]

Such conclusions would become stereotypical denunciations of the old learning by the new. But neither Abelard nor Anselm of Laon could possibly have known the extent of the changes just around the corner.

When he set himself up as a professor, the key quality that Abelard (and all subsequent university scholastics) promised was the ability to teach *how* to think as opposed to just *what* to think.

> It so happened that at the outset I devoted myself to analyzing the basis of our faith through illustrations based on human understanding, and I wrote for my students a certain tract on the unity and trinity of God. This I did because they were always seeking for rational and philosophical explanations, asking rather for reasons they could understand than for mere words which the intellect could not possibly follow, that nothing could be believed unless it could first be understood, and that it was absurd for any one to preach to others a thing which neither he himself nor those whom he sought to teach could comprehend. Our Lord Himself maintained the same thing when He said: "They are blind leaders of blind."[18]

"The blind," of course, referred to the teachers he knew so well—the cathedral schoolmasters. Abelard made his point particularly clear by proposing a lecture on the same topic as a popular cathedral schoolmaster in order to draw away his students; and it often worked.

If we peer behind Abelard's vaunted rhetoric and the clash of personalities, we can see how and why these challenges began to stick—this was not a simple matter of Abelard and other dialecticians like him changing the educational landscape. A major paradigm shift was clearly underway, with its cause deep in the changing political landscape of the late eleventh and early twelfth centuries.[19] Once again, as in Charlemagne's day, a major political change brought with it a shift in educational emphasis.[20] It quickly

17. *Historia Calamitatum* III.

18. *Historia Calamitatum* IX.

19. R. W. Southern, "Schools of Paris and the School of Chartres," in *Renaissance and Renewal in the Twelfth Century*, ed. Robert L. Benson and Giles Constable (Oxford: Clarendon, 1982), compares the success of Paris and the new style of education, and how it came to dominate by as early as 1140.

20. There were significant changes across the board in the twelfth century far beyond just educational emphasis, so many in fact that some have dubbed this era

became apparent that there was immediate practical application for the skills developed by professors and then in the universities which formed around them by as early as the middle of the twelfth century. Much of this demand hearkened, again, to the Investiture Controversy, which not only weakened the competing educational program of the cathedral schools, but actually, and unintentionally, gave the university a reason to exist at the same time.

The Investiture Controversy had definitively clarified the church's role, but it had unwittingly opened up a huge set of questions about the role and function of the "state." As the eminent American medievalist Joseph Strayer eloquently put it,

> Like all victories, the victory of the Church in the Investiture Conflict had unforeseen consequences. By asserting its unique character, by separating itself so clearly from lay governments, the Church unwittingly sharpened concepts about the nature of secular authority . . . In short, the Gregorian concept of the Church [i.e., opposed to Lay Investiture] almost demanded the invention of the concept of the State. It demanded it so strongly that modern writers find it exceedingly difficult to avoid describing the Investiture Conflict as a struggle of Church and State.[21]

And with this definition and subsequent organization of the secular authorities came an increasing demand for political functionaries to make "the state" work—bureaucratic, legal, as representatives in assemblies, etc. It was this niche which the university began to fill; it served to qualify students for careers in secular professions.[22] The students of professors and then universities demanded a new type of higher-level thinking to take

---

"The 12th Century Renaissance." Significant changes in vernacular poetry, liturgy, law, art, architecture, logic, and even in perceptions of the individual have long interested scholars. While scholars agree that all these were going on at the same time, there are many different perspectives on how and on whether there are basic connections among them. Radding and Clark, *Medieval Architecture, Medieval Learning* proposes a picture in which they are not simply part of a web of mutual influence or simply reflections of culture as a whole, products of growing specializations and the emergence of disciplines for focusing on difficult problems in philosophy and architecture. The picture I am presenting here focuses exclusively on higher education and so has to leave out discussion of some of these broader changes going on at the same time.

21. Joseph R. Stayer, *On the Medieval Origins of the Modern State* (Princeton: Princeton University Press, 1970), 22.

22. See Gordon Leff, *Paris and Oxford Universities in the Thirteenth and Fourteenth Centuries: An Institutional and Intellectual History* (New York: Wiley, 1968), for a detailed discussion of the type of preparation they received.

on unprecedented problems, questions, developments—these were indeed uncharted waters. The university emerged as a true model of the practical value of education. This was not, *nota bene*, a narrow pragmatism, but rather an expansive and dynamic preparation for meeting the challenges of rapidly changing times.

Soon, the elites of Europe were being shaped by a standard educational experience. The great leaders who ran Europe, their advisors, and their staffs had a common collegiate background in what became the lecture halls of the new universities. The University of Paris was chartered by Philip II Augustus, king of France, in 1200, thus giving it full and mutually beneficial "state" approval. The dynamic interplay of thought and demand produced an upward spiral; the developing "state" demanded more and more complexity of thought to work, and the new form of higher education, by its very nature, delved deeper and deeper into prevailing questions and problems.

The move to the university was fairly quick, and even with initial resistance from the Church and the cathedral schools, the professor began appearing in most major European cities. The movement toward the university was initially centered in Paris during the lifetime of Abelard (1079–1122) but spread rapidly and far beyond this center. Professors were attracting a solid following by the end of the twelfth century. In these early years, of course, there was no institutional apparatus surrounding and supporting the professor. His professional livelihood, in fact, depended on the number of paying students he could attract through his lectures (imagine if that were the case today . . . ).

Institutionalization followed the early stage of the lone professor, and, by 1170, we can see universities at Paris and elsewhere, just twenty-eight years after Abelard's death in 1142. This time frame coincided with the complete passing of the first generation after the close of the Investiture Controversy. Bishops firmly in place at the time of the Concordat of Worms were now all dead (bishops held office for life). Soon after 1200, the Western university was the dominant intellectual player, and the cathedral schools never really recovered as a new form of higher education took over.

Unlike the old cathedral schools, the universities—Paris, Oxford, Bologna, Cambridge, Pavia, for example—drew students from afar and in spades, attracting an ever-growing number of students from throughout Europe. By 1209, for example, Oxford University had as many as three thousand students. Cathedral schools rarely had boasted more than one hundred, although there were many more of them, usually one in each major city. The gathering together of personnel, students, and universal and local knowledge from far and wide would be a hallmark of the university from that day forward.

In Paris and elsewhere, the professor and university together proceeded to break the power and monopoly of the cathedral school chancellor, paving the way for an unprecedented academic freedom that set the standard for all later expressions of this vital university component.[23] By contrast, in Chartres, the power of the chancellor was not challenged, and there was no significant movement to establish a university there.[24] At Oxford, there was not a cathedral school, and thus no chancellor to challenge the growing strength of the professor, a basic explanation for the meteoric rise of that university. The fact that the university became universally recognized stems from the outside support it also received from emperors, kings, and, in time, popes.[25] As always, where there is support, there are strings attached, and the medieval university often found itself reemphasizing its freedom from ecclesiastical and civil control, often to no avail.

The visible manifestations of the university's growth and complexity—charters, courses of study, rules, degrees—all attest to a remarkably stable institution by the thirteenth century. The professors could now come and go, but the institutions remained. *Universitas*, from which our term derives, means "all"; in a collective sense it could mean any group of people cooperating for a common end. To ensure order and organization to this setting, educational guilds emerged in which professors and students pledged themselves to conform to statutes, cooperating toward the common end. For an odd example, students were at one point forbidden to "bring bows and arrows to class" and, to many a student's relief, professors were fined for beginning class late or going on too long. The university was now a corporation capable of expelling those not conforming and rewarding those who followed through its programs with degrees. By the early thirteenth century, for example, a degree program for a Bachelor of Arts consisted of completing two books on grammar and five on logic. Four to six more years of study of *quadrivium* led to Master of Arts, and seven to twelve for a doctorate.[26]

23. See Leff, *Paris and Oxford Universities*, on the Professors displacing the Chancellor.

24. See Southern, "Schools of Paris and the School of Chartres."

25. See Leff, *Paris and Oxford Universities,* 20.

26. See Leff, *Paris and Oxford Univerities,* for an in-depth look at the nuts and bolts of these degree programs. It almost goes without saying that the medieval sense

Within the universities, the ancient classics continued to be used alongside the Scriptures and church fathers as the school curriculum. The new method of their use, though, produced a very different type of education from what had been seen before.[27] The racy love poetry of Ovid, for example, became basic reading even for the monks trained in this tradition. The Scriptures were meditated and prayed over less and studied more for answers to speculative problems.[28] But it is crucial to note that it was "not the materials they had at their disposal . . . but the ways in which they thought about and ordered their material that set Abelard" and the Scholastics apart from their predecessors.[29] Scholastic thinkers also began searching out texts that had been long lost or forgotten. Stray references in the late Roman Boethius's (480–524) writing and elsewhere had hinted at the existence of the New Logic of Aristotle, unknown to Medieval thinkers up to that time. The text was searched out along with other works of Aristotle, and would serve as an important basis for new types of exploration of the mental and physical universe.[30]

The disciplinary emphasis of the universities followed some long-established patterns at first. Theology, "the queen of the sciences," was initially the major field of study. In fact, to describe this field, Abelard himself coined our term *theology*. But soon theology lost its place as the "driving force behind education," even as it still remained the queen of the sciences. University study was primarily oriented toward this world. While the "juxtaposition of spiritual and temporal was the of essence" of the earliest universities, they existed to train critical thinkers to solve very earthly problems.[31]

---

of "completing" a book was far different from ours, and involved close and careful reading and rereading until the text was truly mastered.

27. See Jean LeClerq, "The Renewal of Theology," in *Renaissance and Renewal in the Twelfth Century*, ed. Benson and Constable.

28. Ibid., 82.

29. Radding and Clark, *Medieval Architecture, Medieval Learning*, 76.

30. Note that Abelard knew only one work of Aristotle when he died in 1142, but was independently coming to some of the same conclusions as Aristotle's works soon to be introduced in the West. This intellectual movement was *not*, as some have claimed, simply a response to diffusion of texts from the Byzantine or Islamic worlds. Humans are not passive receptors of texts. See Radding and Clark, *Medieval Architecture, Medieval Learning*, for a detailed critique of the view that Aristotle's texts caused the changes. Leff, *Paris and Oxford Universities*, takes the diffusion-of-texts-as-agents -of-change perspective.

31. Leff, *Paris and Oxford Universities*, 3; see also 116.

Philosophy became the dominant emphasis, overtaking theology as the dominant field, although the fields could be intertwined. Teaching critical, rational thought, for example, by way of a long-term study of the Old Testament book of Ezekiel was one way Abelard himself brought the fields together early on. Such an approach, though, was bound to foster critical challenges to recognized authorities. Saying something new about Ezekiel or, perhaps worse, about the Trinity (as Abelard did) provoked Church authorities; innovation, prized by the professors and the universities, met much resistance at first. Philosophical and theological learning, which did not necessarily parrot early church writers or have official sanction of the bishops, could be dangerous, and the *Misfortunes* part of Abelard's autobiography title says much about the reactions he received (although we should not forget his bristly, arrogant ways, either). He was hounded by authorities, driven out of teaching posts, and even forced to burn one of his own works.

It is not difficult to see how this new educational method could be so unsettling to a system based almost entirely on affirming older authorities. Not helping matters much was that professors, as people, could be a tendentious lot. Interpret as you see fit the fact that four of the most famous high- and late-medieval names synonymous with contention, debate, and challenge—Peter Abelard, John Wycliffe, John Huss, and Martin Luther—were all university professors. Contentiousness does not have to be the only image of the medieval university scholar, although it does dominate. The renowned Scholastic St. Thomas Aquinas was famous in his own day both for his remarkable erudition and his irenic humility; and he still stands out as a rare example of both. Excesses of the professors rightly earned the rebukes they would receive from later medieval figures. The late medieval mystic Thomas á Kempis (1380–1471) was clearly taking aim at university professors in an introductory line to his famed *Imitation of Christ*:

> Of what use is it to discourse learnedly on the Trinity, if you lack humility and therefore displease the Trinity? Lofty words do not make a man just or holy; but a good life makes him dear to God. I would rather feel contrition than be able to define it. If you knew the whole Bible by heart, and all the teachings of the philosophers, how would this help you without the grace and love of God?[32]

32. Thomas a Kempis, *The Imitation of Christ*, trans. Leo Sherley-Price (New York: Viking, 1952), 27.

Petrarch (1304–1374), the so-called father of Italian Renaissance humanism, was clearly challenging university Scholasticism with one of his favorite lines: "it is better to will the good than to know the truth." Indisputably, in the university movement, gaining knowledge and getting the better of opponents in disputation often became ends in themselves.

Such problems aside, not long after the university charters were in place, leading churchmen and then friars were seeking out the universities to sharpen their minds and abilities. The results across the social, cultural, and intellectual landscape are difficult to overestimate. Arenas far afield from politics were shaped by and expressed the new Scholastic learning. The Western world, even the Roman Empire, had never seen such volume and diversity of higher-educated men. The study of law, for example, veritably exploded. Lawyers, working both with secular law and with newly emerging canon law, developed a new jurisprudence, which could be studied at the Universities of Bologna and Pavia—these could in turn help make the new law states function.[33] Twelfth-century jurisprudence showed unprecedented complexity as the Scholastically trained mind took it to new levels.[34] Medical schools also expanded, incorporating the new Scholastic methods into traditional modes of teaching that field.

The university was, by definition, universal, and was fueled by a broad vision to reclaim lost human knowledge and push the frontiers of understanding indefinitely outward. It continued to recruit the best minds from far and wide to cooperate in this task. On the whole, the university represented a passionate quest to understand the natural and supernatural order, the likes of which the world had never before seen. The past provided the fragments, the university setting aimed at integration and synthesis of the whole.[35]

The Scholastic thinking that emerged from this moment was felt in nearly every crevice of the high- and late-medieval worlds and beyond. Viewed positively, the Scholastic program was "an attempt to make the created universe and its relationship to the eternal being of God and the heavenly hierarchies as fully intelligible as the limitations of fallen human

33. The best study to date remains Charles Radding, *The Origins of Medieval Jurisprudence: Pavia and Bologna, 850–1150* (New Haven: Yale University Press, 1988). Radding explains how schools of law emerged over the early twelfth century in terms of their continuity and growing complexity.

34. See Stephen Kuttner, "The Revival of Jurisprudence," in *Renaissance and Renewal in the Twelfth Century*, ed. Benson and Constable; and Knüt W. Nörr, "Institutional Foundations of the New Jurisprudence," in ibid.

35. See Kuttner, "Revival of Jurisprudence."

nature allow."[36] Viewed negatively, it was an arcane dispute over how many angels could dance on the head of a pin (a hackneyed caricature not actually leveled at Scholasticism until centuries later). In fact, it represented a relentless search for truth, and one that did not simply stare wistfully at the past. In the words of the eminent English medievalist R. W. Southern, "The practical application of this intellectual programme produced a reorganization of medieval society along lines which were very generally operative until the eighteenth century. It was the abandonment of this programme . . . which caused the great crisis of belief in the existence of any attainable body of knowledge about an eternal state of Being."[37]

So, what exactly can the modern university, post-Enlightenment, learn from its medieval counterpart? What can we learn about faith and freedom from this origin story? Faith, of course, undergirded higher education from its very inception in the cathedral schools. These schools in fact were designed to help produce "full and worthy members of the *communitas fidelium*," the community of the faithful ones. With the birth of the university, faith continued to dominate discussion and undergird the Scholastic disputes. The venerable tradition exemplified by such gems as St. Augustine of Hippo's "I believe in order that I may understand" (*credo ut intelligam*) and St. Anselm's "faith seeking understanding" (*fides quarens intellectum*) was carried into the new institutional setting of the university. In stark contrast, it bears saying, although no one says it as definitively as George Marsden, that "contemporary university culture is hollow at its core. Not only does it lack a spiritual center, but it is also without any real alternative."[38] But as D. G. Hart asks us, is this necessarily a bad thing? Can the university continue to function, separate from its roots, in a postmodern world?

Freedom, won by the university, was central to that institution from its inception. The cathedral schools were beholden to the Church and State from the start—staffed by bishops and training church/state functionaries, there was no room for free and open inquiry. Challenge and disputation, the hallmark of the university, were the mainstays of an environment of free and open inquiry, the passionate pursuit of truth. Not always welcome, then or now, truly open inquiry was a pillar of the medieval university.

36. R. W. Southern, *Scholastic Humanism and the Unification of Europe*: Volume 1, *Foundations* (Oxford: Blackwell, 1995).

37. Southern, *Scholastic Humanism*, v.

38. George M. Marsden, *The Outrageous Idea of Christian Scholarship* (New York: Oxford University Press, 1997), 3.

One might ask if and where these venerable traditions might be alive and well today? In truth, many a "faith-based" institution in modern America either simply blushes when too closely associated with its own faith tradition or simply exists for the sake of promulgating some narrow and exclusive ideological and/or political vision. It is difficult to find anything in between. Christians and conservatives should be constantly aware of the danger of creating our own little self-affirming worlds, far from the *universal* vision of the university. And while "academic freedom" is proclaimed by all legitimate current institutions of higher learning, faith-based scholarship is in most quarters an "Outrageous Idea," to again invoke Marsden. To pursue it or anything like it can, in some quarters, simply bar one from the halls of academia, or at least relegate one to a closet off the hall. Furthermore, the often stultifying effects of politicized academic consensus-building can likewise restrict free inquiry. In my field of history, and not too long ago, to not pursue research on race, class, and/ or gender, would likewise consign one to a mop and broom closet off the hall of academia. Is this free and open inquiry, passionately devoted to the pursuit of truth?

But let's not play the martyr over much here, as Christians are only too prone to do (not that there is not an ancient tradition to that too . . . ). The medieval university is not finished with us quite yet. In an age when many, many students (here and elsewhere) are motivated primarily by tests, quizzes, and grades, it is worth remembering that at the very foundations of the Western university lay a deep desire for flexible thinking and analytical skills. The scholastic program was never about simply mastering a body of material; learning what to think was not the end-all issue, but rather *how* to think. The program was never about idealizing or even idolizing old classics—but learning how to think with them. This, at its functioning best, was not sterile and flaccid classicism but a vibrant and dynamic dialectic interaction with the best minds of the past, guides for responding to new and unprecedented situations.

My experience has been that most American students today, here and elsewhere, are actually rather uncomfortable with this teaching method in practice—"just give me the answers (and in organized outline form, please), so I can memorize them for the next test. And please stop asking so many questions during class; how am I supposed to take organized notes on discussions?" And far too often, the Professor has been content to play the role of cathedral master—"I am the authority sent here to enlighten you; simply sit and listen to and learn from me, and do not raise challenges and questions except to tap the deep font of my mind." And yes, "just memorize this body of knowledge for the next test . . . and be affirmed." *What* to think. In the uncertain times of the twelfth and thirteenth centuries, no less than our own, the flexible thinking skills of the University need a new lease on life. In fact, are not such venerable and hoary critical thinking skills actually even more needed in our own breathtakingly-changing times?

But there are significant dangers lurking here and paths certainly to be avoided. Higher education came into being at political instigation and was supported and maintained by governments from its earliest years. Today when we protest the politicization of the academy, we might just be striking at a very deep tap root. The freedom from ecclesiastical control soon came to align the University with the State. And, of course, a university supported by the government, as we here at Grove City College know more than most, is one controlled by it; and the medieval university, no less than the modern, often had to struggle for its freedom.

The hubris of the medieval university has also too often been carried into each subsequent age. Late medieval mystics like Thomas á Kempis as well as the Italian and Northern humanists like Petrarch and Erasmus well recognized the medieval university's Achilles' heel. The program to recover all lost knowledge has often descended into a self-confident arrogance or simply arguing for the sake of arguing and striving, above all, to win arguments. St. Augustine recognized these problems, before the Middle Ages ever even dawned, in his timeless *De Doctrina Christiana*:

> All that one has to be on guard against here is a passion for
> wrangling and a kind of childish parade of getting the better of
> one's opponents . . . Never stop reflecting on that maxim of the
> apostle's, "Knowledge puffs up, love builds up."

Finally, what can the medieval university reveal about the purpose of higher education? There are a few idealistic dreamers among us who actually think that higher education is and should be learning for learning's sake (if you have not yet divined this, I'm one). But let's be honest. cathedral schools, medieval universities, and modern universities have existed to meet very practical demands. We can and should not delude ourselves into thinking that learning has ever been about simply the pursuit of knowledge for the sake of the pursuit of knowledge; learning for the sake of learning. That particular Golden Age thrived only, I think, right alongside the fabled El Dorado. Higher education always has been pursued for very practical ends. It has always been an investment of time and money which was expected to "pay off," in one way or another.

In medieval universities, though, such practical ends were never narrowly defined as simple job preparation or vocational training. Such, in fact, was the death of the cathedral schools; they were not flexible enough in changing times. Higher education in medieval universities was never intended to simply put one onto a narrow career path but rather to sharpen broadly applicable thinking skills that could meet changing times and circumstances head-on. The earth-shattering results, intentional or not, were felt at all intellectual, cultural, and social levels and profoundly helped shape the West as we know it. Perhaps it would do the modern American university some good if in some vital areas it strove to "git medieval," at least every once in a while.

# 3

# From "Old Time" Christian College to Liberal Protestant University

*The Forgotten Interlude in the History of the Secularization of Princeton University*

## P. C. Kemeny

IN THE PAST, AS one conservative Presbyterian observed in 1914, Princeton University "sent out men who carried a stalwart evangelical message . . . But the message which to-day goes out from her department of Bible Studies is stoutly antagonistic to the Protestant Evangelical faith." To agitated fundamentalists, the *university's* Bible professor, Lucius H. Miller, was a "devil in cap and gown" proselytizing students with a false religion. Fundamentalist frustration with the spiritual direction of the university grew after President John G. Hibben refused Princeton Seminary professor Charles R. Erdman's request in 1915 to sponsor a Billy Sunday evangelistic service on campus but hosted the liberal Protestant theologian Albert Parker Fitch, president of Andover Seminary, at the university's first Religious Emphasis Week. Conservative Presbyterians believed that while Sunday occasionally showed "bad form" with his coarse language, at least he was "sound on all *the fundamentals*," unlike the "damnable heresies" that Fitch preached. Unable to force the university to revert to the halcyon days of its youth when evangelicalism dominated Princeton, some fundamentalists advocated a position that would have been unthinkable a generation earlier—secularization. In a letter to President Hibben, John DeWitt, one of the more theologically conservative members of the university's Board of Trustees and a professor at Princeton Seminary, argued that the university should "remove Professor Miller" by secularizing the curriculum. "I am thoroughly persuaded," he wrote, "that the interests of the University will be promoted by the abolition of *all theological courses*."[1] Because it remained committed to preserving the historic religious mission of the university, the liberal Protestant administration refused to bow to the fundamentalists' demands.

That certain fundamentalists called for the secularization of Princeton, and that liberal Protestants in many ways proved to be the conservators of the Protestant character of the university, defies conventional wisdom. Historians of American religion and of higher education typically attribute the demise of traditional evangelical interests and practices at colleges and universities such as Princeton to the corrosive results of secularization. To be sure, such interpretations are not entirely misguided when they point to the destructive consequences that the postbellum revolution in higher education had on established educational commitments and conventions.[2] At the same time, many Protestants in the Gilded

---

* I would like to thank Professor Gillis Harp and my student assistants, Katherine Conley, Joel Musser, Sean Morris, and Ben Wetzel, for reading various drafts of this essay.

1. "The Princeton Work in Peking," *Presbyterian*, 1 Apr. 1914, 7; Ford C. Ottman, *The Devil in Cap and Gown* (New York, 1914), 1; Editorial Comment, *Presbyterian*, 15 Apr. 1915, 10; John DeWitt quoted in P. C. Kemeny, *Princeton in the Nation's Service: Religious Ideals and Educational Practice, 1868–1928* (New York: Oxford University Press, 1998), 182.

2. Richard Hofstadter, "The Revolution in Higher Education," in *Paths of American Thought*, eds. Arthur M. Schlesinger Jr. and Morton White (Boston: Houghton Mifflin, 1963), 269–90; Richard Hofstadter and Walter P. Metzger, *The Development of Academic Freedom in the United States* (New York: Columbia University Press, 1955), 320–66; Frederick Rudolph, *The American College and University: A History* (New York: Vintage, 1962), 410–20, 345–8; Frederick Rudoph, *Curriculum: A History of the American Undergraduate Course of Study since 1636* (San Francisco: Jossey-Bass, 1977), 139, 156–57, 174, 177; Laurence R. Veysey, *The Emergence of the American University* (Chicago: University of Chicago Press, 1965), 40–50, 128, 137–38, 203–4; William C. Ringenberg, *The Christian College: A History of Protestant Higher Education in America* (Grand Rapids: Christian University Press, available from Eerdmans, 1984), 114–33; George M. Marsden, *The Soul of the American University: From Protestant

Age were stricken with a "spiritual crisis."[3] Given the academic revolution and the decline of orthodox belief in academic circles, many distinctively evangelical interests and practices disappeared on campuses in the early twentieth century. As Mark A. Noll observes, "In almost every way imaginable the new university undercut the traditional values of Christian higher education in America."[4]

Yet historians, even recent revisionists, have frequently undervalued the ways in which Protestant beliefs and practices continued to play a crucial role in higher education in the twentieth century. This study challenges conventional interpretations by arguing that, at one representative institution, Protestant interests were not abandoned but rather modified to conform to the educational and intellectual values of the modern university. Liberal Protestants, like President Hibben, refused to forsake religious education because they believed, like their nineteenth-century predecessors, that the university had a responsibility to mold the Christian character of students and ultimately to shape the Christian character of American culture. In other words, before historically evangelical Christian colleges and universities became secular institutions, they became liberal Protestant institutions. Liberal Protestants still adhered to the cultural mandate to nurture religious faith in students because they deemed it part of the college's historic mission to American society. Increasingly alienated conservative Protestants simply discarded that mandate.

---

*Establishment to Established Nonbelief* (New York: Oxford University Press, 1994), 101–356; D. G. Hart, "Faith and Learning in the Age of the University: The Academic Ministry of Daniel Coit Gilman," in *The Secularization of the Academy*, eds. George M. Marsden and Bradley J. Longfield, Religion in America Series (New York: Oxford University Press, 1992), 107–45; L. Bruce Leslie, *Gentlemen and Scholars: College and Community in the "Age of the University," 1865–1917* (University Park: Pennsylvania State University Press, 1992); Warren A. Nord, *Religion & American Education: Rethinking a National Dilemma*, H. Eugene and Lillian Youngs Lehman Series (Chapel Hill: University of North Carolina Press, 1995), 63–86, 96–97.

3. Paul Carter, *The Spiritual Crisis of the Gilded Age* (Dekalb: Northern Illinois University Press, 1971); D. H. Meyer, "American Intellectuals and the Victorian Crisis of Faith," *American Quarterly* 27 (1975) 585–603; James Turner, *Without God, Without Creed: The Origins of Unbelief in America*, New Studies in American Cultural and Intellectual History (Baltimore: Johns Hopkins University Press, 1985).

4. Mark A. Noll, "Christian Colleges, Christian Worldviews, and an Invitation to Research," introduction to *The Christian College*, by William C. Ringenberg, 29.

## EDUCATIONAL ORIGINS OF THE CONFLICT: COMPETING VISIONS OF PRINCETON

The influential trustee and fundamentalist John DeWitt's argument for the secularization of the undergraduate curriculum marked a dramatic reversal from the high view of religious education that conservative Protestants had previously held. In the nineteenth century, evangelicalism provided a unifying center to collegiate education and played a pivotal role inside and outside the classroom. Princeton, like many other church-related institutions established before the Revolutionary War, was technically a nondenominational college. Although founded by Presbyterians in 1746, it could only get its charter approved by the British governor by pledging to grant "free and Equal Liberty and Advantage of Education" to "those of every Religious Denomination." Throughout its history, many looked upon Princeton as a de facto Presbyterian school devoted to meeting the educational needs and upholding the intellectual ideas of Presbyterians and the larger Protestant community.[5] During James McCosh's presidency, 1868 to 1888, evangelicalism played a central role in the discipline-and-piety philosophy of higher education that McCosh and other educators espoused in the late nineteenth century. The traditional liberal arts curriculum, McCosh believed, contained that body of knowledge derived from natural revelation and learned through reason. Required Bible classes, daily chapel, and two Sunday worship services taught that body of higher truths supernaturally disclosed. The six mandatory natural theology courses reconciled any "apparent" conflicts between the two.[6] The college curriculum, in short, harmonized a traditional Protestant faith with the moderate Scottish Enlightenment.

The annual Day of Prayer for Colleges, the activities of the Philadelphian Society, the campus YMCA, and occasional revivals complemented the formal elements of the college's program of Christian education. No student, said McCosh, "passes through our College without being addressed from time to time, in the most loving manner, as to the state of his soul." The most memorable revival came in 1876 when the evangelistic team of D. L. Moody and Ira Sankey held a service on campus.

---

5. "Charters of the College of New Jersey," in Thomas Jefferson Wertenbaker, *Princeton, 1746–1896* (Princeton: Princeton University Press, 1946), 396–97. On the founding purposes of the college, see Mark A. Noll, *Princeton and the Republic, 1786–1822: The Search for a Christian Enlightenment in the Era of Samuel Stanhope Smith* (Princeton: Princeton University Press, 1989), 16–22.

6. *Catalogue of the College of New Jersey, 1875–76,* 17–20, 30.

At the spring meeting of the trustees, McCosh proudly reported that one hundred students had been converted, seventy "backsliders" had been aroused, and another hundred had gotten "some heat from the burning fire."[7]

In a widely-publicized debate in 1886 with Harvard University president Charles W. Eliot, McCosh contended that religious education prevented students from becoming intellectually "narrow-minded" and kept the "chilling and deadly influence" of agnosticism from settling upon campus and, consequently, upon the nation.[8] McCosh's commitment to mandatory religious education simply mirrored the traditional Whiggish conception of higher education. It rejected the Jeffersonian insistence on a strict separation of religion and civic life and insisted that the nation needed a common set of values—nonsectarian Protestant values—in order to avoid the turmoil associated with the French Revolution.[9] Since conservative Presbyterians in the late nineteenth century valued mandatory religious education so highly, the willingness of their heirs in the early twentieth century to surrender these convictions is all the more striking.

A key reason for some fundamentalists' shifting position on mandatory religious education was that the university's program of religious instruction had taken on a very new orientation in the early twentieth century. Woodrow Wilson, president of the university from 1902 to 1910, transformed Princeton into a genuine research university. In the process, he adjusted its program of religious instruction to this newfound vision of Princeton as a national educational institution. As expressed in his famed 1896 sesquicentennial address, "Princeton in the Nation's Service," and later in his inaugural address, "Princeton for the Nation's Service," Wilson stressed in a new way the institution's mission as a public institution.

7. James McCosh, "The Place of Religion in College," in *Minutes and Proceedings of the Third General Council of the Alliance of the Reformed Churches holding the Presbyterian System, Belfast, 1884* (Belfast: Alliance of Reformed Churches, 1884), 468; James McCosh, *Twenty Years of Princeton College* (New York: John Scribner's Sons, 1888), 54–55; "Messrs. Moody and Sankey in Princeton," *Princeton Press*, 12 Feb. 1876.

8. James McCosh, *Religion in a College: What Place It Should Have. Being an Examination of President Eliot's Paper, Read before the Nineteenth Century Club, in New York, Feb. 3, 1886* (New York: Armstrong, 1886), 13–14, 21.

9. The terms *Jeffersonian* and *Whig* are used in a typological as opposed to a strictly historical sense. In the mid-nineteenth century, Whiggery was not only a political party but also a larger cultural tradition with distinctive political and social ideas. See Robert Kelley, *The Cultural Pattern in American Politics: The First Century* (New York: Knopf, 1979); Daniel Walker Howe, *The Political Culture of the American Whigs* (Chicago: University of Chicago Press, 1979).

Wilson undertook a variety of major reforms to enable the university to meet the nation's educational needs more effectively. Most important, he built a major graduate school. As he dramatically expanded the faculty, he gave priority to hiring faculty members distinguished by their scholarship and educational credentials instead of Princeton alumni status. Also important, Wilson dropped the informal orthodoxy tests for prospective faculty members because most elite academics had come to see such theological standards as parochial and contradictory to the national educational ambitions of genuine universities. Given a choice between a bona fide scholar and a theologically orthodox dilettante, Wilson's national goals gave priority to the legitimate academic over the theologically safe candidate. Under Wilson the faculty grew from 98 in 1902 to 162 in 1909. Wilson had little trouble hiring faculty with prestigious academic qualifications. A large number of the new hires had little sympathy with Princeton's evangelical past. The fact that few evangelical Protestants pursued advanced degrees at prestigious universities also made it easy for Wilson to look beyond the Presbyterian Church for competent scholars. Because of Princeton's newfound national aspirations, Wilson was open to hiring professors who were not even Protestant. Wilson hired Princeton's first Jewish scholar, Horace Meyer Kallen, in 1904 and its first Roman Catholic, David A. McCabe, in 1909. Some new professors, such as the philosopher Frank Tilly, did not even have a religious affiliation.[10]

With liberal cosmopolitan elites now in charge of the university, Wilson had allies capable of empowering him to make the changes necessary to realize his dream at Princeton. He reduced the number of seats on the board of trustees designated for clergy. This move allowed him to replace clerics with laymen who had the financial resources to fund Wilson's vision to turn Princeton into a legitimate research university. Wilson also expanded the university's community of support well beyond the narrow confines of the Presbyterian Church. There was simply not enough interest or money among Presbyterians to underwrite his national hopes for Princeton. Moreover, Wilson persuaded the trustees to declare Princeton an officially nondenominational institution in order to qualify for Carnegie Foundation pension funds. Many of the changes that Wilson undertook were typical of those at other church-related schools.

As Wilson reconfigured the university's mission, he accommodated the religious aspect of Princeton's heritage to the institution's newfound public mission. Like his nineteenth-century predecessors, Wilson believed

---

10. Kemeny, *Princeton in the Nation's Service,* 140–41.

that Protestantism, through its moral influence upon civic institutions such as universities, was essential to the public good. He implemented what historians describe as a "liberal culture" philosophy of higher education.[11] Wilson had little sympathy for the Presbyterian orthodoxy, however, that had dominated Princeton in the past. Conservative Presbyterians had driven Wilson's uncle, James Woodrow, from his position as a professor at Columbia Theological Seminary in the 1870s for offering a theistic interpretation of evolution in response to the purely atheistic model offered by Darwinists. Although Princeton University professors, not to mention those at Princeton Seminary, had deemed a theistic view of evolution perfectly compatible with Scripture, Wilson nevertheless nurtured a longstanding grudge against conservatives within the Presbyterian Church. Wilson's predecessors as Princeton's president, McCosh and Patton, as well as his colleagues at the seminary, would have never described religion as a matter of emotion or sentiment. For them, Christianity entailed truth that could be easily expressed in propositional form. Although he was the son of a Southern Presbyterian minister and educated at Princeton, Wilson's views of religion echoed the liberal Protestantism of Horace Bushnell and Henry Ward Beecher. In 1902 Wilson abolished the compulsory Bible courses taught by the former president's son, the theologically conservative George S. Patton, and reduced chapel attendance requirements to twice weekly and Sunday mornings. Religion, Wilson insisted, "cannot be handled like learning. It is a matter of individual conviction and its source is the heart." To advocates of liberal culture, the curriculum—the natural revelation side of McCosh's educational formulation—possessed the most catholic human values of Western civilization.[12]

Although Wilson did not believe that biblical instruction was essential to a liberal education, neither did he think it was incompatible so long as Bible classes avoided the supernatural dogmatism of evangelicalism. In 1905, Wilson reintroduced Bible instruction to the curriculum as elective courses and hired Lucius H. Miller, a university alumnus, to teach the courses instead of the conservative Patton. Hiring Miller was a bold slap in the face of Princeton's conservative Presbyterian tradition. Not only had he replaced the son of Wilson's orthodox Presbyterian predecessor, but

11. Woodrow Wilson, "Princeton in the Nation's Service," 21 Oct. 1896, "Princeton for the Nation's Service," 25 Oct. 1902, in *The Papers of Woodrow Wilson,* ed. Arthur S. Link, 69 vols. (Princeton: Princeton University Press, 1966–1994), 10:11–31; 14:170–85.

12. On Wilson's Princeton presidency, John M. Mulder, *Woodrow Wilson: The Years of Preparation* (Princeton: Princeton University Press, 1978), 158–228; 74–106.

Miller had recently graduated from the liberal Union Theological Seminary in New York. Miller wholeheartedly embodied the newfound spirit of liberal Protestantism. In his lectures to Princeton students, as he wrote Woodrow Wilson, he hoped to nurture their faith through "those intellectual explanations of the Old Faith that are necessitated by the changes in our modern life and thought." Miller believed that modern theology, unlike the implacable faith of the conservatives who "put God into their pocket with their printed creed," offered students "a secure foundation for their religious faith" and yet also kept "a perfect openness toward those changes of thought," especially in science.[13] Although Miller's liberal faith contrasted sharply with the beliefs previously taught at Princeton, the Bible professor, like his predecessors, still hoped to shape the Christian character of American society and, by extension, the world. Continuity with many of Princeton's traditional religious practices made the transition from a conservative to a liberal piety an easy one. The campus ministry of the Philadelphian Society, which flourished in this decade, played a critical role in this transition. At least at Princeton in the early twentieth century, liberal Protestantism was still very much a "lived" religion.

## CONTROVERSY AT PRINCETON

By the second decade of the twentieth century, however, Miller and his liberal Protestant theology had become a *casus belli* in Princeton. In the eyes of the *Presbyterian*, a religious weekly published in Philadelphia (a stronghold of Princeton alumni and conservative Old School Presbyterians), "Professor Miller is one of the brood produced by Union Seminary who have been permitted to stealthily creep into the church and Christian institutions, and in the name of 'advanced views' introduce their detestable and vicious teachings."[14]

The new aggressiveness that both Miller and the fundamentalists exhibited was a result of the growing sense that America in the 1910s was in the midst of a cultural crisis. The outbreak of war in Europe among the world's most "civilized" nations precipitated this widespread fear

13. Lucius H. Miller, "Modern Views of the Bible and of Religion," *South Atlantic Quarterly* 7 (1908), 311, 309; P. R. Colwell, ed., *Duocennial record of the Class of Eighteen Hundred and Ninety-Seven Princeton University* (Princeton: Princeton University Press, 1907), 138–39.

14. "The Devil in Cap and Gown," *Presbyterian,* 9 Sept. 1914, 5; *New York Times,* 30 Aug. 1914, 15.

that Victorian culture was breaking down.[15] While fear over allegedly degenerative trends in education and American culture at large neared hysteria in the second decade of the twentieth century, during the war years conservative Princetonians became steadily more alarmed at the liberal direction of Princeton's program of religious education. Once convinced that one of America's leading universities, like the nation itself, was teetering on the verge of chaos and that theological liberalism was the source of this peril, fundamentalists attacked Miller and the university ferociously. According to one fundamentalist, the theological liberalism espoused by Miller was "the real cause of the European war" and suggested that "bad instruction in American universities will end in some similar break-out in our own land."[16]

## COMPETING REVIVALS AND CONFLICTING COALITIONS

While the war raged in Europe, rival pieties battled for supremacy in Princeton. This conflict was set in bold relief when conservatives and liberals conducted competing religious revival services in early 1915. As the end of the age of innocence drew to a close, the evangelist Billy Sunday had the message that conservative Presbyterians wanted Princeton students to hear. Princeton Seminary Professor of Practical Theology Charles R. Erdman, a graduate of the college, asked President Hibben for permission to hold an evangelistic service at his alma mater. Despite a student petition, Hibben refused Erdman's request, explaining that "the university authorities feel that the place to hear him is a religious edifice rather than a college building" and thus, they would "withhold their official auspices." Undaunted, the seminary faculty voted unanimously to sponsor the evangelist themselves and made arrangements to hold services at the First (now Nassau) Presbyterian Church, located conveniently adjacent to the campus.[17] The cooperation of the populist fundamentalist Billy Sun-

15. Henry F. May, *The End of American Innocence: A Study of the First Years of Our Own Time, 1912–1917* (1959; repr., Chicago: Quadrangle, 1964), ix; George M. Marsden, *Fundamentalism and American Culture: The Shaping of Twentieth-Century Evangelicalism, 1870–1925* (New York: Oxford University Press, 1980), 153–64.

16. "Religious Instruction at Princeton," *Presbyterian*, 14 Oct. 1914, 4.

17. "Princeton Students Will Study Billy Sunday Here," n.p., n.d.; *Philadelphia Inquirer*, 3 Jan. 1915, 1; "Billy Sunday and His Work as Viewed by the People," *North American* [Philadelphia], 7 Feb. 1915, n.p., The Papers of William and Helen Sunday, Microfilm Edition, Scrapbook 6, Box 18, Reel 22, Collection 61, Archives of the Billy

day and scholarly Old School Presbyterian theologians at the seminary demonstrates the fact that before the end of the World War, populist fundamentalists and scholarly denominational conservatives were eager to cooperate in efforts to thwart the spread of modernism.

Billy Sunday arrived in Princeton in March 1915 with an entourage of more than twenty-five reporters to document his reception in the Ivy League town. An estimated 850 to 1000 undergraduates (out of a total of 1455) squeezed into the church to hear Sunday preach his well-known sermon "Dr. Jekyll and Mr. Hyde." Unlike D. L. Moody in 1876, Sunday cast his evangelistic message in negative terms. All, he argued, were Mr. Hydes who suppressed their Dr. Jekylls because of the love of sin. "You may not like the doctrine of an original sin," he asserted, "but unless you are a moral idiot you can't deny the fact that there is an inborn tendency on the part of men to sin—I don't give a rap who you are." While Sunday's crude slang did not disappoint his critics, his blatant Arminianism may have annoyed the Calvinistic sensibilities of his hosts. Despite human wickedness, the evangelist counseled, "You've got the power to decide whether you will go to heaven or hell." Afterwards, some reporters declared the revival a grand success while others observed that students regarded him as "more interesting than a travelling medicine show."[18]

One week after Sunday visited, President Hibben and the Philadelphian Society inaugurated the university's Religious Emphasis Week. Hibben clearly did not want Sunday to upstage his efforts to arouse religious beliefs in the university students. Albert Parker Fitch, like Sunday, aimed his message at that class of students who, as an editorial in the Daily Princetonian suggested, had "no religious beliefs" or "many grave doubts."[19] Faith, Fitch explained, cannot be "imposed upon us from without by churches or creeds or ministers or parents." In response to the challenges of Darwinism, higher criticism, scientific positivism, and historicism,

Graham Center, Wheaton College; "Theological Seminary Invites Evangelist Sunday," *Princeton Press*, 27 Feb. 1915, 1–2; Kemeny, *Princeton in the Nation's Service*, 188.

18. Samuel H. Hays to W. M. McPheeters, 4 Apr. 1915, W. M. McPheeters Papers, Archives, John Bulow Campbell Library, Columbia Theological Seminary; H. W. Myers, Jr., "Billy Sunday at Princeton," *Continent*, 18 Mar. 1915, n.p., Sunday Papers, Scrapbook 6, Box 18, Reel 22, Collection 61; "Mr. Sunday's Princeton Visit," *Princeton Press*, 13 Mar. 1915, 1; "Sermon of the Rev. Wm. A. Sunday, 'Dr. Jekyll and Mr. Hyde,'" 4, 8, 17–18, Sunday Papers, Box 8, Reel 11, Collection 61 (the quotes are from a stenograph copy of a sermon that Sunday preached in his New York City campaign in May 1917).

19. "Dr. Fitch Will Discuss Problems of Religion," *Daily Princetonian*, 2 Mar. 1915, 1; Editorial, "Dr. Fitch's Meetings," *Daily Princetonian*, 2 Mar. 1915, 2.

more thoughtful fundamentalists, such as those at the seminary, redoubled their commitment to orthodox Protestantism and the Scottish philosophy that supported it. Other Protestants, like Fitch and Professor Miller, took another path. They found in the philosophical tradition of Kant and German idealism, and in the theological work of Friedrich Schleiermacher as refined by Albrecht Ritschl, a new foundation for constructing a religious system impervious to the criticisms of scientific naturalism. Religion, Fitch argued, was "the sense" that "the significance and power of the universe" are hidden within "its visible and temporal expressions." According to Fitch, the authority of this religion rests not on the supernatural revelation of the Bible but on this "veritable and undeniable" experience.[20]

Hibben's refusal to welcome Sunday to campus and his decision to invite Fitch scandalized conservatives within the university's community of support. The *Presbyterian* lamented the fact that the university kept Billy Sunday, a Presbyterian minister, off campus but planned to host a liberal like Fitch who "shred[s] the Bible to pieces."[21] The once-respected conservatives now found their views politely ridiculed in the university. Like their nineteenth-century predecessors, they assumed that the truths of nature and the Bible were fixed and immutable. The university, they believed, should uphold truth, not promote falsehoods that contradicted their common-sense reading of the Bible. One of the most astute critiques of Fitch's lectures came in an anonymously published review penned by the university trustee and seminary professor John DeWitt. Because Fitch blurred the fundamental distinction between nature and grace, DeWitt complained, he "lands in all . . . grievous errors." According to DeWitt, Fitch denied the fundamentals of the faith because he had reconstructed the faith on an erroneous philosophical foundation.[22] The difference between their theology and Fitch's theology, according to critics like DeWitt, was simply the difference between Christianity and liberalism.

Critics of fundamentalism in the university community were not slow in responding to the conservative Presbyterians' attacks upon the university. Dean West, the son of a controversial Presbyterian minister who was a leader in the late nineteenth-century premillenarian movement—an important precursor to and component of the early twentieth-century

20. Albert Parker Fitch, *Religion and the Undergraduate: Four Addresses Delivered at Princeton University, March 1915*, with an introduction by John G. Hibben (Princeton: Princeton University Press, 1915), 6–7, 8, 12.

21. "The Princeton Spectacle," *Presbyterian*, 18 Feb. 1915, 4.

22. "Dr. Fitch's Teachings at Princeton," *Presbyterian*, 29 Apr. 1915, 3; [John De-Witt], "Baal's Priests in Alexander Hall," *Presbyterian*, 25 Mar. 1915, 7.

fundamentalism—was the first to answer fundamentalists in the town paper with a list of some vulgar quotes from Sunday. Such "shameless statements" made "in the name of Christ," West concluded, "ought not to be favored here." Both before and during the controversy, fundamentalists readily agreed that Sunday "is odd, eccentric, volatile, and conforms to none of the common 'Rules for Preachers.'" But, they maintained, he was effective because he spoke the language of the "common people."[23]

To be sure, Sunday's sacrilegious language made him a Philistine among the respectable Protestant elites of the university. When Moody preached in Princeton in 1876, the college was almost exclusively Protestant in religious composition. In the subsequent forty years, Princeton remained religiously homogeneous.[24] Over the same period, however, Princeton became more socially exclusive. One indicator of this development is the growth of the eating clubs, and another is the dramatic rise in the number of students who had attended private schools. In the Class of 1876, for example, approximately six percent of the students came from boarding schools. By 1909, seventy-eight percent of the student body had attended one of the elite secondary schools, such as Andover, Exeter, or Lawrenceville.[25] Princeton fundamentalists, who tolerated the evangelist's crass language because of his evangelistic success, charged West with

23. Andrew F. West, "Mr. Sunday's Utterances," *Princeton Press*, 27 Feb. 1915, 2; "Billy Sunday," *Presbyterian*, 23 Dec. 1914, 11.

24. Although not an exact indicator of religious composition because it excludes students who did not graduate, the *Nassau Herald* provides useful survey information on religious composition. Of the 118 students in the class of 1876 who identified their religious affiliation in the senior yearbook, 72 percent were Presbyterian, 12 percent Episcopalian, 5 percent Baptist, 5 percent Methodist, 2 percent Dutch Reformed, and the remaining 4 percent Congregationalist, Lutheran, Christian, or Brethren in Christ. Only one student gave "none" as a response. *Nassau Herald, 1876*. In the class of 1915, 80 percent of the students were church members, including 37 percent Presbyterian, 22 percent Episcopalian, 5 percent Methodist, and 3 percent Catholic. *Nassau Herald, 1915*.

25. By comparison, only 65 percent of Yale students, 47 percent of Harvard students, and 9 percent of Michigan students had the advantage of such an education. The 1876 estimate is based on a survey of the alumni files of each member of the class of 1876. Kemeny, *Princeton in the Nation's Service*, 165; *Fourth Annual Report of the Carnegie Foundation for the Advancement of Teaching . . . October, 1909* (New York 1910), 148, as cited in James McLachlan, *American Boarding Schools: A Historical Study* (New York: Scribner, 1970), 206. On the social and ethnic milieu of early twentieth-century Princeton, see Marcia Graham Synnott, *The Half-Opened Door: Discrimination and Admissions at Harvard, Yale, and Princeton, 1900–1970* (Westport, CT: Greenwood, 1979), 160–98; Leslie, *Gentlemen and Scholars*, 117–25, 189–209.

"snobbery."[26] West's explanation not only suggested that the dean had repudiated the uncouth pietism of his youth but also reflected the growing perception that fundamentalism conflicted with values of "liberal culture." To those outside the conservative camp, Sunday was not merely a militant version of the irenic D. L. Moody, as the fundamentalists saw him, but an uncultured parody of him. The cultural elitists dominating Princeton had left behind the evangelicalism of their predecessors.

Others in the Princeton community defended the decision to ban Sunday by drawing upon the university's religious mission. These were liberal Protestants who opposed Sunday because the fundamentalists' theology conflicted with the university's religious mission. The university, the editors of the *Princeton Alumni Weekly* warned, "must be careful to respect the faith of all faiths and creeds, and as students and investigators, however closely allied we personally may be to any one sect or doctrine, leave a free field to all, lest in the words of the poet, one good custom should corrupt the world." Since a "university's business is with truth only," Princeton could not propagate religious views that would meet the approval of the "*sectarians*." Hibben, who was the son of an Old School Presbyterian minister as well as a graduate of Princeton Seminary and a Presbyterian minister, also responded to the fundamentalists' attacks. Contrary to the charge of the fundamentalists, he insisted that Princeton had not given up on its religious mission. "I wish it to be clearly understood that I, both as a minister of the Presbyterian Church and as President of Princeton University stand ready to defend" Fitch's lectures as "essential elements of Christian belief."[27] For Hibben, Fitch's message met the criteria for the kind of religion a public, nonsectarian institution should advocate. But fundamentalism—be it the anti-intellectual version espoused by the populist Sunday or the scholarly orthodoxy favored by the seminary faculty—conflicted with Princeton's civic mission.

---

26. Editorial Comment, *Presbyterian*, 15 Apr. 1915, 10; "The Sunday Meetings in Philadelphia," *Presbyterian*, 11 Feb. 1915, 18; "Why the Exclusion Was Unwise," *Presbyterian Banner*, 15 Apr. 1915, 7; "Princeton and Mr. Sunday," *Herald and Presbyter*, 14 Apr. 1915, 4; "Dean West's Defense of Princeton," *Presbyterian Banner*, 15 Apr. 1915, 6; "Yet the Defense Fails to Convince," *Presbyterian Banner*, 15 Apr. 1915, 6–7; "Dean West's Denial," *Presbyterian Banner*, 29 Apr. 1915, 7.

27. Editorial, *Princeton Alumni Weekly*, 24 Feb. 1915, 475; John G. Hibben, letter to the editor, *Presbyterian*, 22 Apr. 1915, 11.

## MILLER AND THE ONGOING CONTROVERSY
## BETWEEN RIVAL PIETIES

The conflict between the rival pieties soon became intertwined with questions of academic freedom. The resolution of this conflict not only helped liberal Protestantism secure its place as the established religion of the university but also left fundamentalists as outsiders to the university. In the first decade of the twentieth century, conservative Presbyterians were still important to the university, and early in his career Miller went out of his way to avoid antagonizing them. Before he published his article on modern views of the Bible, for example, he got Wilson's approval lest he arouse the wrath of conservatives. Wilson appreciated Miller's loyalty and assured him that he "did not see how any reasonable person could object to the article." But by the mid-1910s, fundamentalists were appalled to learn that their views no longer had a home in the university. While Princeton was "not required to become sectarian," the *Presbyterian* insisted, to be "true to her history and traditions . . . she ought not to supplant the teachings of such men as McCosh . . . and Patton with bald Unitarianism."[28] Miller, not surprisingly, feared that conservative Presbyterians in the university's larger community of support would get him fired. One leading modernist, Shailer Mathews of the University of Chicago, tried to bolster a nervous Miller by telling him that he could not "imagine how the University should be in any way exercised over the matter." "If liberty of teaching means anything," he added, "it certainly means such temperate writing as your articles."[29]

As criticisms of Miller mounted in the fall of 1914, the trustees created an informal committee to find a way to end the conflict. On one side stood fundamentalist Presbyterians on the Board of Trustees and in the university's larger community. On the other were liberal Protestants on the faculty and in the administration with more secular-minded scholars on the faculty. The recent furor over academic freedom at Lafayette College between two Princeton graduates probably gave the committee plenty to consider. In the spring of 1913, the president of Lafayette College, Ethelbert Warfield, had forced a philosophy professor, John Mecklin, to resign because of his alleged unorthodoxy. The events at Lafayette helped precipitate the creation of the American Association of University Professors in January 1915. In fact, three Princeton University professors,

28. Wilson quoted in Kemeny, *Princeton in the Nation's Service*, 154; "Prof. Lucius Miller Denies Christian Resurrection," *Presbyterian*, 25 Feb. 1915, 6.

29. Mathews quoted in Kemeny, *Princeton in the Nation's Service*, 177.

Edward Capps, Edward M. Kemmerer, and Howard C. Warren, joined Johns Hopkins University Professor Arthur O. Lovejoy on its organizational committee.[30]

The fundamentalist threat to Miller's academic freedom helped to create a liberal Protestant and cultural modernist alliance. Professor Howard C. Warren, who had just helped write the AAUP policy on academic freedom, wanted to guard the advancements achieved in the university's public mission during Wilson's presidency against fundamentalist attacks. Like many professors in the early twentieth century, Warren had become a cultural modernist during his academic career. Raised in a conservative Episcopalian home, Warren had become a thoroughgoing agnostic. In 1915, he led the effort to persuade Princeton's trustees to adopt the AAUP's policy on academic freedom.[31] Ironically, while fundamentalists loathed the implications of academic freedom, they unwittingly aided Warren in achieving his goal.

Just days after the creation of the AAUP, Princeton's trustees met to hear from the informal committee created to resolve their dilemma. The first option was to "remove Miller" by abolishing all Bible courses in the curriculum. Trustee DeWitt favored this option. "I think," as he later repeated in a letter to President Hibben, "that the sooner the university abolishes" all Bible courses "and confines itself to teaching courses in the Humanities, Philosophy, and Sciences, the sooner it will relieve itself of the difficulties and criticisms for which Mr. Miller's conduct is largely responsible."[32] Some conservative critics had also called for voluntary chapel because they did not want their sons subjected to the "infidelity" of liberalism. Some were even threatening to boycott the university.[33] Despite DeWitt's effort, the board rejected his recommendation to eliminate Bible courses just as they had rebuffed the pleas of certain fundamentalists to eliminate mandatory chapel services.

The second option open to the trustees, the committee reported, was simply to fire Miller. This move, the committee believed, "would at once

30. Kemeny, *Princeton in the Nation's Service*, 181–82; "Chapel Undiscussed in Fall Trustee Meeting," *Daily Princetonian*, 23 Oct. 1914, 1. On the Lafayette Controversy and the founding of the AAUP, see Marsden, *Soul of the American University*, 296–316.

31. Howard C. Warren, "Howard C. Warren," in *History of Psychology in Autobiography*, ed. Carl Hurchison (Worcester, MA: Clark University Press, 1930), 456; Howard C. Warren, "Academic Freedom," *Atlantic Monthly*, Nov. 1914, 689–99.

32. DeWitt quoted in Kemeny, *Princeton in the Nation's Service*, 182–83; "Professor Lucius H. Miller's Book," *Presbyterian*, 28 Jan. 1915, 7.

33. Editorial, *Presbyterian of the South*, 8 Dec. 1915, 1.

49

precipitate a violent and protracted discussion as to the privileges of academic freedom." Because the university's primary purpose was to serve national educational interests, and since academic freedom had become a defining characteristic of such public institutions, terminating Miller was simply unthinkable because it would have represented catering to what had come to be seen as a sectarian agenda representing the interest of just one faction within the university community. Consequently, the majority of liberals among the faculty and trustees along with the more secular-minded faculty took a third path, preferring academic freedom over the institution's past commitment to evangelical Protestantism.[34]

Predictably, the decision outraged fundamentalists but pleased many professors, especially the cultural modernists on the faculty.[35] The policy of academic freedom guaranteed that Protestantism, evangelical or liberal, would no longer provide a unifying center for undergraduate education at Princeton, and so long as professors abided by professional standards in meeting their academic responsibilities, the faculty had the freedom to subvert, or for that matter to champion, Protestant values.

Although they had been unable to force Miller's dismissal or revert to a time when evangelicalism dominated the institution, fundamentalists had successfully created a climate so antagonistic that Miller, as he wrote Woodrow Wilson, found teaching "intolerable." He resigned in the spring of 1917. Because he left voluntarily, his departure did not technically involve a direct violation of the university's policy of academic freedom. The faculty, however, saw the strong arm of fundamentalism giving Miller a firm shove toward the door. The faculty sent a letter to the trustees, signed by fifty-five of the university's sixty-eight full professors, protesting Miller's resignation.[36]

Yet Miller's departure proved to be a pyrrhic victory for the fundamentalists. Not only had academic freedom been established within the university but the faculty became vigilant to guard Princeton from the undue influence of fundamentalists. While many historical studies note that fundamentalism lost its influence within the elite centers of American culture, the Miller controversy reveals exactly how and why fundamentalists were quickly becoming outsiders to the modern university. Conservatives now found themselves strangers in their own culture.

34. Trustees Minutes quoted in Kemeny, *Princeton in the Nation's Service,* 182.

35. "Professor Lucius H. Miller's Book," 7; Warren quoted in Kemeny, *Princeton in the Nation's Service,* 184.

36. Miller quoted in Kemeny, *Princeton in the Nation's Service,* 192.

In the letter protesting Miller's resignation, the faculty asked the trustees to find a way to retain him or to replace him with someone else with his "scientific attainment and sympathy with the modern methods of investigation that prevail in Princeton University."[37] To the scholars inside the university, fundamentalists threatened the most basic values of a university—reason and science—and challenged the professional expertise of the faculty. Fundamentalist criticisms of Miller not only furthered their intellectual marginalization in Princeton but also led to a reduction of their presence in positions of power within the university. When conservative trustees like DeWitt retired, Hibben and the board replaced them with others who more fully shared their new vision of Princeton. Presbyterian fundamentalists came to be seen as strangers to the educational mission of the university. Although they may have still represented a sizeable minority, if not a majority, in the larger Princeton community of support, they were a cognitive minority inside the university. Unable to win their way in the affairs of the university, fundamentalists eventually withdrew from the community.

## LIBERAL PROTESTANT HEGEMONY IN THE MODERN UNIVERSITY

After the United States entered the war in Europe in the spring of 1917, the administration was too busy helping to make the world safe for democracy to find a replacement for Miller. But with the establishment of a policy of academic freedom, the declining influence of fundamentalists, and preoccupations with the war effort, the administration had time to develop a new rationale for the inclusion of religious instruction in the undergraduate curriculum. In the nineteenth century, Bible and apologetics courses were intended to proselytize students in the evangelical faith. In the 1920s, Princeton, like many other institutions, was slowly coming to the position that the Bible had its legitimate place within a liberal arts education if it was studied as literature or history.[38] The university also opened a magnificent chapel and hired a full-time chaplain.

37. Letter to the Curriculum Committee of the Board of Trustees quoted in Kemeny, *Princeton in the Nation's Service*, 193.

38. Charles Foster Kent, "Order and Content of Biblical Courses in College Curriculum," *Religious Education* 7 (1912) 42–49; Charles Foster Kent, "The Bible and the College Curriculum," *Religious Education* 8 (1913) 453–58.

A trustees' curriculum committee report in 1924 expressed the new educational rationale for the inclusion of the study of religion. These courses involved "the *presentation* of Christianity" as "a basic element in the education," "not as a religious *propaganda*," which is "not the function of an educational institution." The "failure to draw this line of demarcation," the report added, had left many students "largely ignorant of Christianity" and "indifferent to religion." This new rationale for the academic study of religion, it was hoped, would indirectly "remove" students' "indifference to religion."[39] Although the religion courses added to the curriculum in the mid-1920s still had a decidedly Protestant orientation and the unambiguous, if subordinate, goal to cultivate the Protestant faith of students, they did not constitute—at least to Hibben, the trustees, and faculty—a return to the dogmatic Christian education of the previous generation. Because the university's leadership still hoped that the academic study of religion would nurture faith, they saw themselves as conserving the traditional Protestant mission of the university. Religion at Princeton, as President Hibben put it, would help teach students to be "benefactors of mankind" and contributors to the "coming of the Kingdom of God upon earth."[40]

## CONCLUSION

This brief review of some of the activities and interests at Princeton in the late nineteenth and early twentieth centuries suggests that the relationship between religion and modern higher education in the early twentieth century was more complex than has been previously assumed. Although evangelicalism no longer provided the unifying center to collegiate education and many conventional religious convictions and customs vanished, traditional Protestant interests reappeared in new ways and in other places on campus. While liberal Protestants at Princeton had begun the modernization process on their own initiative, fundamentalists in some ways unwittingly hastened the adaptation of the historic religious mission of collegiate education to the educational and intellectual values of the modern university. In retrospect, liberal Protestant theology's détente with secularism proved to be short-lived. But for liberal Protestants at

39. Trustees Minutes, quoted in Kemeny, *Princeton in the Nation's Service*, 193; "President Hibben's Alumni Day Address," *Princeton Alumni Weekly*, 23 Feb. 1923, 430.

40. Galen M. Fisher, ed., *Religion in the Colleges* (New York: Association Press, 1928), 5.

Princeton in the early twentieth century, the adjustment of orthodox theology to modernity gave a spiritual power to their piety. The living out of liberal Protestant beliefs, moreover, in a variety of conventional religious practices, such as the Bible classes, the chapel program, and the campus YMCA, provided continuity with Princeton's traditional religious mission. It may have also made the transition from an evangelical to a secular institution a slow but not necessarily easy one. While liberal Protestant religious and cultural hegemony started to fall prey to secular liberalism beginning in the 1920s, the controversies at Princeton also demonstrate how liberal Protestants preserved hegemony over one significant social institution. Since mainline Protestants continued to believe that Christianity was critical to the public good, they could tolerate a certain degree of religious diversity, but the need for social order and stability required cultural uniformity. The criticisms of certain fundamentalists jeopardized the religious unity of the university and ultimately threatened its religious mission. With the aid of cultural modernists, the liberal Protestant administration successfully checked fundamentalist dissent within the university. In the subsequent generation, new pressures—namely cultural pluralism and, more importantly, secularism—would make liberal Protestantism as passé and parochial as fundamentalism appeared in the early twentieth century and would produce another reevaluation of the role of religion in the university. But for Hibben and many in his generation, the university had found a way to avoid the sectarianism of fundamentalism while at the same time attempting to mold the Protestant character of the student body and thereby shape the national culture.

# 4

# Christianity and Higher Education

*Why Exclusion Is a Compliment*

## D. G. Hart

MOST CONTEMPORARY CHRISTIANS WHO are serious about their faith agree that the university—a catchword for all of American higher education—needs religion and is unnecessarily hostile to faith. Arguably, the most forceful and sustained argument among the recent debates about God and the university is George Marsden's highly acclaimed 1994 book, *The Soul of the American University: From Protestant Establishment to Established Nonbelief.* His story of religion in American higher education attempts to show how the university, which once thrived upon the religious zeal of liberal Protestants in establishing research and academic specialization as ideals, banished religion from its educational and social mission. "While American universities today allow individuals free exercise of religion in parts of their lives that do not touch the heart of the university," Marsden reasoned, "they tend to exclude or discriminate against relating explicit religious perspectives to intellectual life."[1] Marsden added that the

1. George M. Marsden, *The Soul of the American University: From Protestant Establishment to Established Nonbelief* (New York: Oxford University Press, 1994), 6.

university's commitment to pluralism was incredibly inconsistent regai∟ ing religion. To be sure, he was not advocating Bible studies or campus-wide prayer meetings. Marsden insisted that expressions of religion on campus needed to "pass muster academically." Still, "there is no reason why it should be a rule that *no* religious viewpoint shall receive serious consideration."[2]

Not everyone was persuaded by Marsden's argument—his history was fine, but his analysis of the relationship between the university and belief was less so. Among secularists, for instance, David Hollinger has argued that "universities should not surrender back to Christianity the ground they have won for a more independent, cosmopolitan life of the mind." He agrees with Christian critics of modern higher education that plenty of things are wrong with colleges and universities. But "a deficiency of Christianity is not one of them." Hollinger's reason is epistemological. Modern universities operate according to epistemic rules that are better than faith for understanding truth about the world. "In that bygone era," he writes, "the boundaries of the epistemic community and the boundaries of the community of faith were largely coterminous." This is no longer so, and it is a good thing. In fact, for Hollinger the issue raised most forcefully by critiques of the secular university is not "whether learned communities should be tolerant or intolerant, pluralistic or nonpluralistic, flexible or inflexible." The issue is "the specific direction the always ongoing revision of the epistemic rules of these communities should take." Hollinger's point is that the university once tried to operate according to the rules of faith, inspiration, and divine revelation. Those rules no longer make sense of contemporary advanced learning.[3]

Lost in this academic version of Miller Lite commercials—more faith, less intolerance—is the question of how including faith within the university actually affects belief itself. For most of religion's advocates, the task of instilling more religion into the university is a win–win; religion itself, and Christianity specifically, is a cultural good that has heaped untold benefits upon Western civilization and liberal democracy. Consequently, putting more religion into a religiously deprived environment could only be an improvement. According to Warren A. Nord, the director of the humanities program at the University of North Carolina and the author

2. Ibid., 429–44, quotation on 431.

3. David A. Hollinger, "Enough Already: Universities Do Not Need More Christianity," in *Religion, Scholarship & Higher Education: Perspectives, Models, and Future Prospects*, ed. Andrea Sterk (Notre Dame: University of Notre Dame Press, 2002), 49, 43.

of another important book on religion and American education, because of the "massive importance of religion," because public institutions must be open to "the full range of ideas in our marketplace of ideas," because the Constitution requires neutrality "between religion and nonreligion," and because "the truth has become elusive even for intellectuals," religion "must be taken seriously in public schools and universities." Specifically, the curriculum must equip students to understand "religion from the 'inside'" and allow religious ideas to contend with secular outlooks.[4]

The reality that contemporary religion itself is not without difficulties—from the crisis within the Anglican Communion to the evaporation of church members in the Christian West, and that it hardly has the resources to fix itself, let alone the six-hundred-pound gorilla of American higher education—never receives much attention from the advocates of a religion-friendly university. But even if no one has actually considered the effects of advanced learning on religion itself, the subject deserves consideration. The reason is that the record of religion's performance throughout the past four centuries in public spaces, whether in government or the university, has not been stellar. Invariably, the requirements of civility and tolerance in public settings force religion to become something either unrecognizable as real religion or turn it into something that generates more critics of secularization (i.e., faith turns liberal).

What follows is an exploration of the negative consequences of including religion in the university. As much as religion's advocates can recount the history of higher education's secularization to make their case for faith's positive influence on, say, the colonial or denominational colleges of the past, few pay attention to the one specific instance where Protestants proposed religion as the cure for secular higher education. What this particular episode from twentieth-century American academic life reveals are a couple of lessons that those who advocate a greater religious presence should spend more time pondering. The first concerns the nature of religious discourse or faith that the university permits. The faith of higher education, even when conducted with the best of intentions and the smartest proponents, is too exclusive for the religiously mixed and epistemically diverse environment of the university. The second lesson has to do with higher education itself and why it tolerates one kind of religion but excludes others. Universities tend to favor faiths that are liberal and

4. Warren A. Nord, *Religion and American Education: Rethinking a National Dilemma* (Chapel Hill: University of North Carolina Press, 1995), 2, 5, 378–79.

hence unsatisfying to those believers most alarmed by secularization. The point of these reflections is to suggest that the university's intolerance of serious and devout faith is a blessing, not in disguise, but in reality.

## WHEN THE UNIVERSITY GOT RELIGION

Faith-based learning advocates seldom remember that American higher education was never a hospitable environment to theology per se. In fact, the formal study of Scripture or Protestant divinity had never been as central to liberal education or to the institutions that offered such a course of study as the critics of the secular university assume.[5] For the British Protestants who founded the colleges of Harvard, William and Mary, Yale, and Princeton, formal instruction in the Christian religion—that is, the study of Scripture and theology—was almost exclusively reserved for students training for the Christian ministry. Theological education as such was not part of British university instruction. Posts in explicitly religious subjects were not established in British higher education until the nineteenth century. Of course, prospective ministers needed to have university training, but their education there was primarily literary—a familiarity with ancient languages, texts, and authors. For theological training students supplemented undergraduate studies with an apprenticeship under the oversight of a settled minister. Only in this informal setting would future pastors become acquainted with church teaching, biblical interpretation, ecclesiastical polity, and pastoral experience. This was the pattern for seventeenth-century English-speaking Protestants on both sides of the Atlantic.

The absence of theology in liberal arts education persisted into the nineteenth century even as the denominational college emerged as the established means for transmitting Western civilization and Christian culture to adolescent American males. The ethos of these schools was explicitly religious. But Greek, Latin, and knowledge of the ancient world dominated the curriculum and held the key to unlocking the gates of wisdom and virtue. In their senior year students were required to take a course in moral philosophy with the college president, who was invariably

5. On the place of religion in college education before the advent of the research university, see Michael F. Perko, "Religion and Collegiate Education," in *Encyclopedia of the American Religious Experience*, ed. Charles H. Lippy and Peter W. Williams, 3 vols. (New York: Scribner, 1988), 3:1611–25; and Bruce Kuklick, *Churchmen and Philosophers: From Jonathan Edwards to John Dewey* (New Haven: Yale University Press, 1985).

a minister in the college's sponsoring denomination. Still, this course did less to communicate Scripture and Christian doctrine than it did to defend Christianity from attacks by skeptics and acquaint students with the demands of Christian morality. Consequently, nineteenth-century Protestant students who wanted to study theology formally needed to go to seminary, a new academic institution begun as early as 1808 with the founding of Andover Seminary in Massachusetts. The seminary formalized the education that prospective ministers had received as apprentices to established clergy but was still separate from the liberal arts college. Andover was a stand-alone institution, Princeton Seminary was located in Princeton but had—and still has—no formal tie to Princeton University. Harvard and Yale would counter with divinity schools, but these were professional or vocational institutions again separate from the core undergraduate program in the liberal arts.

If American undergraduate education was intentionally Christian during the colonial and antebellum eras, it appeared to diverge considerably with the advent of the research university, a development that significantly altered American learning during the decades after the Civil War.[6] This so-called revolution in higher education was responsible, according to the secularization-of-higher-education thesis, for dissolving the Christian roots and character of America's colleges. It established the scientific method as the chief means of knowing. Still, because the study of Scripture and theology took place outside the college and the university, the revolution inaugurated by the research university did not unseat theology as the queen of the sciences. For the entirety of America's history, theology was a means toward the end of being a minister, not an academic discipline in its own right. After all, the chief branches of the university were the humanities and the social and natural sciences. Theologians studied divinity, a subject distinct from either literature or nature and society.

What was revolutionary, though, about the research university was its sacrifice of curricular integration and personal formation for academic specialization. The trail-blazing institutions of the research university, for instance, Cornell, Johns Hopkins, and Stanford, were sponsored by big business rather than the churches. This made it easier for the new universities to abandon the rules for hiring and recruiting that had helped to

6. Two different perspectives on the so-called revolution in American higher education come from Laurence Veysey, *The Emergence of the American University* (Chicago: University of Chicago Press, 1965); and James Tunstead Burtchaell, *The Dying of the Light: The Disengagement of Colleges and Universities from Their Christian Churches* (Grand Rapids: Eerdmans, 1998).

perpetuate a school's Christian identity. At the same time, the curriculum of the university expanded to include new areas of study, such as the natural sciences and the social sciences. For instance, the old denominational college course in moral philosophy taught by the college president now required a host of new professors to cover the range of subjects involved—namely, philosophy, sociology, history, anthropology, and ethics. Indeed, one of the most significant changes in American higher education caused by the research university was the professionalization of knowledge. Unlike an earlier era when the learned gentleman (most often a minister) could teach a variety of subjects in the undergraduate curriculum, in the research university (and in the colleges that sought to emulate them), scholars specialized in a narrow field of study as experts.

These changes make plausible the contention that American universities secularized after 1870. Christianity had been the orientation that gave collegiate studies coherence as a system of knowledge and morality. To be sure, academic theology was not responsible for this integration and coherence. Instead, it was a conviction that all truth added up to God's truth, no matter how general or insubstantial those truths might be. Even so, by unleashing the quest for detailed and specialized knowledge, the research university destroyed the older liberal arts and Christian ideal of integration. And the older ideal of curricular coherence was not simply across different subjects; it also involved the integration of knowledge and character.[7]

Protestant leaders took a while to respond to the new academic environment, but when they did the banner under which they marched was integration.[8] By the 1930s specifically, the sheen on science and its accomplishments had begun to fade thanks to world war and economic failure. Various leaders in the American academy along with Protestant scholars began to criticize the university's myopic concentration on material and technical problems without considering questions of meaning and value. The crisis of another world war that pitted the forces of liberal democracy against those of tyranny, followed by the Cold War's duplication of those same foes, reinforced a growing sense among educators that the secular direction of the university had been a mistake and needed correction. A major part of this solution came in the form of more attention to the

7. Marsden's account of these changes in *The Soul of the American University* is well worth reading.

8. The following paragraphs are adapted from D. G. Hart, "Christian Scholars, Secular Universities, and the Problem with the Antithesis," *Christian Scholar's Review* 30 (2001) 383–402.

humanities, such as that proposed by Harvard University's *General Education for a Free Society* (1945) and the President's Commission on Higher Education's *Higher Education for American Democracy* (1947).

Mainline Protestant theologians responded in turn by arguing that theology was the necessary corrective to the university's scientific excesses. The most vigorous Protestant defense of theology in the university came from the unlikely place of Union Theological Seminary in New York City, an institution known more for its liberal theology than for defending Christian verities in the face of a hostile culture. As early as 1937 William Adams Brown, longtime professor of theology, was arguing for the inclusion of theology in the university in cadences that echoed his former fundamentalist foes. His book, *The Case for Theology in the University*, made arguments that foreshadowed contemporary critics of the secular university. Like so much of the twentieth-century literature on Christianity in American higher education, Brown's book made two main points, the first countering the secularist assumption that faith had no place in a world of learning dominated by reason, the second answering the question about what Christianity had to offer to the modern academy.

On the first score, Brown asserted that the separation between church and state in America's political order was no model for the relation between religion and education. But the lack of parallels between American government and education did not mean that Brown was comfortable with secularism in the former while hoping for a different relation in the latter. "The separation of church and state," he wrote, "so far from being designed by our fathers was not even anticipated by them." The founding fathers were "Christians" and "desired to be known as such." In fact, "the last thing they desired to do" was to form a "purely secular" state. The force of Brown's logic, then, was to claim for the university what the founding fathers intended for the United States. Universities in America, accordingly, were originally Christian but had turned secular thanks to the removal of theology to specialized schools of divinity and to academic specialization that made no room for theology's generalizations. Even so, "Harvard was established by Christian men for the purpose of providing an educated ministry."[9] The same could be said of Yale and any number of New England schools, which, by implication, were the backbone in Brown's view of American higher education. Secular education, accordingly, was a novelty in human history, and the presence of Christianity in America's earliest

9. William Adams Brown, *The Case for Theology in the University* (Chicago: University of Chicago Press, 1938), 24, 32.

colleges had not prevented them from becoming academic institutions of the first rank. In other words, Brown would have none of the idea that religion was out of place in the university.

After clearing the hurdle of academic secularism, Brown raced to show that Christianity offered precisely what American universities needed. Here he argued that the aspect of theology that appeared to be a weakness was actually its strength. Brown believed that many academics had dismissed theology because it could not compete with other disciplines at the level of specialized research. But specialization was actually responsible for the fragmentation of American learning. In fact, by removing Christianity as the unifying vision for the university, academic reformers had broken up "an educational system controlled by a single consistent philosophy" and pointed American higher education on the long road toward "what we may call the bargain-counter theory of education." Theology could reverse this trek by furnishing "the organizing principle" the university needed, and by making Christianity the "rational foundation for the ideal of freedom." And the way theology could accomplish this seemingly monumental undertaking was by providing a unified outlook for study:

> [Theology's] central thesis is that this is a meaningful world because it has God for its author, and God is essentially a rational being and has endowed man with reason, by which he can know him. It is, further, a moral world because God is essentially a moral being and has created man a moral being in order that he may serve him. Man, therefore, as made in God's image has essential dignity, and personality is not only the key to the meaning of the universe but the highest end it is designed to promote. This is the philosophy which alone can supply a religious basis for our democratic tradition, and it is this philosophy which in the past has supplied it as a matter of fact.[10]

The need for meaning and values in the university was also part of the argument from another Union Seminary theologian, Henry Van Dusen. At the forefront of the fundamentalist controversy in the northern Presbyterian Church because of his unwillingness to affirm the virgin birth of Christ, by 1951, Van Dusen had become a prominent spokesman for Protestantism as president of Union. This was also the year that Scribners published a series of lectures he had given at Rice University on religion and higher education. Fourteen years after Brown's case for theology in

10. Ibid., 13, 119, 112.

the university, the situation was even more dire, according to Van Dusen. *"The knowledge and skill of Modern Civilization,"* he declared on the first page, *"have outrun the moral and spiritual resources for their direction and control."* The only way out of this crisis was through theological renewal. To prove the point, Van Dusen quoted General Douglas MacArthur, not the typical authority on religion or culture, who said *"Our problem is basically theological."*[11] Of course, Van Dusen did not propose to solve all of Western civilization's woes, but only one aspect, namely, the place of God in higher education.

In a manner that would have pleased fundamentalists and anticipated the apologetics of conservative Protestants such as Francis Schaeffer, Van Dusen blamed the moral and spiritual crisis of American education on the philosophy of Descartes and Kant. Even though each thinker, Van Dusen conceded, had intended to defend religious truth, both ended up subverting the faith because each isolated the sacred from the secular. Religion, however, could not be locked away in a secure box. According to Van Dusen, "God . . . must be the Sovereign of *all* Reality. He must be so discerned. And He must be so confessed. Therefore the truth concerning Him . . . must be, *a fortiori*, the controlling principle of all knowledge."[12] From here the rest of Van Dusen's argument was downhill. American colleges and universities, he complained, had drifted from their Christian origins thanks to the expansion of the student body, the specialization of knowledge, and the secularization of the United States. Van Dusen even threw in a clarifying chapter on what the founding fathers intended about religion within the nation's polity. But the thrust of his position, once he had diagnosed the philosophical foundations of secularism, was to overcome the dualism that Descartes had sown and that Kant watered. And the way to do this, though the specifics might involve a few wrinkles, was to recover the assumption that "Truth is an organic unity," and that each segment of knowledge will not be properly understood unless it is seen in relation to "the Unity of Truth." Such a unified approach to learning could only proceed through "fidelity to the Sovereign which all learning acknowledges as liege Lord."[13]

Arguments like these persuaded university leaders to include religion as an academic discipline. Between 1945 and 1970, religious studies was

---

11. Henry P. Van Dusen, *God in Education: A Tract for the Times* (New York: Scribner, 1951), 17, 19, italics original.

12. Ibid., 38.

13. Ibid., 81–82, 84.

a growth industry in American higher education. Undergraduate enrollments, majors in religion, and doctorates awarded to professors responsible for teaching all of these religion courses increased significantly. What is more, the curriculum of religion departments was decidedly Protestant. Students majoring in religion received instruction in the Bible, ethics, church history, and a form of doctrinal teaching that combined the angst of existential philosophy with the *Anfechtungen* of Karl Barth. So respectable did religion become as a field of study that when Princeton University's Council of the Humanities teamed up with the Ford Foundation to give an overview of humanistic scholarship in American learning, the scholars responsible devoted two of the thirteen volumes to religion. One of these books, Clyde Holbrook's *Religion: A Humanistic Field* (1963) showed the close links between the study of Protestant divinity and the broader postwar effort to correct scientism with a search for meaning and values. The second volume in the Princeton Humanities series, *Religion* (1965), was a multi-author collection of essays on the different fields in religion edited by the Princeton University ethicist, Paul Ramsey. This book surveyed the subjects typically taught in religion departments, which coincidently mirrored the curriculum of Protestant seminaries minus courses in pastoral theology and ministerial training.[14]

And yet, for all of the resources bestowed in Protestant divinity, religious studies could not maintain its own coherence—let alone bring coherence to the entire range of subjects taught in the university. Signals of religious studies' own confusion came in the 1960s when the professional organization to which religion faculty belonged changed its name. Until 1964 this organization had been called the National Association of Biblical Instructors (NABI)—surely an antiquated name since religion involved more than Old and New Testament studies, but still plausible in a culture that honored a Protestant establishment. But in 1964 NABI changed its name to the American Academy of Religion (AAR). The new name signaled that the study of religion would no longer be absorbed with religious questions within the United States (*American* instead of *National*), that it would be professionally rigorous (*Academy* instead of *Instructors*), and that it would include faiths beyond Christianity (*Religion* instead of *Biblical*). To be sure, the implications of this change in name would take time to surface. But the emergence of the AAR did reveal that the one area of

14. On the emergence of religious studies as an academic discipline after World War II, see D. G. Hart, *The University Gets Religion: Religious Studies in American Higher Education* (Baltimore: Johns Hopkins University Press, 1999).

study that many Protestants believed would fix the university had itself fallen prey to the trends of academic specialization. Instead of trying to bring a larger and normative perspective to bear on the arts and sciences, religion scholars felt the need to prove themselves in the university by carving out their own specialized area of investigation.

Equally important for religion faculty to acquire stature in the university was their loss of a Protestant identity. The timing of the de-Protestantization of academic religion occurred not coincidently at the same cultural moment that Protestantism lost its hegemony within America's public schools. From roughly 1800 to 1965, American Protestants of English descent functioned as an informal religious and cultural establishment, the point of which assumed that American norms were synonymous with Protestant convictions. In sum, Protestantism of a fairly generic kind, with latitude to encompass both rank liberals and raving fundamentalists, was the nation's faith. In this sense, Protestantism was a public religion; other faiths, especially Roman Catholic and Jewish, needed to find institutions outside the glare of public funding and work with expectations that presumed non-Protestant religions were not serving a public or national purpose. Sydney Alhstrom put the reversal of American Protestant fortunes well when he wrote of the 1960s,

> [T]he exploration and settlement of those parts of the New World in which the United States took its rise were profoundly shaped by the Reformation and Puritan impulse, and . . . this impulse, through its successive transmutations, remained the dominant element in the ideology of most Protestant Americans. To that tradition, moreover, all other elements among the American people—Catholic, Orthodox, Lutheran, Jewish, infidel, red, yellow, and black—had in some way, negatively or positively, to relate themselves. Or at least they did so *until the 1960s*, when the age of the WASP, the age of the melting pot, drew to a close.[15]

The consequences for religious studies were enormous. All of a sudden, religious studies had its academic rationale pulled out from under its institutional feet. Protestant divinity, once regarded as the culmination of Western progress and the common religious idiom of the American people, now appeared to be elitist, exclusive, intolerant, and almost as sectarian as Roman Catholicism.

15. Sydney E. Ahlstrom, *A Religious History of the American People* (New Haven: Yale University Press, 1972), 1079, italics original.

Only in the 1960s did Americans, especially Protestants themselves, realize that Protestantism was not a public or universal faith, but that in fact national interests and even Western cultural achievements were distinct from Protestant Christianity. Supreme Court rulings that culminated in *Abington v. Schempp* provided one incentive for this discovery in the context of America's public education and its legal system. Changes within the teaching of religion at colleges and universities were less consequential and affected fewer Americans but still demonstrated what arguments first in school districts and then in Washington had shown, namely, that Protestantism was no less partisan than other religions. Certainly, Protestants believed their pedigree to be purer and their history more firmly established in the national record than other faiths. But no longer was it possible to think that Protestant prayers at public functions were appropriate. Nor was it possible to act as if the doctrines of one part of the American people, the Protestant sector, could speak for and unify all Americans.

Consequently, the reorientation of religious studies during the 1960s revealed the fundamental weakness of older arguments for including religion in the university. That rationale assumed that the university lacked intellectual coherence and was becoming increasingly fragmented. Theology, many Protestants believed, would fix the problem. The 1960s showed otherwise. Real theology, the doctrine of one branch of Christianity, was too narrow for all groups. At the same time, theology that could speak to all Americans could not do justice to the particular truths of one branch of the church. In other words, the 1960s revealed that theology in the university will inevitably rest between a rock and a hard place. Religion in the academy cannot satisfy the demands of both the university and the church. What invariably happens, then, is that to foster academic credibility theologians jettison those aspects of theology that make it most salient to believers and academic theology becomes merely the study of religion.

## IS ACADEMIC THEOLOGY THEOLOGY?

If the recovery of religion in American higher education overestimated the capacity of theology to unite scholars and even citizens, it did so precisely because of a confusion about the norms governing scholarly inquiry and theological reflection. To put the differences between advanced learning and theology simply as the Enlightenment rivalry between open-ended reason and authoritarian dogma borders on being simplistic. But to suppose that theology conducted in the setting of the university is the same as theological reflection carried out for the sake and within the context of the church is naive. Until the nineteenth century, theology proper was a dogmatic enterprise, meaning that the theologian's task was to explain and elaborate the teachings—that is, the dogma—of the church. And even when theology took a liberal turn toward the end of the nineteenth century, the reasons stemmed from the large overlap among the state, the state church, and the state that functioned as patron of the university. In other words, because theology was a public enterprise, for a state-sanctioned church, the confusion of public and private spheres was inevitable.

Seldom recognized was that the standards for membership in the church were different from and more selective than those for citizenship. Once the religious wars of the seventeenth century and the revolutions of the eighteenth century (United States and France) revealed the difference between church membership and citizenship, the impropriety of dogmatic or catechetical theology for a religiously mixed setting was easier to see. Even so, Christians living well after these pivotal turning points in the history of the West, both Protestant and Roman Catholic, continued to believe that theology held a proper place within the university because faith, they believed, played a valuable role in society. This explains why Protestantism in the United States, even after religious disestablishment, remained an informal religious establishment. It also accounts for the efforts of twentieth-century Protestants to use theology as a solution to the problem of a specialized, scientific, and secular university.

The history of biblical and theological studies within the university after 1800 gives very little comfort to those who think that the university needs more religion, not less.[16] In fact, one could construct a fairly plausible case that the modern study of Christianity in the academy, especially biblical studies, has yielded a body of knowledge consistently hostile to the church and its members. An important factor here is the interpretive community for which a scholar works and writes. If a student of the Bible or theology is writing chiefly for other academics in his or her academic discipline, the result is generally a product at odds with the teachings and practices of Christian churches (e.g., the Society of Biblical Literature and

16. See, for instance, Ernest W. Saunders, *Searching the Scriptures: A History of the Society of Biblical Literature, 1880–1980,* Society of Biblical Literature Biblical Scholarship in North America 8 (Chico, CA: Scholars, 1982); Mark A. Noll, *Between Faith and Criticism: Evangelicals, Scholarship, and the Bible in America,* Confessional Perspectives Series (San Francisco: Harper & Row, 1986); and Gerald P. Fogarty, *American Catholic Biblical Scholarship: A History from the Early Republic to Vatican II* (San Francisco: Harper & Row, 1989).

the University of Chicago provide distinct readers and arguments from Concordia Theological Seminary and the Reformed Presbyterian Church of North America). The exception to this trend would appear to be academic settings in which the overlap between the academy and the church is wide, such as a Christian college or seminary where the academic mission serves the church. But because a prominent theme in the history of higher education is emancipating the academy from nonacademic authorities, whether the state or the church, under the banner of academic freedom and open-ended inquiry, institutions that still maintain a religious or churchly mission are generally considered inferior to ones where solely academic standards prevail. For example, as good as Wheaton College may be, it is not in the league of Swarthmore, Williams, or Dartmouth.

Lest readers think this is a prejudiced reading of the academic study of religion, consider a few recent examples of academic theology. In an article for the *Journal of the American Academy of Religion*, the premiere scholarly journal for religious studies in the United States, Ellen T. Armour, who teaches religion at Rhodes College in Memphis, Tennessee, a school with historic ties to the Presbyterian Church, yields a glimpse of the concerns that prevail among academic theologians. Her aim is to consider the contribution that theologians can make to the postmodern world. She even calls this work an "obligation." Armour describes her own work as a theologian as highly indebted to Martin Heidegger, who constructed a fourfold makeup of man, that is, as "his raced and sexed others, his divine other, and his animal other." The task of a theologian is to explore the place of religion in the modern construction of human identity, and add guidance. What is interesting about Armour's article is that she also mentions her experience while teaching Sunday school at a Presbyterian church in Memphis and how it reinforced an awareness of a deep divide between church and academy. Church members were eager to learn but knew little about Karl Barth or Rudolf Bultmann, let alone the theological implications of Stanley Fish or Jacques Derrida. Still, unclear in Armour's reflections was the point of her work with respect to the historic object of theology—namely, the knowledge and worship of God—or how her work fit meaningfully within the Reformed tradition of theological reflection. Hers is largely a humanistic project in which the contours of academic religious reflection explore the modern construction of the self. For this reason, she concludes that the greatest contribution theology can make to both academic theology and to religion in the pews is scholarship "that pursues the making and unmaking of the ties that bind our fields to modern man and his doubles."[17]

Another example of the sort of humanistic-centered and confusing character of modern theology comes from the scholarship of John D. Caputo. A professor of theology at Syracuse University, Caputo won the 2007 AAR prize for excellence in the study of religion with his book, *The Weakness of God: A Theology of Event* (Indiana University Press). The following is the publisher's description of Caputo's contribution:

> Applying an ever more radical hermeneutics (including Husserlian and Heideggerian phenomenology, Derridian deconstruction, and feminism), John D. Caputo breaks down the name of God in this irrepressible book. Instead of looking at God as merely a name, Caputo views it as an event, or what the name conjures or promises in the future. For Caputo, the event exposes God as weak, unstable, and barely functional. While this view of God flies in the face of most religions and philosophies, it also puts up a serious challenge to fundamental tenets of theology and ontology. Along the way, Caputo's readings of the New Testament, especially of Paul's view of the Kingdom of God, help to support the "weak force" theory. This penetrating work cuts to the core of issues and questions—What is the nature of God? What is the nature of being? What is the relationship between God and being? What is the meaning of forgiveness, faith, piety, or transcendence?—that define the terrain of contemporary philosophy of religion.

To be sure, comparing the theology of either of these professors to the teaching of the English and Scottish divines who wrote the Westminster Shorter Catechism may be unfair. But it does underscore the point that theology in the university is a far cry from theology in the church. Caputo and Armour undoubtedly have lots of good reasons for thinking that the first answer to the Shorter Catechism, "Man's chief end is to glorify God and enjoy him forever," is inadequate for the modern university. The catechism, for starters, is sexist, antiquated, naive, doctrinaire, and perhaps even anti-intellectual. But the point of this comparison is not to judge superior theology.

---

17. Ellen T. Armour, "Theology in Modernity's Wake," *Journal of the American Academy of Religion* 74 (2006) 8, 11, 13.

Instead, the aim here is to remind those who want more religion in the academy of the dangers inherent in allowing the university to conduct and regulate the study of the Bible and theology. As flawed as a secular university may be, and as much as colleges and universities might be truly tolerant if they welcomed believing scholars and provided a forum for theological reflection, critics of the secular university seldom remember that the academy has not excluded religion. Only for a brief period, say from 1870 to 1940, were theologians in exile. Since the middle of the twentieth century, however, American universities and colleges have been awash in a sea of religious studies and their supporting cast of theologians and biblical scholars. More often than not, modern religious scholarship is precisely what believing critics of the university lament—a form of religion that is unfaithful either to Scripture or to a particular religious tradition. In which case, the problem of the modern academy is not one of secularization but of orthodoxy. The modern academy has plenty of religion, but it is generally too irreligious for modern believers. Maybe the real solution is to exclude religion rather than find ways to insert more.

So instead of faulting the university for its lack of religion, those who want more room for faith within the university need to figure out a way to conduct and sponsor all the disciplines and lines of inquiry that modern higher education fosters while still making room for orthodox faith. One way to do this is actually to abandon the modern project of the arts and sciences and go back to a Great Books or classical-education model. Some Protestant and Roman Catholic colleges have tried this. But retaining the edifice of modern learning with the humanities, natural and social sciences, and the variety of professional schools while also hoping the university will be a source of sound religious teaching is tantamount to betting that the proverbial snowball in hell will not melt.

The other solution to the predicament of religion in the modern university, then, is simply to let theology flourish where it thrives best, namely, in nonacademic settings such as churches, families, and private schools. Indeed, one of the lessons of American church history is that Christianity prospered unbelievably well once freed from the oversight and the sponsorship of public institutions. After disestablishment the churches found remarkable ways of pursuing their missions and turned the United States into one of the most observant nations in the history of the world—maybe even more so than ancient Israel and Judah. Conversely, churches in Europe flagged under the weight of state control and regulation. If faith does better apart from the support of public institutions

69

like the state, then the same logic may hold for religion in an academic context. To be sure, faith's advocates today still have trouble accepting a secular state and want government to be more openly supportive of faith and traditional morality. Many of these critics of a secular state also lament secular higher education. But again, if the history of Christianity in the United States is in any way instructive, faith does best when it is a private initiative. For that reason, by excluding Christianity from public life, whether in politics or education, a secular academy, whether it intends it or not, pays the Christian faith a high compliment.

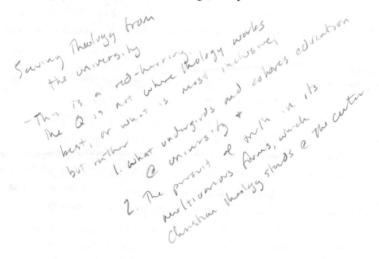

Saving Theology from the university.

-This is a red-herring. The Q is not where Theology works best, or what is most inclusive but rather

1. What undergirds and coheres education @ university?

2. The pursuit of truth in its multitudinous forms, which is @ the center Christian theology stands

*5*

# *God and Man at Yale* Revisited

## George H. Nash

IN EARLY 2008, WILLIAM F. Buckley Jr.—the "patron saint" of American conservatives[1]—died at the age of 82 at his home in Connecticut. Best known as the founder and longtime editor of *National Review*, and as the host for more than thirty years of the television show *Firing Line*, he had led one of the most productive lives in the history of American journalism. During his nearly sixty years in the public eye, he published more than fifty books (both fiction and nonfiction); dozens of book reviews; more than 800 editorials, articles, and remarks in *National Review*; several hundred articles in periodicals other than *National Review*; and approximately 5,600 syndicated newspaper columns. He gave hundreds of public lectures around the world (often at the rate of seventy or more a year), conducted 1,429 separate *Firing Line* programs, and may well have composed more letters than any American who has ever lived.

Conservatives like to say that "ideas have consequences." Certainly the aphorism is applicable to the sizzling writings of William F. Buckley Jr. Of all his books, undoubtedly the most consequential was his very first, *God and Man at Yale*. Written when he was barely twenty-five years old, it has stayed in print almost continuously for nearly six decades. For the

---

1. See John Judis, *William F. Buckley, Jr.: Patron Saint of the Conservatives* (New York: Simon & Schuster, 1988).

student of faith, freedom, and higher education in America, the story of *God and Man at Yale* remains a tale worth knowing.

William F. Buckley Jr. was born in 1925 into a large and rambunctious Roman Catholic family presided over by his wealthy, ultraconservative father, an oilman from Texas. From an early date it was evident that he was going to make his mark upon the world. Upon entering Yale University in 1946 (after military service in the Second World War), he quickly became a Big Man on Campus, a formidable member of the debating team, a ubiquitous conservative polemicist, and, in his senior year, a member of the prestigious Skull and Bones society. From early 1949 to early 1950 he served as the chairman (editor-in-chief) of the undergraduate *Yale Daily News*, from which perch he fired conservative editorial fusillades at liberal targets, much to the discomfiture of the faculty and administration.

By his senior year, Buckley—although personally popular—was increasingly distressed by the pedagogical drift of things at Yale. Brought up to be a devout Christian and staunch "individualist" (in today's parlance: a free-market conservative or libertarian), he was appalled by the rampant secularism, atheism, and socialistic sentiments that he discerned inside and outside the classroom—and by official Yale's seeming indifference to these threats. He therefore responded eagerly when Yale's administration invited him to become the undergraduate speaker at the university's annual Alumni Day ceremonies on February 22, 1950.

Buckley prepared a speech depicting Yale as a university that had lost its moorings and "mission." So long as Yale persisted in its "fanatical allegiance to *laissez-faire* education," he wrote, "she will lead her students nowhere." It was time, he argued, for Yale's trustees to define their institution's purpose and to take measures to "imbue her students with that same purpose."[2]

When President Seymour of Yale and his advisers saw an advance copy of Buckley's text, they were aghast. In the president's words, it was nothing less than "an attack upon the Yale faculty" and totally inappropriate for the occasion. The administration promptly requested Buckley to revise his draft. Buckley reluctantly agreed to tone it down a little but refused to alter its substance. Instead, he offered to withdraw from the program completely if his text were still deemed unacceptable. To his astonishment, just one day before the event President Seymour accepted his

2. The text of Buckley's proposed Alumni Day address of February 22, 1950 is printed in William F. Buckley Jr., *God and Man at Yale* (Chicago: Regnery, 1951), 222–27, as well as in subsequent editions of this book.

offer. The alumni audience, he told Buckley, would have been "upset" by his proposed speech.[3]

In Buckley's later word, Yale's suppression of his Alumni Day address was the "catalyst" for what happened next.[4] Shortly after his graduation in 1950, he embarked upon a systematic, book-length case study of the educational environment at Yale as it had impinged upon his faith and political philosophy. The informal motto of the university was "For God, for Country, and for Yale." With the daring and aplomb that had helped to make him an undergraduate luminary, he entitled his book *God and Man at Yale: The Superstitions of "Academic Freedom."*

In his foreword, Buckley came swiftly to the point. "I myself believe," he wrote, "that the duel between Christianity and atheism is the most important in the world. I further believe that the struggle between individualism and collectivism is the same struggle reproduced on another level. I believe that if and when the menace of Communism is gone, other vital battles, at present subordinated, will emerge to the foreground. And the winner must have help from the classroom."[5]

Alas, he reported, neither orthodox Christianity nor traditional American beliefs in free enterprise and limited government were receiving much help from the classrooms of his alma mater. He had entered Yale looking to it "for allies against secularism and collectivism."[6] Instead, despite its façade of "detached impartiality," the "net impact" of Yale's educational offerings was distinctly *anti*-Christian and scornful of the free market philosophy pioneered by Adam Smith. Acting under the "protective label" of "academic freedom," Yale had become an example of "one of the most extraordinary incongruities of our time: the institution that derives its moral and financial support from Christian individualists and then addresses itself to the task of persuading the sons of these supporters to be atheistic socialists."[7]

In two bluntly worded chapters Buckley attempted to substantiate his claims. He asserted that Yale's department of religion was neither "a source of pervasive Christian influence" nor, indeed, of *any* influence upon most undergraduates. He charged that some of Yale's most popular

---

3. Ibid., 129–30; Buckley, *Miles Gone By: A Literary Autobiography* (Washington, DC: Regnery, 2000), 106; Judis, *William F. Buckley, Jr.*, 76–78.

4. Buckley, *Miles Gone By*, 106.

5. Buckley, *God and Man at Yale*, xii–xiii.

6. Ibid., ix.

7. Ibid., xi–xiii, xv.

professors (whom he named) were publicly hostile to Christianity, even in the classroom. One noted professor of religion had even called himself "80 per cent atheist and 20 per cent agnostic."[8] In many of the social-science departments, Buckley continued, secularist biases were pervasive. In fact, he asserted, not a single department at Yale was "uncontaminated with the absolute that there are no absolutes, no intrinsic rights, no ultimate truths."[9] Although a Christian presence could be found in Yale's extracurricular activities, much of it was of a nondoctrinal, do-good variety—no substitute for "classroom exposition and guidance."[10] Christian *students* there certainly were at Yale, wrote Buckley, but they received little sustenance from either the faculty or the administration.

In the realm of economics, Buckley reported, the intellectual climate was more disturbing still. Citing chapter and verse from the pro-Keynesian textbooks and teachings of Yale's department of economics, he portrayed a department committed to a "revolution": "one that advocates a slow but relentless transfer of power from the individual to the state."[11] Not only was Yale's economics curriculum riddled with Keynesian biases and critiques of traditional capitalism; the favored textbooks completely ignored critiques of the liberal Keynes by distinguished free-market scholars like Friedrich Hayek, author of *The Road to Serfdom*. To Buckley, it was proof that Yale—its pious protestations of neutrality notwithstanding—was deliberately and dangerously tilting to the Left. The "net influence of Yale economics" was "thoroughly collectivistic," he charged. "Individualism is dying at Yale, and without a fight."[12]

Buckley did not stop with documenting "Yale's intellectual drive toward agnosticism and collectivism."[13] In an audacious display of counterrevolutionary fervor, he called upon the university's alumni—if they agreed with him—to "interfere" and set Yale's "educational policy" aright.[14] Invoking a consumer-sovereignty model for university governance, he argued that the university's alumni—its "consumers"—were the ultimate "governing body" and "ultimate overseers" of Yale's product.[15] He

8. Ibid., 9.

9. Ibid., 25.

10. Ibid., 26–34.

11. Ibid., 46–57.

12. Ibid., 46, 113.

13. Ibid., 114.

14. Ibid., 114–15.

15. Ibid., 116, 134–35, 175, 185. According to Buckley, "every citizen of a free

reminded his readers that Yale was a *private* educational institution and that its graduates had both a right and a duty to insist that their alma mater instill the "value orthodoxy" that they themselves believed in.[16]

To achieve this objective, Buckley knew that he must pierce the carapace of Yale's protective ideology: what he provocatively called the "superstitions" of "academic freedom." It was "the shibboleths of 'academic freedom,'" he thundered, which had thwarted efforts to "Christianize Yale" for many years.[17] It was the "hoax" of "academic freedom" that had provided a convenient smokescreen for incoherent "laissez-faire education." At one point he asserted that Yale already possessed a "value orthodoxy"; *he* proposed only to "narrow" it. In place of the secularist and collectivist tendencies currently ascendant at Yale, he would implant an orthodoxy grounded in the truths of Christianity and individualism. And he would enforce it: if a socialist were found to be teaching at Yale he would be barred from doing so because he was "inculcating values that the governing board at Yale consider to be against the public welfare."[18] If the "overseers" of a university "have embraced democracy, individualism, and religion," he said, then "the attitudes of the faculty ought to conform to the university's."[19]

The fearless controversialist conceded that some professors would be discharged (and some "ought to be discharged") if he succeeded. But "no one apathetic to the value issues of the day," he countered, could "in good conscience contribute to the ascendancy of ideas he considers destructive of the best in civilization." "If the majority of Yale graduates believe in spiritual values and in individualism" (as Buckley assumed), "they cannot contribute to Yale so long as she continues in whole or in part to foster contrary values." As for the dogma of "academic freedom": "in the last analysis" it "must mean the freedom of men and women to supervise the educational activities and aims of the schools they oversee and support."[20]

To the young alumnus, these concerns were not trivial. The "educational institutions" of the West are "the nerve center of civilization," he

---

economy, no matter the wares that he plies, must defer to the sovereignty of the consumer" (*God and Man at Yale,* 185). Colleges and universities were no exception.

16. Ibid., 175, 194.

17. Ibid., 43.

18. Ibid., 151, 154–55, 186.

19. Ibid., 181.

20. Ibid., 197, 195–96, 195, 190.

contended. All too often, the "guardians of this sustaining core of civilization" had "abdicated their responsibility to mankind."[21]

*God and Man at Yale* was published on October 15, 1951, by the Henry Regnery Company, a small, conservative publishing house in Chicago. Within a week the first printing of 5,000 had sold out.[22] In its first six months the volume sailed through four more printings and sold 25,000 copies—an extraordinary feat for a little-known author writing about a seemingly obscure topic.[23] The volume's sales were fueled by lively publicity in the press. *Time, Life,* and *Newsweek* ran articles about it.[24] *The Saturday Review*—a highly influential, literary weekly—gave the book *two* reviews (one pro, one con).[25] In all, something like one hundred periodicals weighed in with articles and commentaries. Clearly Buckley had touched a sensitive nerve.

Several adventitious factors contributed to the book's astonishing sales. With the assistance of his father, Buckley poured $16,000 (a substantial figure) into publicity; the fund enabled Regnery to advertise the book aggressively and to mail a circular to 40,000 Yale alumni.[26] John Chamberlain's laudatory introduction to the book also gave it a boost; Chamberlain (Yale Class of 1925) was a respected journalist and former daily book reviewer of the *New York Times*. Partly it was a matter of felicitous timing: *God and Man at Yale* was launched just four days before Yale celebrated its 250th anniversary, a milestone much noted in the press. The timing was no coincidence: Buckley and his father successfully pressured Henry Regnery to speed the book into print in time to benefit from Yale's publicity.[27]

---

21. Ibid., 193.

22. *New York Times*, October 30, 1951, 27.

23. Regnery to William F. Buckley Sr. (Buckley's father), April 14, 1952, Henry Regnery Papers, Box 11, Hoover Institution Archives, Stanford University; copyright page for the December 1968 paperback edition of Buckley's book (for the listing by date of the various printings between 1951 and 1968).

24. "Secular, Collectivist Yale?" *Newsweek* 38 (October 22, 1951) 70; "Rebel in Reverse," *Time* 58 (October 29, 1951) 57–58; "God, Socialism and Yale," *Life* 31 (October 29, 1951) 32.

25. "Isms and the University," *Saturday Review* 34 (December 15, 1951) 18–19, 44–45.

26. See Judis, *William F. Buckley, Jr.*, 89, and the following correspondence: Regnery to William F. Buckley Jr., September 24 and 29, 1951 and October 22, 1951; and Regnery to William F. Buckley Sr., January 8 and 28, 1952. All in Regnery Papers, Boxes 10 and 11.

27. Henry Regnery, *Memoirs of a Dissident Publisher* (New York: Harcourt Brace Jovanovich, 1979), 168; Judis, *William F. Buckley, Jr.*, 88–89.

Interest in Buckley's broadside was also stimulated by its sheer novelty and effrontery. Here was a dashing young alumnus of Old Eli—and a member of Skull and Bones, no less!—publicly skewering his alma mater for straying from true religion and sound economics. No one had ever seen anything quite like it. *Life* magazine compared the book to the "brat who comes to the party and tells the guests that their birthday boy is secretly a dope addict."[28] *Time* dubbed Buckley a "Rebel in Reverse": "a fire-eating youthful conservative."[29]

There was more to the story, however, than that. In his Foreword Buckley prophesied that his volume would evoke "bitter opposition."[30] Barely a month after publication, he confessed that he had been "naïve beyond recognition." The opposition had been more vituperative than he had ever dreamed. "I should have known better, of course, for I had seen the Apparatus go to work on other dissenters from the Liberal orthodoxy, and I respected the Apparatus and stood in awe of it."[31]

Instead of loftily ignoring Buckley's polemic, official Yale reacted to it (in one journalist's words) "with all the grace and agility of an elephant cornered by a mouse."[32] Even before the book was published, President Griswold of Yale (who had not yet read it) privately condemned it and attempted to induce Buckley to withdraw it.[33] Three months before the publication date, Yale's trustees secretly created a committee of alumni to investigate "the intellectual and spiritual welfare" of the university—an obvious preemptive act of damage control. The existence of the committee was disclosed four days before Buckley's book appeared. Early in 1952, without once mentioning Buckley by name, the committee announced triumphantly that all was well at Yale: its investigation had found not a single faculty member who was "trying to undermine or destroy our society" or to "indoctrinate" students with "subversive theories." Nor was Yale encouraging irreligion or atheism; religious life at the university was said to be "deeper and richer than it has been in many years." For good measure

28. "God, Secularism and Yale," 32.

29. "Rebel in Reverse," 57.

30. Buckley, *God and Man at Yale,* xii.

31. Buckley to the editor, *Yale Daily News,* November 26, 1951, William F. Buckley Jr. Papers, Yale University Library.

32. Dwight Macdonald, "God and Buckley at Yale," *Reporter* 6 (May 27, 1952) 36.

33. Buckley to the editor, *Yale Daily News,* November 26, 1951; Judis, *William F. Buckley, Jr.,* 93; Buckley, introduction to the 1977 reissue of *God and Man at Yale.* This lengthy (46-page) introduction can be found in his *God and Man at Yale* (South Bend, IN: Gateway Books, 1986), v-l. It is reprinted also in Buckley, *Miles Gone By,* 57–94.

the committee ringingly extolled the principles of academic freedom and affirmed that a university's "business" was "to educate, not to indoctrinate its students."[34]

McGeorge Bundy (Yale class of 1940 and now a Harvard professor) was not so inclined to beat around the bush. In a blistering review essay in the November 1951 *Atlantic*, Bundy excoriated *God and Man at Yale* as "dishonest in its use of facts, false in its theory, and a discredit to its author." He labeled Buckley "a twisted and ignorant young man whose personal views of economics would have seemed reactionary to Mark Hanna."[35] Bundy subsequently denied that Yale's administration had designated him to "deliver the counterattack," or that he had been "approached" by Yale's administration "in any way whatever." He did not reveal that after accepting the assignment from the *Atlantic*'s editor (a Yale man), he himself had approached Yale and had spent a day with President Griswold discussing the forthcoming review point by point.[36] Delighted by Bundy's scathing assault (which he confessed to a "kind of savage pleasure" in composing), Yale's administration promptly ordered 2,000 reprints, which it handed out to inquiring alumni.[37]

Bundy's "intemperate performance" (as Buckley soon labeled it)[38] was but one cloudburst in a torrent of vituperation that rained down upon the young Yale graduate in the months ahead. Even today, nearly six decades later, one is startled by the vehemence of many of the rejoinders to Buckley's criticisms. In the *Yale Daily News,* Professor of Religion Theodore M. Greene—one of Buckley's targets—called the book "pure fascism": "he would transform Yale into the most dogmatic, hidebound institute for orthodox propaganda."[39] In the *Saturday Review,* Chad Walsh asserted that what Buckley "really proposes is that the alumni of Yale should turn themselves into a politburo, and control the campus exactly

34. *New York Times,* October 12, 1951, 25, and February 18, 1952, 1, 12; Buckley, introduction to *God and Man at Yale,* 1977 edition, xxvii.

35. McGeorge Bundy, "The Attack on Yale," *Atlantic* 188 (November 1951) 50–52.

36. William F. Buckley Jr., "The Changes at Yale," *Atlantic* 188 (December 1951) 78–82; Bundy, "McGeorge Bundy Replies," ibid., 82–83; Judis, *William F. Buckley, Jr.,* 93.

37. Judis, *William F. Buckley, Jr.,* 93; Buckley, introduction to *God and Man at Yale,* 1977 edition, xxvii.

38. Buckley, "Changes at Yale," 78.

39. Theodore M. Greene, quoted in *Time* 58 (October 29, 1951) 58, and in Buckley, introduction to *God and Man at Yale,* 1977 edition, xxxv.

as the Kremlin controls the intellectual life of Russia."[40] A reviewer in the *New Republic* accused Buckley of advocating "precisely" the "methods" used in Fascist Italy, Nazi Germany, and Communist Russia.[41] A reviewer in the *Journal of Bible and Religion* worried that Buckley's book might become "the campaign pamphlet of a totalitarian movement to assume control of all American higher education."[42] Irate reviewers compared him to Torquemada, Savanarola, and Joseph Goebbels (Adolf Hitler's minister of propaganda).

At Yale itself a professor of economics assailed the book as "authoritarian" in its educational theory and as "scurrilous and boorish in its reference to individuals."[43] In *The Progressive*, Yale professor of law Fred Rodell, a militant liberal, called it (among other things) "dishonest," "balderdash," and a "barbarian bleat" by "one bigoted boy" against his alma mater.[44] In the scholarly *Yale Law Journal*, Vern Countryman—another very liberal Yale law professor—began his review this way: "Once upon a time there was a little boy named William Buckley. Although he was a little boy, he was much too big for his britches." In the ensuing, twelve-page review essay, Countryman never again referred to Buckley by his surname. Instead, the professor condescendingly called him "Willie" and "little Willie."[45]

It was Frank Ashburn, however—respected headmaster of the Brooks School and a trustee of Yale University—who hurled the most sensational accusation. *God and Man at Yale,* he wrote in the *Saturday Review,* "stands as one of the most forthright, implacable, typical, and unscrupulously sincere examples of a return to authoritarianism that has appeared . . . This book is one which has the glow of a fiery cross on a hillside at night. There will undoubtedly be robed figures who gather to it, but the robes will not be academic. They will cover the face."[46]

Why was the liberal reaction to *God and Man and Yale* so extravagantly antagonistic? Why the heated, even hysterical allusions to Nazis,

---

40. Quoted in Buckley's 1977 introduction to *God and Man at Yale,* xxxi.

41. Robert Hatch, "Enforcing Truth," *New Republic* 125 (December 3, 1951) 19.

42. S. Vernon McCasland in *Journal of Bible and Religion* 20 (April 1952) 135.

43. Quoted in Regnery, *Memoirs,* 169.

44. Fred Rodell, "That Book about Yale: The Attack on Free Universities," *Progressive* 16 (February 1952) 14–16.

45. Vern Countryman review in *Yale Law Journal* 61 (February 1952) 272–83.

46. Frank Ashburn review in *Saturday Review* 34 (December 15, 1951) 44–45.

the Spanish Inquisition, and the Ku Klux Klan? Why, in particular, in Buckley's later words, the "remarkably virulent" response by Yale itself?[47]

In the case of Yale's administration, the immediate motivation was financial. Shortly before *God and Man at Yale* was published, one of the university's trustees told John Chamberlain that the book would cost the institution a million dollars.[48] It was not an irrational apprehension. Buckley's treatise contained an explicit summons to Yale's alumni to rise up and assert control of their alma mater—and a stern warning that they should not "support" it if it encouraged values they deemed "inimical to the public welfare."[49] If Buckley's factual case against Yale's gained credence, the university might suffer a crippling decline in alumni giving.[50]

If Yale's administration feared a financial backlash, Yale's liberal professors (and, by extension, liberal and leftist professors elsewhere) feared something else: a loss of academic power—and conceivably employment—if Buckley's challenge to "academic freedom" and his theory of consumer (alumni) sovereignty took root. Again, this was not an entirely implausible specter. In 1951 and 1952 the cold war against Communist Russia and China was raging. At home growing numbers of Americans, championed by Senator Joseph McCarthy (among others), feared that Communists and their fellow travelers had penetrated the U.S. government and other institutions, including the universities. At the University of California professors had been required by authorities to sign "loyalty oaths" (swearing that they were not Communists) as a condition of holding their jobs. (One of the California dissenters who refused to sign—and was then fired—soon received an honorary degree from Yale.[51]) In this highly charged context, Buckley's stentorian call for new "value orthodoxy" at his alma mater—and for the dismissal of professors who deviated too far from it—seemed genuinely alarming. More irritating still to many liberal professors, "this little Neanderthaler" (as Countryman called him)[52] was mocking *their* "religion," *their* orthodoxy—the sacred creed of academic

---

47. Buckley, *Miles Gone By,* 106.

48. Henry Regnery to Buckley, September 24, 1951.

49. Buckley, *God and Man at Yale,* 194. See also 195.

50. In the fiscal year 1950–51, which ended on June 30, 1951, contributions to Yale University's Alumni Fund exceeded $1,000,000—a record for Yale and apparently "an all-time record for any university." *New York Times,* July 9, 1951, 23; Macdonald, "God and Buckley at Yale," 37. A possible loss of $1,000,000 in donations (because of Buckley's book) would have been a humiliating blow to Yale's fundraisers.

51. *New York Times,* June 12, 1951, 1, 25.

52. Countryman review, 283.

freedom—in the name of—of all people—the alumni. The alumni! It was a horrifying thought. Liberal academia was filled with *refugees* from the philistine world that alumni supposedly inhabited. If Buckley was disgusted by the perceived intolerance and hypocrisy of liberal Yale, many a liberal professor in 1952 was equally vexed by the perceived anti-intellectualism of "McCarthyite" America.

Even some Yale alumni shared this negative perception of their own fellow graduates. Not long after *God and Man at Yale* appeared, Buckley chanced to meet the Reverend Henry Sloan Coffin, chairman of Yale's alumni committee that had been set up to evaluate Yale's health (and refute Buckley's book). Said Coffin gruffly to his youthful nemesis: "Why do you want to turn over Yale education to a bunch of boobs?"[53]

The rancor of the controversy intensified further when some of Buckley's fiercest critics took aim at what they considered the key to the entire controversy: his Roman Catholicism.[54] To McGeorge Bundy, writing in the *Atlantic*, it seemed "very strange," even impudent, for an "ardent" Catholic like Buckley to "offer a *prescription*, pretending to speak for Yale's true religious tradition" (which was Protestant). It was "stranger still," Bundy added darkly, for Buckley to offer "no word or hint" in his book of his "special allegiance."[55] In a similar vein, Fred Rodell accused Buckley of dishonestly concealing his "very relevant church affiliation."[56] To Bundy there were "pronounced and well recognized differences between Protestant and Catholic views on education in America"—differences that disqualified Buckley from trying to reform historically Protestant Yale.[57]

Bundy's "religious" criticism of *God and Man at Yale* found echoes among Yale's defenders. According to Henry Sloan Coffin (a former president of Union Theological Seminary), Buckley's book was plainly "distorted by his Roman Catholic point of view." Yale—said Coffin—was a "Puritan and Protestant institution by its heritage." Buckley "should have attended Fordham or some similar [i.e., Catholic] institution."[58] Behind

53. Buckley, introduction to *God and Man at Yale*, 1977 edition, xxviii.

54. In a private letter that came to Buckley's attention, Yale's president claimed that Buckley's forthcoming book (which he had not yet seen) was an attack on academic freedom from a "militant Catholic viewpoint" (a charge Buckley stoutly denied). Buckley, letter to the editor, *Yale Daily News*, November 26, 1951.

55. Bundy, "McGeorge Bundy Replies," 84; Bundy, "The Attack on Yale," 50.

56. Rodell, "That Book about Yale," 15.

57. Bundy, "The Attack on Yale," 50.

58. Quoted in Buckley, introduction to *God and Man at Yale*, 1977 edition, xxi and in Buckley, *Nearer, My God: An Autobiography of Faith* (New York, 1997), 30 n.

the scenes, Yale's president and his allies disparaged the book as the work of a Catholic zealot far outside Yale's Protestant mainstream.[59] In the words of one of President Griswold's closest associates: Buckley's proposed reforms would turn Yale into "a small town parochial academy."[60]

What was going on here? Why these angry allusions to Buckley's religious faith? In 1951, Yale had come far from its eighteenth-century origins as a college for Congregational ministers, but it remained generically Protestant in its ambience. To the mainline Protestant custodians of Yale's image and self-understanding, Buckley's untimely manifesto was a retrograde, Catholic attack on their cherished Protestant values: Protestants, they believed, stood for individual freedom of conscience (and its supposed derivative, academic freedom); Catholics stood for "indoctrination" and "a religion of external authority."[61] From this perspective, Buckley's appeal for a new "value orthodoxy" looked like nothing less than a disguised attempt to impose a "Catholic" model of education upon "Protestant" Yale.

It is difficult to know how deeply Yale's advocates believed this. Invoking anti-Catholic biases was an easy way to marginalize their accuser among most Yale alumni. But the early 1950s were not the post-Vatican II, ecumenical era with which we today are familiar. The late 1940s and early 1950s, in fact, were a time of considerable tension between Roman Catholics and other religious groups in the United States. These were the years when Francis Cardinal Spellman and Eleanor Roosevelt argued vehemently in public about government aid to parochial schools and when President James B. Conant of Harvard urged the abolition of all private schools in the country. This was the era when the philosopher Sidney Hook asserted that "[t]here is no academic freedom in Catholic colleges."[62] Perhaps most revealing of the intellectual climate of this period was the publication in 1949 of Paul Blanshard's muckraking *American Freedom and Catholic Power*, which depicted the Roman Catholic Church hierarchy as an authoritarian threat to American liberty and democracy.[63] (Coincidentally, Blanshard's brother, who was not an orthodox Christian, taught philosophy at Yale; Buckley labeled him "an earnest and expansive

59. Buckley, letter to the editor, *Yale Daily News*, November 26, 1951; Judis, *William F. Buckley, Jr.*, 93–94.

60. Quoted in Judis, *William F. Buckley, Jr.*, 93.

61. George M. Marsden, *The Soul of the American University: From Protestant Establishment to Established Nonbelief* (New York: Oxford University Press, 1994), 13–14.

62. Sidney Hook, *Heresy, Yes; Conspiracy, No* (New York: John Day, 1953), 220.

63. Paul Blanshard, *American Freedom and Catholic Power* (Boston: Beacon, 1949).

atheist.")[64] Blanshard's bestselling broadside was hugely popular in liberal academic circles.[65]

It was into this stormy religious environment that Buckley strode in October 1951 with his stunning appeal for a creedal university.

Rather ironically, under the circumstances, Buckley soon found himself under attack from prominent Roman Catholics as well—not for his strictures on secularism in education but for the other foundation of his critique of Yale: his procapitalist, economic "individualism." Both *Commonweal* and *The Pilot* charged him with advocating socioeconomic "heresy." Catholic commentators claimed that his laissez-faire economic philosophy flagrantly contravened the social teachings of the Church, as encapsulated in recent encyclicals by the popes.[66]

To Buckley it must have seemed at times that most of the intelligentsia was against him. Pilloried by Bundy and others as a "violent," "unbalanced," and "twisted" ignoramus, and chastised by liberal Catholics as a heretic in his economics, the young author discovered that even some of his allies on the Right were less than enamored of his views. While *God and Man at Yale*'s factual findings evoked many plaudits in conservative circles,[67] conservative academics were cool about his proposed cure. Friedrich Hayek, from whom Buckley badly wanted a blurb for the book, declined to give him one; the great economist objected strenuously to Buckley's chapter on academic freedom.[68] Russell Kirk, another rising conservative luminary, was also unpersuaded. In his book *Academic Freedom* (1955), he condemned Buckley's "individualism" as anti-Christian and asserted that Buckley's "program of indoctrination" would be "ruinous to his aims": "the preservation of American religious faith, constitutional government, and free economic institutions." Attempting to steer clear both of "indoctrinators" and "doctrinaire liberals," Kirk asserted that

64. Buckley, *God and Man at Yale*, 18.

65. John T. McGreevy, *Catholicism and American Freedom: A History* (New York: Norton, 2003), 166–68.

66. Christopher E. Fullman, "God and Man and Mr. Buckley," *Catholic World* 175 (May 1952) 104–8; Macdonald, "God and Buckley at Yale," 36; "Yale vs. Harvard," *Commonweal* 56 (June 27, 1952) 285.

67. Such right-wing publications as the *Chicago Tribune*, the *Freeman*, *Barron's*, and the *American Mercury* published favorable reviews. Around the beginning of 1952 Buckley compiled a dossier of these and other positive responses to his book. A copy of this document is in the Regnery Papers, Box 11. Buckley did not lack for sympathizers in the popular press.

68. Regnery to Buckley, November 20 and 30, 1951, Regnery Papers, Box 10.

Buckley's remedy would be "worse than the disease."[69] Other conservatives expressed similar qualms.[70]

Both then and later, Buckley fought back hard against his critics. To those who furiously accused him of advocating "fascism," he rejoined that "irresponsible, irreproachable education by an academic elite" was itself a kind of fascism.[71] What, he wondered, was "fascistic" about "a summons to free citizens freely associated, exercising no judicial or legislative power, to communicate their ideals at a private college through the appropriate selection of texts and teachers"? What was authoritarian about the ideals he professed and "sought to serve": "the ideals of a minimalist state, and deference to a transcendent order"?[72] He continued to hold that "academic freedom" was the doctrine "that most successfully impedes the growth of Christianity in precisely the culture where it could most efficaciously take root and spread, the student mind."[73]

As for supposedly slyly and dishonestly concealing his Catholicism, he insisted that the matter was irrelevant. In his book he had evaluated Yale's religious condition using a carefully nondenominational understanding of Christianity. Moreover, he had submitted a draft of his chapter on religion in advance to an interfaith group of religious counselors at Yale, everyone of whom had agreed that there was nothing peculiarly Catholic about his treatment of the subject.[74] As for the "fashionable Catholic journals" which had condemned him as a "heretic," the antistatist libertarian was unrepentant. Too many "Christian modernists," he later observed, believed that "the road to Christianity on earth lies through the federal government."[75]

Nor did Buckley back down after the bitter brouhaha subsided. When he published a 25th anniversary edition of *God and Man at Yale* in

69. Russell Kirk, *Academic Freedom: An Essay in Definition* (Chicago: Regnery, 1955), 118–26. See also Kirk's introduction to Buckley, *Rumbles Left and Right* (New York: Putnam, 1963), 14.

70. Macdonald, "God and Buckley at Yale," 36. Years later Buckley noted, "I think it is safe to say that no fully integrated member of the intellectual community associated himself with my position on academic freedom" (Buckley, introduction to *God and Man at Yale,* 1977 edition, xxxix).

71. Buckley, "Changes at Yale," 82.

72. Buckley, introduction to *God and Man at Yale,* 1977 edition, xlv, xxxix.

73. Buckley, "Father Fullman's Assault," *Catholic World* 175 (August 1952) 332.

74. Buckley, "Changes at Yale," 80; Buckley, introduction to *God and Man at Yale,* 1977 edition, xxi–xxii.

75. Buckley, introduction to *God and Man at Yale,* 1977 edition, xix.

the mid-1970s, he prepared a comprehensive new introduction in which he again lambasted Yale's loss of "mission" and rebutted the arguments and slurs of his enemies. "I cannot come to terms," he confessed, "with a university that accepts the philosophical proposition that it is there for the purpose of presenting 'all sides' of 'any issue' as impartially and as reasonably as possible."[76] Again and again in his later years, he insisted that the "teaching part of a college" should be "animated by certain values" and that the alumni "should have the final voice on the values that a college seeks to promote and cherish." It was "nihilistic," he averred, "to assume that all values are exactly equal, which is what the concept of academic freedom tells you." If any university that he had attended had on its faculty "more than a fair share of professors who taught error," he remarked in 1978, he would withhold his financial contributions and "even campaign aggressively against it."[77]

In 1952, after more than six months of acerbic commotion, the tempest over *God and Man at Yale* tapered off. But the fault lines persisted, with long-term consequences. For Yale itself, the immediate consequences were surprisingly few. Contrary to its panicky fears (and Buckley's hopes), there was no insurrection by the Yale alumni to reform their alma mater along Buckleyite lines. "Yale's challenge," Buckley wrote sardonically, "has always been to flatter its alumni while making certain they should continue impotent," and, so far as he was concerned, it succeeded.[78] What another conservative rebel, M. Stanton Evans (Yale class of 1955), called "the monumental lethargy of the alumni" seemed undisturbed.[79] In the fiscal year in which Buckley's book appeared, alumni contributions to Yale actually increased.[80]

The failure of Yale's alumni to mobilize and "proceed to govern the university"[81] exposed a serious chink in Buckley's armor. What if the alumni were not reliable reformers? What if they bought into the ideology of academic freedom and the anything-can-be-taught practices of "laissez-faire education"? Even worse, what if, over time, a majority of

76. Buckley, introduction to *God and Man at Yale,* 1977 edition, xlvi and xlvii.

77. Interview of Buckley in *Civil Liberties Review* 4 (March–April 1978) 48–49; interview of Buckley in *Prospect* (March 1984) 12.

78. Macdonald, "God and Buckley at Yale," 37; Buckley, introduction to *God and Man at Yale,* xxviii.

79. M. Stanton Evans, *Revolt on the Campus* (Chicago: Regnery, 1961), 2.

80. *New York Times,* July 5, 1952, 23; Regnery, *Memoirs,* 170.

81. Buckley, introduction to *God and Man at Yale,* 1977 edition, xxviii.

graduates of Yale and other elite universities turned out to be secular, collectivistic liberals?

In his book and elsewhere, Buckley conceded that if secular collectivism was what Yale's alumni truly wanted, that was "their privilege." In that case, he said, he would have "nothing more to say."[82] But in 1951, at least, he considered Yale's existing educational "emphases" to be "directly opposed to those of her alumni."[83] As the cold-war era of the 1950s gave way to the tumultuous sixties, he had reason to reconsider. In 1968 he ran as an insurgent conservative for a seat on the Yale Corporation (board of trustees). The contest aroused tremendous excitement. Yale alumni voted in record numbers. Buckley lost decisively—to a liberal.[84]

So in 1951–52 Yale repulsed the perceived Torquemada at its gates. Outwardly, at least, little changed in New Haven. For Buckley, however, the consequences of the battle were both immediate and enormous. With an inadvertent assist from Yale's wrathful "apparatus," a star was born: within weeks he was a national celebrity. Much more important, a *conservative* star was born: the controversy catapulted the debonair debater to the forefront of the emerging conservative intellectual and journalistic community in the United States. Without the *succès de scandale* of *God and Man at Yale*, Buckley might never have successfully founded the conservative *National Review* in 1955. It quickly became the preeminent conservative publication in the United States. Without Buckley, the movement might have floundered indefinitely in its search for sophisticated leadership.

In 1982 John Chamberlain, who had lent his considerable prestige to Buckley's maiden effort, observed that Buckley, "more than any single figure, has made conservativism a respectable force in American life."[85] Ideas have consequences, and so do books. *God and Man at Yale* set Buckley on the road to becoming arguably the most important public intellectual in American life in the past half century.

For Buckley, then, despite the immediate pain, the outcome was exceedingly positive. Not so, at first, for the two men who had helped to launch his intrepid volume. After John Chamberlain contributed his

82. Buckley, *God and Man at Yale*, 114; Buckley, "Changes at Yale," 80.

83. Buckley, Foreword to *God and Man at Yale*, 1951 edition, xiv.

84. *New York Times*, October 21, 1967, 1, 35; ibid., October 29, 1967, E9; ibid., March 9, 1968, 31; ibid., June 17, 1968, 1, 26. See also Buckley, "What Makes Bill Buckley Run," *Atlantic* 221 (April 1968) 65–69. Buckley lost to Cyrus R. Vance, who later became President Jimmy Carter's secretary of state.

85. John Chamberlain, *A Life with the Printed Word* (Chicago: Regnery Gateway, 1982), 147.

supportive introduction, he never again received an invitation to write for the prestigious *Yale Review*, to which he had contributed for many years. The mild-mannered man of letters was "nearly ostracized" by the Yale academic community.[86] Henry Regnery also felt the sting of those who (in Buckley's words) "preached the virtues of an open mind."[87] Angered by Regnery's dissemination of *God and Man at Yale*, the Great Books Foundation at the University of Chicago canceled his lucrative contract to publish its Great Books series.[88] Chamberlain was unfazed and later wrote regularly for Buckley's magazine. Regnery too recovered and became for a generation the leading publisher of conservative books in the United States.

*God and Man at Yale* had even broader consequences for American conservatism. Although not the first twentieth-century book to voice conservative criticisms of liberalism in higher education,[89] it was the first to become a *cause célèbre* and bestseller. Six decades later *God and Man at Yale* remains the locus classicus for what is now a burgeoning genre of conservative social criticism: the exposure of liberal bias and hypocrisy in American higher education. Soon Buckley's volume had successors and imitators in books and articles with titles like *Collectivism on the Campus* and "God and Woman at Vassar."[90] In more recent years, books like *Poisoned Ivy* (a book about Dartmouth College), *Tenured Radicals*, and *Illiberal Education* have owed something of their inspiration to Buckley's pioneering exposé.[91]

86. Buckley, *Let Us Talk of Many Things* (Roseville, CA: Forum, 2000), 249–50. Professor Fred Rodell, who called himself an "old friend" of Chamberlain, nevertheless publicly charged that it had been "irresponsible" of Chamberlain to write an introduction to Buckley's book. Rodell alleged that is was "tragic" that "men like John Chamberlain . . . should lend their influence to what is essentially a know-nothing campaign" against the "spirit of free inquiry." Rodell, "That Book about Yale," 16. The passions surrounding the Buckley book ran deep.

87. Buckley, *Let Us Talk of Many Things*, 249.

88. Regnery to Buckley, December 5, 1951, Regnery Papers, Box 10; Regnery, *Memoirs*, 170–73; *New York Times*, June 23, 1996, 33; Buckley, *Let Us Talk of Many Things*, 192.

89. George H. Nash, *The Conservative Intellectual Movement in America Since 1945*, 30th anniversary edition (Wilmington, DE: ISI Books, 2006), 69–70.

90. Nash, *The Conservative Intellectual Movement in America Since 1945*, 213.

91. Benjamin Hart, *Poisoned Ivy* (New York: Stein & Day, 1984), with a Foreword by Buckley; Roger Kimball, *Tenured Radicals: How Politics Has Corrupted Our Higher Education* (New York: Harper & Row, 1990); Dinesh D'Souza, *Illiberal Education: The Politics of Race and Sex on Campus* (New York: Free Press, 1991).

*God and Man at Yale* and the ensuing brouhaha had another, more subtle influence on conservative intellectuals: it introduced a permanently populist dimension into their critique of academe. Although conservatives have long decried the decadence and degradation of standards in higher education, it was Buckley who first argued that the problem inhered in a power structure controlled by a self-serving elite. In 1951 he referred to it as the "Apparatus." The epithet of choice, for conservatives, soon became the "liberal establishment": preaching freedom but practicing a monopoly; preaching tolerance but all too often willing to demonize conservative dissenters as bigoted and "fascist." Although Buckley himself was a highly intelligent individual, the *God and Man at Yale* experience gave him a lifelong distrust of liberal intellectual arrogance: "these haughty totalitarians who refuse to permit the American people to supervise their own destiny."[92] It was Buckley who in 1963 mordantly remarked: "I am obliged to confess that I should sooner live in a society governed by the first two thousand names in the Boston telephone directory than in a society governed by the two thousand faculty members of Harvard University."[93]

Buckley's proposed solution to liberal academic malfeasance, however, never caught on. With the partial exception, in recent years, of Dartmouth College (where conservative alumni have elected several of their number to the college's governing board), there have been few, if any, successful efforts by conservative college graduates to exercise effective supervision over their alma maters. In the years since 1951 conservatives and libertarians have developed other strategies to counter the perceived liberal stranglehold on higher education. They have tried going around entrenched faculties and biased courses by circulating conservative literature through organizations like the Intercollegiate Studies Institute and the Collegiate Network of alternative student newspapers. Here and there they have created beachheads in the form of academic centers at certain universities; the James Madison Program in American Ideals and Institutions at Princeton is a notable example. They have built an impressive array of think tanks in Washington, DC and elsewhere, where conservatively inclined scholars can pursue advanced studies—and influence public policy—outside the inhospitable confines of academic institutions. They have built the National Association of Scholars into a powerful voice for "reasoned scholarship" and standards of excellence in colleges and universities. They have established the Foundation for Individuals Rights in

92. Buckley, "Changes at Yale," 82.
93. Buckley, *Rumbles Left and Right,* 134.

Education (FIRE) which has come to the legal defense of college students oppressed by the ravages of political correctness. And they have cultivated such faith-friendly outposts as Grove City College—an institution William F. Buckley Jr. admired.[94]

Nearly sixty years after its publication, *God and Man at Yale*'s historical significance is clear. For Yale, the book offered an unwelcome snapshot of an institution in slow recessional from the Christian matrix formed by earlier generations. The ensuing altercation was a noisy episode in the creeping secularization and de-Protestantization of America's elite universities, a process definitively traced by George Marsden in *The Soul of the American University*.[95] For Buckley and his fellow conservatives, it was a critical moment in forging an intellectual resistance to these and other trends sanctioned by the statist and secularizing ideology called modern liberalism.

Nearly sixty years later, *God and Man at Yale* has gone through three distinct editions and continues to sell: quite an achievement for a *livre de circonstance* in 1951. But then, as events proved, it was not a *livre de circonstance* at all. Today the book lives on because its courageous author, in his admittedly "callow" way,[96] raised enduring questions concerning faith, freedom, and education that continue to roil American public life. When all is said and done, what is the purpose of a college or university? Who should define and oversee the fulfillment of its goals? Its faculty? Its students? Its administrators? The parents and alumni who foot most of the bills? The federal government, which now, nearly everywhere, intrudes?

And what are the solemn responsibilities of a university—to its scholars, to its matriculants, to its heritage, and to the surrounding civil society that permits it to be free?

Perhaps the final lesson of *God and Man at Yale* is this. Just as it has been said that war is too important to leave to the generals, so is education too serious a pursuit to entrust to any single, unaccountable authority.

---

94. Buckley gave a commencement address at Grove City College on May 18, 1991 and received an honorary degree.

95. Cited in note 61.

96. Buckley, interview in *Civil Liberties Review* 4 (March–April 1978) 49.

# 6

# The Mission of Christian Colleges Today

## Gary Scott Smith

WHY DO CHRISTIAN COLLEGES exist? What purposes do they serve in twenty-first-century America? Do they have a valuable mission? Why should individual Christians, congregations, denominations, and Christian foundations support them? Why should parents send their children to them? Why should students attend them? Do they offer anything distinctive?

Christian colleges do have a vital mission today. They should offer an education that is fundamentally different from their secular counterparts in numerous ways. Some of their goals are the same as those of other colleges and universities: they strive to provide a high-quality education, prepare students well for vocations and graduate studies, aid them in developing their gifts, inspire them to think about life's most important questions, and help them improve their interpersonal skills. On the other hand, many of their other aims differ sharply from those of secular institutions. What should distinguish Christian colleges is their promotion of commitment to Christ and his church and their emphasis on calling, character, and community. They should also seek to help students constructively engage with culture and develop a passion for service and justice while providing a Christ-centered curriculum and informal curriculum that integrate faith and learning. The posture of Christian colleges should not be defensive, but offensive: to equip their graduates to serve God energetically, enthusiastically, and effectively in today's world, to be winsome ambassadors of Jesus Christ who labor diligently to advance his kingdom. While discussing all these aspects of the mission of Christian colleges, this essay will focus on the importance of teaching all courses from a distinctively Christian perspective.

The United States currently has 4,200 institutions of higher education; 1,600 of them are private, and 900 identify themselves as "religiously affiliated." For many of these nine hundred colleges and universities, this religious affiliation is much more connected with their historical identity than their present approach to education. Although they were founded by Christian denominations and groups, over the years they have abandoned their distinctive Christian commitment, identity, and mission. Today one hundred and ten institutions belong to the Council for Christian Colleges and Universities. Although Grove City College has chosen not to participate in this organization, it shares the CCCU's mission of advancing the "cause of Christ-centered higher education," "faithfully relating scholarship and service to biblical truth," and hiring faculty and administrators who have a "personal faith in Jesus Christ."[1]

Christian colleges should have mission statements that express their commitment to a biblical worldview and seek to implement them in all aspects of their program. They should employ faculty who are guided by that same worldview in their teaching, scholarship, and relationships with students inside and outside the classroom. The mission of a Christian college

---

1. "About CCCU," Council for Christian Colleges and Universities; online: http://www.cccu.org/about/; Duane Litfin, *Conceiving the Christian College* (Grand Rapids: Eerdmans, 2004), 19. Some argue that institutions that only employ faculty who espouse a common religious commitment are intolerant and inhibit the academic freedom of faculty. Alan Wolfe, for example, denounces such institutions as closed-minded, defensive, and prejudiced. See "The Opening of the Evangelical Mind," *Atlantic Monthly*, Oct. 2000; online: http://www.theatlantic.com/issues/2000/10/wolfe.htm/. On the history of Christian colleges in America, see William C. Ringenberg, *The Christian College: A History of Protestant Higher Education in America* (Grand Rapids: Baker Academic, 2006); Arthur deJong, *Reclaiming a Mission: New Direction for the Church-Related College* (Grand Rapids: Eerdmans, 1990); Merrimon Cuninggim, *The College and the Church* (Nashville: Abingdon, 1994); James T. Burtchaell, *The Dying of the Light: The Disengagement of Colleges and Universities from Their Christian Churches* (Grand Rapids: Eerdmans, 1998); Stephen R. Haynes, ed., *Professing in the Postmodern Academy: Faculty and the Future of Church-Related Colleges* (Waco, TX: Baylor University Press, 2002); and Robert Benne, *Quality with Soul: How Six Premier Colleges and Universities Keep Faith with Their Religious Traditions* (Grand Rapids: Eerdmans, 2001).

should permeate everything it does, including its classrooms, scholarship, student life, administration, and relations with alumni, the community, and the world.[2] In its *Bulletin,* Grove City College, for example, declares its intention "to provide an excellent education" in a college that strives to "be thoroughly Christian and evangelical." It seeks to present "a Christian perspective of life" "in all fields of learning" and to show that the Word of God is significant "for all of life."[3]

Christian colleges in America today face immense economic, ideological, and political pressures. Mark Schwehn, the dean of Christ College in Valparaiso University, argues that very few American colleges "have the self-assurance, the endowment strength, and the depth of spiritual conviction to resist the external constraint placed upon them by accrediting agencies, professional schools, and the modern research university."[4] Its history, fiscal policies, strong leadership, and independence from the federal government give Grove City College a solid foundation for resisting these pressures.

Christian colleges should view "higher education as a God-given vocation, to be enacted on behalf of the Christian community, for the benefit of contemporary society, and to the praise of God's name." They should help their students develop skills in thinking, communicating, and research, prepare them for graduate studies and vocations, and help them exercise responsible citizenship. Moreover, they should strive to "foster a thoughtful and compassionate commitment" to the Christian worldview and faith and "to such values as stewardship, justice, truth, and gratitude," "a strong desire to connect theoretical understanding with Christian conduct," an aspiration "to contribute to church and society in various careers, [and] a dedication to the cause of Christ's renewal of the earth and human life."[5]

While chapel services, campus organizations that worship, fellowship, and/or serve together, and courses in theology and biblical studies are important, they alone do not make a college Christian. What primarily distinguishes a Christian college is that the biblical worldview undergirds and drives the entire institution and that classroom instruction, faculty

2. See Litfin, *Conceiving the Christian College,* 18.

3. Grove City College *Bulletin,* 2009–2010, 7.

4. Mark Schwehn, *Exiles from Eden: Religion and the Academic Vocation in America* (New York: Oxford University Press, 1993), 80.

5. "Appendix: An Expanded Statement of the Mission of Calvin College," in Anthony J. Diekema, *Academic Freedom and Christian Scholarship* (Grand Rapids: Eerdmans, 2000), 170–71.

research, and student life are all based upon Christian presuppositions and commitments.[6] As historian James Bratt puts it, what makes higher education Christian is "not required chapel or Bible courses, not opportunities for extracurricular 'service,' not the cultivation of 'character' or 'citizenship,' not the baptism of middle-class decency with Christian rhetoric or the frosting of Christian conviction with cultural refinement, not the promotion of piety alongside of scholarship or professional preparation; but the classroom as a chapel, scholarship as devotion, Christianity as the base of the curriculum and suffusing all studies, [with] the norms of faith guiding professional development."[7]

The Christian college should design its entire program to help students love the Lord with all their hearts, souls, strength, and minds and to love their neighbors as themselves through a life of constructive, Christ-inspired service. It should help students acquire the knowledge, skills, values, and virtues they need to do God's kingdom work.[8] Christian colleges should not strive to create a safe, sheltered, sanitary cocoon that protects students from the contamination, temptations, and problems of the world, as many of them, especially Bible colleges, have done. Rather, they should actively grapple with the strongest intellectual challenges, the thorniest moral issues, and the most difficult problems the world poses to the Christian faith. Their job is not to protect students from the world but to prepare them to engage the world. The Christian college should help students increase their wisdom, understanding of God, the world, themselves and other people as well as their imagination, appreciation of beauty, sensitivity toward and compassion for others, and commitment to Jesus Christ as savior and Lord.[9]

The goal of a Christian college should be to help all members of its community become more and more like Christ, who modeled servant

---

6. Joel A. Carpenter, "The Perils of Prosperity," in *The Future of Religious Colleges*, ed. Paul Dovre (Grand Rapids: Eerdmans, 2002), 191.

7. James Bratt, "What Can the Reformed Tradition Contribute to Christian Higher Education?" in *Models for Christian Higher Education*, ed. Richard Hughes and William Adrian (Grand Rapids: Eerdmans, 1997), 139.

8. Cornelius Plantinga Jr., *Engaging God's World: A Reformed Vision of Faith, Learning, and Living* (Grand Rapids: Eerdmans, 2002), 126–27.

9. See Nicholas Wolterstorff, "Teaching for Justice," in *Making Higher Education Christian: The History and Mission of Evangelical Colleges in America*, ed. Joel A. Carpenter and Kenneth W. Shipps (Grand Rapids: Eerdmans, 1987), 201–3; Michael Oakeshott, "Education: The Engagement and the Frustration," in *Education and the Development of Reason*, ed. R. F. Dearden et al. (London: Routledge & Kegan Paul, 1972), 19–49.

leadership. As V. James Mannoia, the president of Greenville College, argues, knowing Christ personally "is both intrinsically . . . and instrumentally valuable because it affects who we become and what we do." American society loudly proclaims that personal identity depends not on who we are but on what we do and own. Unfortunately, most students and parents ask, "What can graduates do with a college degree?" rather than the equally important question "What kind of person can a college education enable individuals to become?"[10]

The Christian college should create an atmosphere that conveys excitement, enthusiasm, and expectancy about learning that is evident to anyone who visits campus. It should inform and direct the admissions process, freshman orientation, the residence hall program, extracurricular activities, all the courses that are offered, and faculty and student research.[11]

## CALLING

A central task of Christian colleges is to prepare students for their general calling—to be disciples of Jesus Christ who faithfully love God, their neighbor, and themselves—and to discover and become equipped for their specific callings in life through their jobs, families, churches, and other relationships.[12]

All Christians are called to be devoted citizens of God's kingdom and dedicated agents of redemption. Our primary vocation is to be faithful to God in all aspects of life and to advance his work on earth, while remembering that our true citizenship is in heaven. To promote God's reign on earth we should actively engage in the life and ministry of a church and participate in government by "voting intelligently, praying for leaders faithfully, and paying taxes willingly." The general calling of most Christians also includes having a Christ-centered marriage and nurturing children to know and follow Christ. Christians should seek to promote shalom—integral wholeness, peace in all is aspects, universal flourishing,

---

10. V. James Mannoia, *Christian Liberal Arts: An Education that Goes Beyond* (Lanham, MD: Rowman & Littlefield, 2000), 33, 38; quotations in that order.

11. Arthur F. Holmes, *The Idea of a Christian College* (Grand Rapids: Eerdmans, 1987), 49.

12. Quentin J. Schultze, *Here I Am. Now What on Earth Should I Be Doing?* (Grand Rapids: Baker, 2005), 15. See also Leland Ryken, *Redeeming the Time: A Christian Approach to Work and Leisure* (Grand Rapids: Baker, 1995).

and delight—where "natural needs are satisfied and natural gifts fruitfully employed, all under the arch of God's love."[13]

In seeking to determine their specific callings, Christian students should ask: What gifts has God given me? What are my greatest interests and passions? What work will I enjoy? What are the world's greatest needs? Where are kingdom workers inadequate? With whom will I be working? Can I handle the temptations of this type of work? How important to human well-being are the goods or services I will provide?[14] Christian colleges must help students appraise their aptitudes, abilities, temperaments, circumstances, and opportunities and discern God's call for their vocations. While training students to work in the pastoral ministry, evangelism, the mission field, and Christian education, we must recognize that all work done to glorify God and benefit others is kingdom work.[15]

We must also teach students that while they are in college they are not simply preparing for a vocation; they have a vocation. They should view their education as "an act of love, of worship, of stewardship, [as] a wholehearted response to God."[16]

Christian colleges prepare their students for a war. God's kingdom wages continual battle with the world, the flesh, and the devil. Kingdom workers are part of God's army. They can fight effectively only if they are appropriately armed. Christ came to defeat the powers and principalities of this world, to transform this world. Christian higher education prepares students to be agents of the kingdom, models of the kingdom in their communities, and winsome witnesses wherever God sends them. Those who are devout, determined, dedicated, and properly equipped can best advance the kingdom's agenda.[17]

Today's Christian colleges face immense challenges. They are surrounded by a secular culture that exalts feeling good, wealth, success, speed, convenience, consumption, and instant gratification and offers

13. Plantinga, *Engaging God's World*, 111, 15; quotations in that order. See also Nicholas Wolterstorff, *Until Justice and Peace Embrace* (Grand Rapids: Eerdmans, 1983), 69–72.

14. Plantinga, *Engaging God's World*, 118; Leland Ryken, "The Heart of the Matter: Work and Play as Christian Calling," in *Confronting Life's Challenges*, ed. Gary Scott Smith and P. C. Kemeny (Acton, MA: Copley, 2008), 248–52. See also Lee Hardy, *The Fabric of This World: Inquiries into Calling, Career Choice, and the Human Design of Work* (Grand Rapids: Eerdmans, 1990).

15. Wolterstorff, "Teaching for Justice," 202.

16. Holmes, *The Idea of a Christian College*, 49.

17. Plantinga, *Engaging God's World*, 145.

enticing idols for people to worship in place of God. Students who come as freshmen have usually been thoroughly immersed in this secular, hedonistic culture even if they are committed Christians who have devout Christian parents, a solid church experience, and attended private Christian schools or been home schooled. And after they graduate they will return to this same world. Christian faculty members live in this same world and are subject to the same temptations as students. Therefore, the Christian college must constantly emphasize its countercultural mission of preparing students to live in a world that is at war against God and to do the work to which God calls them heartily as unto the Lord. We can do this by making the concept of vocation central to the mission of the career services department, holding seminars on the idea of calling, and continually challenging students in the classroom to prayerfully analyze their gifts in light of the priorities of Scripture and the needs of our world.

## 2. CHARACTER DEVELOPMENT

Character development—helping students become a particular kind of people—should also be a major distinctive of Christian liberal arts education.[18] The Christian college should care as much about the kind of people they graduate as what kinds of jobs they take and as much about how they do their jobs as which jobs they do. An essential part of the calling of a Christian college student is to develop the best character and skills for serving God winsomely in the postcollege world.[19]

Classical education has always sought to help students acquire virtue—firm "dispositions to feel and act in certain ways"—as well as knowledge and skills to enable students to serve others and improve the world. Therefore, the Christian college should labor diligently to help students develop character, compassion, integrity, diligence, and patience and to understand and better use their God-given talents and the world's resources.[20] Classroom instruction, special courses, chapel programs, residential-life policies, and modeling by administrators and faculty can all promote character development. Hopefully administrators and faculty will act in

---

18. Mannoia, *Christian Liberal Arts*, 39. See David Brooks's provocative essay, "The Organizational Kid," *Atlantic Monthly*, April 2001; online: http://www.theatlantic.com/doc/200104/brooks.

19. Plantinga, *Engaging God's World*, 117.

20. Ibid., 132–33; quotation from 132.

such exemplary ways that students will want to be like them and seek to emulate their attributes and dispositions.

## 3. COMMUNITY

The task of Christian colleges is communal. Fulfilling their mission requires cooperation and collegiality among numerous groups and individuals of different ages who have different gifts, interests, and specialties. The Christian college is called to be a community of believers whose intellectual, social, and cultural life is shaped by Christian values.[21] The root of the word *community* means to communicate or to make common, which should be at the heart of a Christian college's mission of "sharing of knowledge, wisdom, and understanding."[22] Shared values and purposes and common tasks help create community. While athletics, chapel services, social life, and vocational preparation can all contribute to a sense of camaraderie, community needs to be grounded first and foremost in the college's educational mission.[23]

Community does not happen automatically or easily, especially in settings where almost one quarter of the members change each year. Community rests upon shared commitments, values, and experiences and transparency and trust. Christian colleges need to make community a priority and work vigorously to achieve it by providing ample opportunities for professors and students to work, think, play, and pray together.[24] Strong community is built upon loyalty, compassion, justice, integrity, and discipline. Therefore, Christian colleges must intentionally foster these values through their classrooms, chapel programs, residential life, and extracurricular activities, and administrators and faculty must embody them in their work and interactions with one another and students. Recognizing this, Grove City College has taken a variety of important steps in the recent years to promote community, including involving faculty, students, and in some cases, alumni in decision making and strategic planning and in accentuating the importance of integrity in all aspects of

21. Holmes, *The Idea of a Christian College*, 77.

22. Douglas Jacobsen and Rhonda Hustedt Jacobsen, "Epilogue: Campus Climate and Christian Scholarship," in *Scholarship and Christian Faith: Enlarging the Conversation*, ed. Jacobsen and Jacobsen (New York: Oxford University Press, 2004), 181.

23. Holmes, *The Idea of a Christian College*, 80–81.

24. See Elton Trueblood, *The Idea of a College* (New York: Harper, 1959). See also Rodney Clapp, *A Peculiar People* (Downers Grove, IL: InterVarsity, 1996), 186.

campus life. "Maintaining community requires rituals, celebrations, worship, traditions, and experiences in which the members of the community remember the past, honor the present, and give promise to the future."[25] Programs that allow students to work together or with faculty to achieve a common goal and that include discussion of and reflection on their shared experience especially promote community.

Philosopher Arthur Holmes argues that the two primary dangers confronting Christian college communities are the same ones any community faces: "excessive individualism and excessive administrative control."[26] Consequently, Christian colleges must structure their life and programs to avoid these perils. Thus wherever appropriate, decision making should be shared among various college constituencies—trustees, administrators, faculty, staff, students, and alumni.

Developing community is important for many reasons. It gives individuals a sense of identity and purpose. Communities can also nurture, support, encourage, challenge, and lovingly correct their members. Moreover, a strong, compassionate community that models the teachings of Christ provides the most powerful witness to the world. Finally, research shows that learning is "more effective when it takes place within a supportive community of learning."[27]

## COMMITMENT TO SERVICE AND JUSTICE

Christian higher education should seek to promote God's kingdom, not simply prepare students "to become standard evangelical Christian American yuppies." Because Christian values differ sharply with those of the world, it is imperative to equip graduates with kingdom values and commitments. The task of Christian colleges is not only to discuss the major issues of life and educate students to think carefully and critically about them but also to promote social justice and remedy social ills and to produce graduates committed to doing the same.[28] As philosopher Nicholas Wolterstorff argues, Christian education should lead to "responsible action."[29]

25. "Appendix: An Expanded Statement of the Mission of Calvin College," 190.

26. Holmes, *The Idea of a Christian College,* 78.

27. Jerry G. Gaff, "The Resurgence of Interdisciplinary Studies," *National Forum* (March 22, 1989), 4.

28. Mannoia, *Christian Liberal Arts,* 8–9, 112; quotation from 8–9.

29. Nicholas Wolterstorff, *Educating for Responsible Action* (Grand Rapids, MI:

Christian education must integrate theory and practice. Too often Christian colleges "introduce students to broad perspectives, strong principles, and clear thinking" and exhort them to make a difference in the world without helping them understand how to do so, without directly connecting their education to specific actions. As Mannoia maintains, "Christian liberal arts colleges should be at the cutting edge of solving the world's real problems." They should train students to help remedy these problems and serve as important resources for the church as it strives "to be light and salt in the world."[30] Kingdom ambassadors should constantly look for ways to improve social institutions and cultural practices, heal society's wounds, and eradicate its deformities.[31]

Christian colleges especially need to help our students develop a love and passion for justice. Arthur Holmes urges professors to examine "the intrinsic relationship between . . . justice and love" by exploring facts, the purposes God intends for various areas of human activity, and policies or actions that situations demand.[32] Professors can trumpet this concern in the classroom, promote it through student organizations they advise, and incarnate it through their work outside the classroom, as Dr. Tim Mech has done through his partnership with Deep Springs International in Haiti and various ministries in India. Presently many Grove City College students participate in ministries that help sensitize them to the needs of the poor, handicapped, and troubled youth. About one hundred and fifty of our students serve each year with New Life, which holds Bible studies in two dozen group homes at George Junior Republic, a resident facility for delinquent youth. Each year several hundred students participate in mission trips to inner cities, Appalachia, the Gulf Coast, or developing nations where they evangelize, teach children, build homes, schools, and churches, serve in soup kitchens, and aid the less fortunate in other ways. Many other Grove City College students participate in ministries in nearby cities such as Urban Impact in Pittsburgh or City Rescue Mission in New Castle or work with the blind, elderly, or people with intellectual disabilities in Grove City and other communities. This service helps them better understand the struggles of the downtrodden, recognize and develop their own gifts (especially leadership, organizational, and communication skills), and confirm their callings to full-time vocations in these

---

Eerdmans, 1980).

30. Mannoia, *Christian Liberal Arts*, 113, 123; quotations in that order.

31. Plantinga, *Engaging God's World*, 120.

32. Holmes, *The Idea of a Christian College*, 51–52; quotation from 51.

areas or make them more likely to volunteer with similar ministries after graduation. Many colleges today require students to participate in some form of community service as a graduation requirement.[33]

## 4. THE CURRICULUM

Christian colleges should base all their academic endeavors—their classroom instruction, research, publications, and other scholarly products on a biblical worldview.[34] To achieve their mission, Christian colleges need to employ Christian scholars, not scholars who are Christians. That is, they need to have professors who are deeply rooted in God's Word and understand the disciplines they teach within the context of a biblical worldview. This requires professors whose teaching, research, and writing are grounded in a commitment to Christ and whose approach to their academic areas is based on biblical presuppositions and perspectives, who strive to integrate faith and learning. Christian colleges should employ professors who say with Dutch philosopher and statesman Abraham Kuyper: "In the total expanse of human life there is not a single square inch of which the Christ, who alone is sovereign, does not declare, 'Mine!'"[35] Christian colleges seek

33. See B. W. Carpenter and J. S. Jacobs, "Service-Learning: A New Approach in Higher Education," *Education* 115/1 (1994) 97–99; R. L. Carver, "Theoretical Underpinnings of Service-Learning," *Theory into Practice* 36/3 (1997) 144–49; Edward Zlotkowski, "Mapping New Terrain: Service-Learning across the Disciplines," *Change* 33/1 (2001) 24–33; and Bruce W. Speck and Sherry L. Hoppe, eds., *Service-Learning: History, Theory, and Issues* (Westport, CT: Praeger, 2004).

34. Holmes explains that a worldview is holistic (it approaches things systematically as a whole), exploratory (it is not a closed, finished system but an ongoing process), confessional and perspectival (it is rooted in a confession of faith, a set of presuppositions), and pluralistic (diversity exists even within particular Christian traditions—Reformed, Arminian, Anabaptist, and Catholic) (*The Idea of a Christian College*, 58–59). Wolterstorff argues in *Reason within the Bounds of Religion* (Grand Rapids: Eerdmans, 1976) that three types of belief are inevitably involved in intelligently choosing among competing theories: data beliefs, data-background beliefs, and control beliefs. Data beliefs are testable assertions about reality; a theory must be consistent about this to be accepted. Data-background beliefs are the kind of evidence individuals are willing to accept as either confirming or disconfirming their data beliefs. Control beliefs are convictions about what makes a theory acceptable—logical consistency; aesthetical appeal; moral consequences; compatibility with one's own ideas, values, and practices. Because all scholars have control beliefs that help shape their thought, Christians can "admit their own control beliefs and take them seriously" (67, 82). The quotation is from Douglas Jacobsen and Rhonda Hustedt Jacobsen, "More Than the 'Integration' of Faith and Learning" in *Scholarship and Christian Faith*, 22.

35. Abraham Kuyper, "Sphere Sovereignty," in James Bratt, ed., *Abraham Kuyper:*

to help students attain a solid biblical and theological knowledge, understand all of life from a Christian perspective, and receive the knowledge and skills they need to effectively, engagingly, and energetically serve God in a world with colossal needs and immense challenges.[36]

Christian colleges should seek to integrate faith and learning, not to add Christianity on to a secular, neutral education. The biblical worldview is not icing on the cake; it is a central ingredient of the cake that cannot be separated from it. It holds the cake together. Faith and learning must be complementary, completely intertwined. The biblical worldview must inform, undergird, and direct learning at Christian colleges.

Christian colleges should strive to teach students to think biblically, which involves thinking holistically, clearly, deeply, and sensitively. What a person thinks about a particular subject is not as important as the mind with which she thinks. Therefore, we must help students develop a Christian mind that is deeply grounded in Scripture, theology, and church history. Students must be aware of various alternative paradigms and ways of thinking in the contemporary world and deliberately seek to develop the mind of Christ.[37]

Shirley Mullen, the president of Houghton College, argues that "integration of faith and learning must be more than integration of piety and learning"; it involves more than professors praying or offering devotional thoughts to begin class. Guided by Jesus' use of parables as a teaching technique, faculty should facilitate, witness to, create curiosity about, and ask questions that help their students think Christianly. "Integration of faith and learning or a life of wholeness of mind and heart ultimately happens inside a person." Because Christian truth is incarnational, the integration of faith and learning must fundamentally occur in an individual's mind and heart.[38]

Christian colleges should help their students understand and embrace a biblical worldview that directs all their thinking and acting. This holistic perspective of life provides them a distinctive lens for viewing art,

---

*A Centennial Reader* (Grand Rapids: Eerdmans, 1998), 488.

36. Holmes, *The Idea of a Christian College*, 7–8.

37. See William Harry Jellema, "Calvinism and Higher Education," in H. Henry Meeter, ed., *God-Centered Living: Calvinism in Action: A Symposium* (Grand Rapids,: Baker, 1951), 120ff.

38. Shirley A. Mullen, "Faith, Learning, and the Teaching of History," in Arlin C. Migliazzo, ed., *Teaching as an Act of Faith: Theory and Practice in Church-Related Higher Education* (New York: Fordham University Press, 2002), 280–82; quotations from 280.

literature, the social sciences, the natural sciences, the media, marriage, family, politics, education, and all other aspects of life. We must remember that what students typically retain from their classroom experience is much more of an orientation, a viewpoint, a set of impressions than specific content.[39]

In some ways, "the task of Christian scholarship within the academy" is "the same as the task of scholarship in general: to ask well-crafted questions about the world, to formulate creative and well-reasoned answers to those questions," and then to vet those answers to determine which are the most promising for further investigation. Like other scholars, Christian ones strive "to think clearly about the world and to reflect critically on our varying interpretations of the world."[40] However, in numerous other ways, the approach of Christian scholars differs sharply from that of their secular counterparts.

The biblical worldview differs from non-Christian ones in its "pretheoretical first principles [and] presuppositions."[41] Truly integrative Christian thinking refuses to accept a compartmentalization that confines Christianity to the world of subjective values that has nothing useful to say about the objective world.[42] Holmes argues that integrative thinking "requires a thorough analysis of methods and materials and concepts and theoretical structures, a lively and rigorous interpenetration of liberal learning with the content and commitment of Christian faith."[43] All disciplines are highly value laden and can help us explore, understand, and appreciate God's character and world.[44] Although "chemical elements

39. See Frances Fitzgerald, *America Revised* (Boston: Atlantic–Little Brown, 1979), 18, and Warren Nord, *Religion and American Education: Rethinking a National Dilemma* (Chapel Hill: University of North Carolina Press, 1995).

40. Douglas Jacobsen and Rhonda Hustedt Jacobsen, "Contours and Contexts of Christian Scholarship," in *Scholarship and Christian Faith*, 156–57, quotations in that order.

41. George Marsden, "The State of Evangelical Christian Scholarship," *Christian Scholar's Review* 17 (1987) 355.

42. See Ralph McInerny, *Characters in Search of Their Authors* (Notre Dame: University of Notre Dame Press, 2001), 91; Stanley Hauerwas, "On Witnessing Our Story: Christian Education in Liberal Societies," in *Schooling Christians: "Holy Experiments" in American Education*, ed. Hauerwas and John H. Westerhoff (Grand Rapids: Eerdmans, 1992), 225.

43. Holmes, *The Idea of a Christian College*, 7.

44. See Leland Ryken, "The Creative Arts," in *Making of Christian Mind: A Christian World View and the Academic Enterprise*, ed. Arthur Holmes (Downers Grove, IL: InterVarsity Press, 1985).

behave the same way" for Christians and non-Christians, Duane Litfin argues, "theistic causal explanations" of chemistry are crucial to Christian thinking. "Only God is truly independent; all created things, including the chemical elements . . . are utterly contingent upon him. They depend for their existence and their properties on him . . . at all points and at every moment. Thus the very chemical properties we study are Christ's handiwork" that can "declare his glory." Although Christian scholars are fascinated with things in themselves, they do not simply want to measure, study, and explain the creation; they seek to explain how various things display the wisdom, power, and artistry of the Creator.[45]

Holmes contends that Christians should pursue "doxological learning."[46] We should glorify God, Litfin adds, by "utilizing our God-given capacities to discover and correlate" truths about God and "the spiritual, moral, and material dimensions of the world he created."[47] All subject matter is connected to Jesus Christ even if the connection is not apparent.[48] Clearly, some disciplines "are more directly impacted by worldview than others"— philosophy more than math and history more than chemistry.[49]

Mathematics and history provide examples of how a Christian worldview can underlie and direct scholarship and learning. In *Mathematics in a Postmodern Age: A Christian Perspective*, Russell Howell and James Bradley explain how their Christian presuppositions shape their understanding of mathematics. God has created people, they assert, with "the capacity to engage in mathematical inquiry." "Mathematical capacity is good," but because humans are fallen, they can use "mathematical exploration for evil ends." Christians strive to "help fulfill God's purposes for creation." Therefore, they should seek to discern why God gave humans the ability "to engage in mathematical activity" and labor to help the mathematical community fulfill his intentions. Scripture does not directly explain why God has given people mathematical capacities so they must be inferred from the broader purposes God has revealed. Genesis 1 and 2 teach that

45. Litfin, *Conceiving the Christian College*, 160–61; quotations from 160.

46. Arthur Holmes, *Building the Christian Academy* (Grand Rapids: Eerdmans, 2001), 2.

47. Liftin, *Conceiving the Christian College*, 173. See Ken Badley, "Two 'Cop-Outs' in Faith-Learning Integration: Incarnational Integration and Worldviewish Integration," *Spectrum* 28/2 (1996) 105–18.

48. Michael Hamilton, "Reflection and Response: The Elusive Idea of Christian Scholarship," *Christian Scholar's Review* 31 (Fall 2001) 21.

49. David Naugle, *Worldview: The History of a Concept* (Grand Rapids: Eerdmans, 2002), 328.

God wants people to develop culture and care for the creation. Because carefully studying the world "often involves forming precise definitions, measuring, and thinking deductively about the way things are and the way they might be," "mathematics is an essential component of co-creating" with God. Mathematics reveals his love of order, variety, and beauty. Those who recognize this can respond to God with greater awe, reverence, and joy. Moreover, mathematics can help humans improve culture, serve others, and protect the earth.[50]

Christian historians also bring certain foundational assumptions to our work. We believe that God directs history. This does not mean that we can know precisely how God is involved in events or how He views them. Without an authoritative revelation—Scripture—to tell us, we cannot be sure about God's role in or judgment of historical developments. Nevertheless, we try to assess events using the tools God has given us—the Bible, reason, historical training, and personal experience. We should evaluate human ideals and actions in light of God's revealed standards in Scripture. Our teaching and research rest upon biblical insights into the nature of human beings, the process of history, the interplay of evil and redemption within history, the meaning of justice, stewardship, and love, and the structure of created reality.[51] As Mullen explains, Christian historians can use history to draw attention to developments, trends, movements, and individuals that are of particular concern to Christians, pose questions that stimulate "moral and theological reflection," and analyze the human condition by studying historical figures and events.[52]

Christian and secular historians share certain commonalities. First, we strive to faithfully follow the accepted canons of our discipline. This involves using sources appropriately, supporting our arguments through facts and solid reasoning, fairly evaluating all groups we study, and acknowledging our biases. Christian historians seek to "see with merciful and gracious eyes" and bring moral and spiritual sensitivities to bear on

50. Russell Howell and James Bradley, *Mathematics in a Postmodern Age: A Christian Perspective* (Grand Rapids: Eerdmans, 2001), 4–5.

51. See Herbert Butterfield, "God in History," in *Herbert Butterfield: Writings on Christianity and History*, ed. C. T. McIntire (New York: Oxford University Press, 1979); David Bebbington, *Patterns in History: A Christian View* (Downers Grove, IL: InterVarsity Press, 1979); Herbert Butterfield, *Christianity and History* (New York: Scribner, 1949); George Marsden and Frank Roberts, eds., *A Christian View of History?* (Grand Rapids: Eerdmans, 1975); Ronald Wells, *History through the Eyes of Faith* (San Francisco: Harper & Row, 1989); and Ronald Wells, ed., *History and the Christian Historian* (Grand Rapids: Eerdmans, 1998).

52. Mullen, "Faith, Learning, and the Teaching of History," 288.

the subjects we study. We also recognize the "complexity, ambiguity, and mystery in the historical process." We believe that "good and evil are inextricably intertwined. There are tensions, paradoxes, and different visions that may never be satisfactorily resolved in this world." Christian historians must strive to discern the presence of good and truth and to assess the role of "human responsibility in the historical process."[53]

Christian historians also seek to illuminate the underlying presuppositions of other scholars, question their moral judgments, and challenge their inferences (such as how well do the facts support their conclusions) in light of our biblical worldview. Moreover, we strive to examine the history of nations and groups, societal structures and institutions, ideas, mores, and patterns of life according to the insights and values provided by a biblical view of God, humanity, society, and the world.

Over against many secular historians, we argue that religion is an important subject for study and significantly influences culture. Thus in teaching survey courses of various historical eras we reject reductionist approaches that portray religion as a dependent variable that masks something deeper—gender, race, or another ideological commitment. We argue that religion is not inert. Although it is influenced by culture, it has affected the economic, political, social, and intellectual aspects of life in substantial ways. For example, we examine topics that are often neglected in academic contexts, such as the work of Christian missionaries in the non-European world.[54]

We contend that historians are never neutral mirrors who simply reflect back the past. We are creatures of time, place, circumstance, interests, predilections, and culture. Although we are trained in the use and evaluation of evidence, we are not exempt from our personal commitments or our desire to read contemporary needs into past events. We are inescapably part of the evidence we attempt to assess. All historians have a set of overarching convictions that influence how they approach the discipline and what they advocate. Each Christian historian selects, arranges, interprets, and reports facts according to his or her presuppositions. We continually make judgments about what events, movements, people, and activities are historically significant. Often what we exclude is as important as what we include. The value judgments historians make are especially important. Christian historians constantly ask: What does God think of this historical development? While we do not profess to know with certainty how

53. Ibid., 281, 290; first quotation from 281, the remainder from 290.
54. Ibid., 283–85.

God views any particular historical event (except where God's response to events is recorded in Scripture), we ask probing questions about events, people's motives, and results. This helps students evaluate important ethical and historical issues. Finally, as Mullen maintains, "integrating faith and the study of history is also a matter of pedagogy—of cultivating in students not only the information that they ought to know as Christians but also the virtues that ought to characterize their lives as Christians."[55]

Although the biblical worldview should undergird the teaching of all the courses in a Christian college's curriculum, we especially promote this at Grove City College through our Humanities core. Many colleges and universities today no longer have a core curriculum. Instead, in the words of former U.S. Secretary of Education William Bennett, on many campuses "the curriculum has become a self-service cafeteria through which students pass without being nourished."[56] At many institutions students can fulfill their general education requirements by taking very narrowly focused courses.[57] We believe that an integrated set of core courses focusing on the major themes of world civilization through the study of the Bible, history, philosophy, political science, sociology, economics, literature, and the arts grounded upon Christian presuppositions better equips students for life and service. Thus all students at Grove City are required to take six courses that constitute our civilization series as well as a course in Studies in Science, Faith, and Technology and a foundations course in some area of the Social Sciences. Our goal is to help our students develop a love of liberal arts learning. We hope they will see general education requirements not as hoops that must be jumped through to earn a degree, but rather as passports to understanding God and his world that provide alluring windows on his nature, actions, and creation.[58]

The Christian college should integrate faith and learning through a variety of other means. In performance areas such as music, art, and physical education and the development of skills in mathematics, the natural

55. Ibid., 289.

56. William Bennett, 1984 NEH report, "To Reclaim a Legacy," quoted in the *Chronicle of Higher Education*, Nov. 28, 1984, 16.

57. See Lynn Cheney, *50 Hours: A Core Curriculum for College Students* (Washington DC: National Endowment for the Humanities, 1989). Also see Alan Bloom, *The Closing of the American Mind* (New York: Simon & Schuster, 1987); Bruce Wilshire, *The Moral Collapse of the University*, SUNY Series in the Philosophy of Education (Albany: SUNY Press, 1990); Dinesh D'Souza, *Illiberal Education* (New York: Macmillan, 1991); and George Douglas, *Education without Impact: How Our Universities Fail the Young* (New York: Carol Publishing/Birch Lane, 1992).

58. Holmes, *The Idea of a Christian College*, 47.

sciences, and engineering, the attitude and motivation of professors and students is crucial. Moreover, the theoretical foundations for all of these areas should be rooted in God's nature and the way he has designed the universe and human beings. The integration of faith and learning operates in three aspects of the classroom experience: the course content, the course management, and the attitude professors have toward their discipline and encourage students to take toward it.[59]

The integration of faith and learning also involves teaching value judgments. This should not simply entail moralizing at the end of lectures, but employing an evaluative process that undergirds the entire course. Value judgments direct the foundational assumptions, goals, and outcomes stated in the syllabus, the selection of topics covered, the readings and papers that are assigned, and the ways particular issues are addressed.[60]

V. James Mannoia urges Christian institutions of higher education to help their students adopt an approach he calls "critical commitment." He complains that Christian colleges often give students answers to questions they never ask. Although these answers are usually good, they rarely sink

---

59. Mullen, "Faith, Learning, and the Teaching of History," 283. Douglas and Rhonda Jacobsen contend that the integration model offers "many valid and insightful ways of construing the goals and purposes of Christian scholarship." However, it is only one vision of Christian scholarship, not a "one-size fits all paradigm that applies equally to everyone or to every field of scholarly endeavor" ("More than the 'Integration' of Faith and Learning," 25). They also note that almost all advocates of this position are Reformed Christians, most notably Arthur Holmes, Nicholas Wolterstorff, George Marsden, and Mark Noll (25). Moreover, they argue that the integration model has several weaknesses: it implicitly claims to be the only valid approach for connecting faith and learning, the one "path all Christian scholars must follow regardless of their own particular understanding of faith" or their specific disciplines. Second, it is a very philosophical approach to Christian scholarship that requires all Christians to temporarily become philosophers no matter what their field of expertise (24). Finally, they question whether Scripture supplies such a complete view of the world as the model suggests. Revelation, they maintain, is "more piecemeal, offering important clues about the origins, meaning, and purpose of the universe but never spelling things out on fine detail" (28). A further problem is that many Christian professors reject this model. For example, Larry Lyon and Michael Beaty report that 42 percent of faculty members at Baylor University believe that faith and learning "are separate tasks and ought not to be integrated." One respondent to their survey declared, "Attempts to integrate faith and learning are, at best treacherous and often lead to dogma and intolerance." For many Baylor professors, "the truth of scientific knowledge and the truths of religious faith are . . . intellectually insulated from one another." See Larry Lyon and Michael Beaty, "Integration, Secularization, and the Two-Spheres View at Religious Colleges: Comparing Baylor University with the University of Notre Dame and Georgetown College," *Christian Scholar's Review* 29 (Fall 1999) 83–84.

60. Holmes, *The Idea of a Christian College*, 51.

in because they do not address the questions students are truly asking. After students leave the "hothouse environment" of the Christian college, these answers often seem irrelevant. Secular institutions, by contrast, frequently provoke students to ask better questions but give them little help in answering them. Many of their faculty are unwilling to profess anything except their personal tastes or ideological preferences. Christian colleges need to encourage students to ask tough questions even if we cannot fully or even satisfactorily answer them. Graduates of Christian colleges, Mannoia insists, should be "neither dogmatists nor cynics." They should "go beyond dogmatism" by using "the best critical tools available" to respond to life's most challenging questions. They should also move beyond cynical skepticism by committing themselves to Christ and biblical teaching despite whatever doubts they have. "Open to new discoveries and changed belief," critical commitment affirms both belief in ultimate truth and the freedom to question.[61]

One of the major challenges that Christian colleges face today is that most of their faculty have received little or no guidance about how to integrate faith and academic life. Because their graduate training has not assisted, and in many cases has "actively discouraged," establishing connections between their faith and their disciplines, many professors see them as two separate and disjointed bodies of knowledge and belief.[62] Christian colleges can help address this problem by providing workshops that teach their faculty how to integrate their faith and their disciplines, by encouraging faculty to join organizations in their fields that promote the integration of faith and learning, and by urging faculty to read the many excellent monographs and articles Christian scholars have produced on the subject in recent years.[63]

61. Mannoia, *Christian Liberal Arts*, 39–43; all quotations from 43.

62. William Hasker, "Faith-Learning Integration: An Overview," *Christian Scholar's Review* 21 (March 1992) 237.

63. These organizations include the American Scientific Affiliation, the Association of Christian Mathematicians, the Christian Association for Psychological Studies, the Conference on Faith and History, the Conference on Christianity and Literature, Christians in the Visual Arts, the Society of Christian Philosophers, the Association of Christian Librarians, the Fellowship of Christian Economists, the Christian Sociological Society, Christians in Political Science, and the Evangelical Theological Society. Helpful books and articles on the integration of faith and learning include Dovre, ed., *The Future of Religious Colleges*; Andrea Sterk, ed., *Religion, Scholarship, and Higher Education* (Notre Dame, IN: University of Notre Dame Press, 2002); Haynes, ed., *Professing in the Postmodern Academy*; Benne, *Quality with Soul*; Hughes and Adrian, eds., *Models for Christian Higher Education*; John Wilcox and Irene King, eds., *Enhancing Religious Identity: Best Practices from Catholic Colleges* (Washington DC: Georgetown

Postmodernists denounce all worldviews that assert belief in transcendent truth and condemn all viewpoints that offer a unified picture of reality. They denounce such metanarratives as "dangerous creeds designed to marginalize and oppress the weak." Secularists of all stripes strive to push Christianity out of academia and relegate it to the private realm; they try to eliminate God or at most grant him a ceremonial role; much of the media heralds this; almost all textbooks assume it; numerous pundits proclaim it. Rejecting these claims and resisting these pressures, Christian colleges must discuss and debate a wide variety of ideas (ruling out none of them immediately), encourage free and open discourse, and not compel students to embrace any particular positions.[64]

To thrive academically, Christian colleges also need to encourage and reward the scholarship of their faculty and students. They can do this through providing faculty sabbaticals, supplying significant amounts of money for faculty and students to attend conferences, travel, and do research, generously funding faculty and student research projects, publicly recognizing scholarly achievement, and considering scholarship a major component in determining faculty promotions and salaries. Unfortunately, many Christian colleges have not done these things because trustees and administrators feared they would detract from their faculty's commitment to quality teaching, failed to recognize how important these policies are to their mission, or felt inhibited by financial constraints. Administrators should inspire both faculty and students to "the highest level of scholarly aspiration." Through the language they employ and the policies they establish they can stimulate the scholarship of both groups. Christian colleges should reward faculty equally for high-quality teaching, excellent scholarship, and significant service to the campus community. Rhonda and Douglas Jacobsen argue that scholarship is important because

---

University Press, 2000); Douglas V. Henry and Bob R. Agee, *Faithful Learning and the Christian Scholarly Vocation* (Grand Rapids: Eerdmans, 2003); Harold Heie and David L. Wolfe, eds., *The Reality of Christian Learning: Strategies for Faith-Discipline Integration* (Grand Rapids: Eerdmans, 1987); Nicholas Wolterstorff, "Educating for Shalom," in *Essays on Christian Higher Education*, ed. Clarence W. Joldersma and Gloria Goris Stronks (Grand Rapids: Eerdmans, 2004); and Mark Schwehn, "A Christian University: Defining the Difference," *First Things* 93 (1999) 25–31. Mannoia also recommends holding workshops for faculty to discuss sound principles of "student cognitive, moral, and faith development" (136) and to explore "the most appropriate techniques for promoting development at different levels" (139). Moreover, colleges should keep these factors in mind in sequencing their courses. The general education curriculum needs to be matched with the development level of students (137).

64. Liftin, *Conceiving the Christian College*, 268, 179, 259; quotation from 268.

it "adds depth and breadth not only to the scholar's life" and to his or her educational community but "also to the academy, the church, and society. Quality scholarship overflows: it produces passion, curiosity, synergy, and community" beyond "the boundaries of any particular institution."[65] It helps to conserve, transform, and enrich.[66]

## THE INFORMAL CURRICULUM

Numerous aspects of the informal curriculum can also help students develop critical commitment. The informal curriculum plays a very important role in promoting dissonance (challenging preconceived notions by presenting students with alternative views), providing role models, and fostering community. Many fear that dissonance may weaken the faith of Christian students, but in the long run, it is likely to strengthen their faith because confronting various perspectives and arguments forces them to reexamine, question, and defend what they believe.

Residence life can play a crucial role in furthering these ends. Unless residential life promotes cognitive, moral, and faith development as well as social development, it is likely to inhibit rather than advance the mission of the Christian college.[67] In fact, in many institutions residential life is inversely correlated with the development of characteristics typically connected with liberal arts learning.[68]

Cross-cultural experiences—inter-city campuses, short-term missions, travel interims, and semester or summer abroad programs—force students to reappraise how they think, how they relate to others, what they value, and what they believe. Mentoring programs are also very valuable. Students and faculty can commit to spend time together regularly for a semester, year, or longer. These relationships enable them to discuss activities, critique each other's work, and socialize and worship together.[69]

College-wide activities—orientation for new students, admission events, baccalaureate, commencement, and chapel—should also promote

65. Jacobsen and Jacobsen, "Epilogue: Campus Climate and Christian Scholarship," 179–80, 182; first quotation from 179, second from 182.

66. Keith Anderson, *What They Don't Always Teach You at a Christian College* (Downers Grove, IL: InterVarsity Press), 183.

67. Mannoia, *Christian Liberal Arts*, 155.

68. See David G. Winter et al., *A New Case for the Liberal Arts* (San Francisco: Jossey-Bass, 1981).

69. Mannoia, *Christian Liberal Arts*, 154

the college's intrinsic and instrumental goals. As much as possible, the whole college community should help to create, implement, and especially participate in these activities. The chapel program should challenge and disturb students and force them to reevaluate their normal ways of thinking and acting. Chapel speakers should be excellent communicators who have godly character. Programs should help students understand the needs of the world and motivate them to consider how God can use them to meet them and how they can best prepare themselves to do so.[70]

Ensuring diversity—ethnic, racial, religious, political, ideological, and/or geographic—can also help produce graduates who are critically committed and can tackle real world problems. Many Christian colleges have little diversity because their students come from the same regions, socioeconomic class, racial group, and denominational background and share the same political perspectives.[71] Diversity makes dissonance and controversy much more likely and helps students develop critical commitment. Exposing students to varied perspectives about all kinds of subjects—politics, media, medical ethics, economics, worship styles, social justice, and theology—is especially important. Faculty panels and debates should be frequent and stimulating on controversial issues such as the death penalty or homosexual marriage. Having students of different races or nationalities may or may not significantly increase diversity, although it often prompts students to reexamine their fundamental assumptions more than they would otherwise. Gender diversity is also helpful because men and women see many issues differently. Interacting with male and female students, faculty, and administrators as well as with people of color and individuals of varied temperament, interests, and experiences can help prepare students to confront postcollege life.[72] Role models who are female, members of racial minorities, or citizens of other countries can especially help provide alternative understandings of the world and life. Short-term visiting professors who are part of other religious traditions or atheists, speakers who represent alternative perspectives, and films, art, and music that offer unconventional views can all enrich the campus environment and experience of students.

70. Ibid., 158, 160.
71. Ibid., 161.
72. Ibid., 162.

## CONCLUSION

The mission of today's Christian colleges is extremely challenging and incredibly important. They are called to prepare well-educated, committed Christians who can serve God lovingly, joyfully, courageously, and diligently in a world with enormous spiritual, material, and physical needs. While churches, parachurch organizations, and Christian professors at secular institutions help in this task, Christian colleges have the primary responsibility of equipping Christians to advance God's kingdom through the professions, the business world, and voluntary organizations. The ability to do this effectively depends in large part on their faithfulness to God's Word and their commitment to basing all aspects of their life and work—their promotion of calling, character development, community, service, justice, constructive engagement with the world, and critical commitment, and their formal and informal curriculum—on biblical norms and principles. Just as the Holy Spirit enables the church's many diverse members to function as one body, so he can empower Christian colleges despite their members' differences in age, ideology, interests, and religious practice, to function as one body that faithfully serves God and advances his kingdom in the world.[73]

73. Ibid., 194.

# 7

# Unpopular Opinions
## *Dorothy L. Sayers on Education*

## Janice B. Brown

*There is only the fight to recover what has been lost*
*And found and lost again and again*

— T. S. ELIOT

SOMETIMES WE NEED TO go back in order to make progress. The need to retrieve what was best in the past is described in the epigraph above as the constant "fight to recover what has been lost." Like T. S. Eliot, Dorothy L. Sayers believed such a return to the past to be necessary in many areas of life. Her view of culture and tradition is conservative, holistic, and relentlessly Christian, and is, therefore, particularly relevant to the consideration of higher education.

Such views are not always popular. But Dorothy L. Sayers did not mind if her opinions were unpopular; in fact, she published one volume of essays under the title *Unpopular Opinions.* The unusually high value she placed on things of the past is reflected particularly in what Sayers had to say about education. In a novel she wrote in 1935, she reminded her readers that Oxford University has been called "the home of lost causes." Though she loved Oxford passionately, she seemed to agree with that designation, and even to delight in it.

The word "lost" is, in itself, a key to Sayers's position on education. But like Eliot, she did not believe that the best things of the past were permanently lost. She saw them as things we must perennially fight to recover.

Clearly, the historical context in which Sayers thought and wrote is relevant to what she had to say on cultural issues. Her most productive years as a writer were the 1940s and 50s—a time when England was in crisis. First there was the Second World War, which ended in 1945, and then the trauma of the recovery period, which lasted from 1945 well into the 1950s. The process of reestablishing a postwar cultural equilibrium involved the rethinking of many basic assumptions of life. The Church of England played a key role in this process because it was still a major influence in British society. Dorothy L. Sayers had become a well-known, though unofficial, spokesperson for the Church's position—or at least for a *Christian* position of the sort that most people expected to be compatible with that of the official Church.

Throughout the 1940s and 1950s Sayers wrote prolifically on many crucial subjects. The titles of some of her publications in the 40s indicate the kind of concerns she addressed: *Begin Here* (her proposed basis for a re-formed society, 1940); *The Church in the New Age* (1941); *A Christian Basis for the Post-War World* (1942); *A Time is Born* (1945); *Making Sense of the Universe* (1946); *Creed or Chaos* (1947); and *The Lost Tools of Learning* (1947). The last of these, "The Lost Tools of Learning," is the most comprehensive statement of Sayers's view of the ills in education and the means of curing them.

## THE LOST TOOLS OF LEARNING

This paper was delivered at a "Vacation Course in Education" held at Oxford. In it Sayers identifies the symptoms of educational failure, diagnoses the cause of the symptoms to be a particular kind of teaching, and proposes the cure—a different kind of teaching.

Although by the middle of the twentieth century literacy was at a higher level than ever before, Sayers saw that people were poorer than ever at critical thinking, and especially susceptible to mass propaganda. Her paper includes many specific examples of this. She notes that people are generally unable to debate a topic competently. She asks, "Have you ever, in listening to a debate among adult and presumably responsible people, been fretted by the extraordinary inability of the average debater to speak to the question, or to meet and refute the arguments of speakers on the other side?"[1] Such incompetency involves many different factors: failure to define terms or respond to terms as defined; careless syntax; failure to keep to the topic. She concedes that many of these things probably are taught in school to some degree, but seem to have been so poorly learned that they are easily forgotten.

These failures in reasoning as applied to discussion are closely linked, she feels, to several other symptoms of educational failure. Though people come through the school system and even college with what might be regarded as a reasonably good reading level, many of them are still "unable to distinguish between a book that is sound, scholarly and properly documented," and one that is quite the opposite.[2] Students generally lack skill in reading critically, and this goes hand in hand with a general inability in research. Much education packages topics in such a way that people never learn how to tackle a new subject for themselves. Indeed, people are especially inept at thinking *across* topics. They tend to compartmentalize their thinking: "a 'subject' remains a 'subject,' divided by water-tight bulk-heads from all other 'subjects,' so that they experience very great difficulty in making an immediate mental connection between [one discipline and another]."[3]

The far-reaching effects of poor writing and logic are evidenced in one particular case that Sayers observed in a weekly paper. A biologist was quoted as actually claiming that the resemblance between variations produced by stock breeders and variations produced by natural selection is evidence against the existence of a divine creator. In such unsound reasoning, Sayers points out, "all that is proved by the biologist's argument is that he was unable to distinguish between a material and a final cause."[4]

She observes, also, that poor reasoning skill is widely apparent on a much more mundane level:

1. Dorothy L. Sayers, *The Lost Tools of Learning* (London: Methuen, 1948), 4.
2. Ibid., 4–5.
3. Ibid., 5.
4. Ibid., 6.

> Has it ever struck you as odd, or unfortunate, that today when the proportion of literacy throughout Western Europe is higher than it has ever been, people should have become susceptible to the influence of advertisement and mass-propaganda to an extent hither-to unheard-of and unimagined? Do you put this down to the mere mechanical fact that the press and the radio and so on have made propaganda much easier to distribute over a wide area? Or do you sometimes have an uneasy suspicion that the product of modern educational methods is less good than he or she might be at disentangling fact from opinion and the proven from the plausible?[5]

The problems that Sayers identified over sixty years ago have only intensified, and as we look closely at what alarmed her in 1947, we can recognize the same basic educational failures that plague our culture today.

Sayers attempted to identify causes of the widespread educational failure that she saw evidence of all around her, especially in newspapers, and even in such prestigious literary papers as the *Times Literary Supplement*. Though she wondered whether the effects of the mass media might be part of the problem, she saw that the inadequate preparation for "disentangling fact from opinion and the proven from the plausible"[6] must have to do with the educational system. She diagnoses the problem as having to do, not with what is taught, but with the way it is taught, and urges educators to "inquire whether, amid all the multitudinous subjects which figure in the syllabuses, [they are] really teaching the right things in the right way."[7] She asks, "Is not the great defect of our education today—a defect traceable through all the disquieting symptoms of trouble that I have mentioned—that although we often succeed in teaching our pupils 'subjects,' we fail lamentably on the whole in teaching them how to think?"[8] Though young people are taught many useful things, they are not specifically taught the most basic thing of all—"the art of learning."[9] When people are taught to do things mechanically, without understanding them, their knowledge is not transferable to a new task. We can certainly recognize some current education practices in Sayers's observation that in the teaching of certain arts and crafts, it is sometimes required that the child simply "express himself" in paint before he is taught how to handle the colors and

5. Ibid., 4.
6. Ibid., 4.
7. Ibid., 2.
8. Ibid., 7.
9. Ibid.

the brush.[10] And yet, as she rightly observes, this "is not the way in which a trained craftsman will go about to teach himself a new medium."[11]

Clearly, the most important thing is to learn *how to learn,* and in her paper on "The Lost Tools of Learning" delivered to educators in 1947, Sayers develops a very concrete scheme through which she thinks this can best be accomplished. She proposes radical reforms—radical because they involve turning back the calendar to the way education was understood and conducted in the late Middle Ages. Proposing this drastic step was, however, something of a facetious ploy. She knew (or thought she knew) that the idea would never be seriously taken up, but she proposed it as a gesture of appreciation, even reverence, for what was best in medieval education:

> This prospect need arouse neither hope nor alarm. It is in the highest degree improbable that the reforms I propose will ever be carried into effect. Neither the parents, nor the training colleges, nor the examination boards, nor the boards of governors, nor the Ministry of Education would countenance them for a moment. For they amount to this: that if we are to produce a society of educated people, fitted to preserve their intellectual freedom amid the complex pressures of our modern society, we must turn back the wheel of progress some four or five hundred years, to the point at which education began to lose sight of its true object, towards the end of the Middle Ages.[12]

One major distinctive of the medieval approach to education was the very early point in a young person's life at which "higher" education actually began:

> When we think about the remarkably early age at which the young men went up to the University in, let us say, Tudor times, and thereafter were held fit to assume responsibility for the conduct of their own affairs, are we altogether comfortable about the artificial prolongation of intellectual childhood and adolescence into the years of physical maturity which is so marked in our own day? . . . The stock argument in favour of postponing the school-leaving age and prolonging the period of education generally is that there is now so much more to learn than there was in the Middle Ages. This is partly true, but not wholly. The modern boy and girl are certainly taught more subjects—but

10. Ibid., 8.

11. Ibid.

12. Ibid., 2.

does that always mean that they are actually more learned and know more?"[13]

Sayers argues, however, that there was something else that was much more important than the age at which serious education began, or the length of time it took. What she admires most is the nature of the medieval *Syllabus*. The way it was organized was key. It was an ordered plan that reflected not only the overall intention of education, but also the way it should be sequenced. Medieval education had two main parts: *Trivium* (which had three divisions) and *Quadrivium* (which had four subjects), taught in that order. The crucial thing, in Sayers's opinion, was that the Trivium was taught first, because it provided the preliminary discipline, or the "tools" needed for all subsequent learning.

The three parts of the Trivium are Grammar, Dialectic, and Rhetoric, taught in that order.[14] But, according to Sayers's application of this medieval educational approach, these are not "subjects" in the ordinary sense of the word: "they are only methods of dealing with subjects."[15] Grammar can, of course, be thought of as a "subject" in the sense that it means learning to read and speak a specific language—in the Middle Ages the first language taught was Latin. Sayers explains the value of "Grammar" (language learning) and the value of the other two parts of the Trivium:

> Grammar . . . does mean definitely learning a language . . . But language itself is simply the medium in which thought is expressed. The whole of the Trivium was, in fact, intended to teach the pupil the proper use of the tools of learning, before he began to apply them to "subjects" at all. First, he learned a language; not just how to order a meal in a foreign language, but the structure of language—*a* language, and hence of language itself—what it was, how it was put together and how it worked. Secondly [when he moved on to Dialectic], he learned how to use language: how to define his terms and make accurate statements; how to construct an argument and how to detect fallacies in argument (his own arguments and other people's). Dialectic, that is to say, embraced Logic and Disputation. Thirdly [when he moved on to Rhetoric], he learned to express himself in language; how to say what he had to say elegantly and persuasively . . . At the end of his course, he was required to compose a thesis upon some theme set by his masters or chosen by himself, and

13. Ibid., 3.
14. Ibid., 8.
15. Ibid.

afterwards to defend his thesis against the criticism of the faculty. By this time he would have learned—or woe betide him—not merely to write an essay on paper, but to speak audibly and intelligibly from a platform, and to use his wits quickly when heckled.[16]

Sayers acknowledges that some continuation of the medieval Trivium had filtered down to the British education system of the mid-twentieth century. She points out, though, that a lot of these processes—like learning the structured patterns of a foreign language, learning to write a tightly reasoned essay, and learning to debate formally—are "cultivated more or less in detachment, as belonging to the special subjects in which they are pigeon-holed rather than as forming one coherent scheme of mental training to which all 'subjects' stand in a subordinate relation."[17] It is unsound educationally to teach thinking skills in a casual, haphazard way, and to separate activities pertaining to the development of mental acuity, rather than working toward coherence in mental training. Dialectic, for example, may be learned through participating in debates, but this is chiefly an extracurricular activity taken up by very few, and one which receives little emphasis.

Sayers sums up the main differences between the medieval way of laying an educational foundation through the Trivium and what we have in modern times:

> Taken by and large, the great difference of emphasis between the two conceptions holds good: modern education concentrates on *teaching subjects*, leaving the method of thinking, arguing and expressing one's conclusions to be picked up by the scholar as he goes along; mediaeval education concentrated on first *forging and learning to handle the tools of learning*, using whatever subject came handy as a piece of material on which to doodle until the use of the tool became second nature.[18]

In contrast, Sayers observes the ill-preparedness of modern young people for the challenges they will face:

> [W]e let our young men and women go out unarmed, in a day when armor was never so necessary. By teaching them all to read, we have left them at the mercy of the printed word. By the invention of the film and the radio, we have made certain that

16. Ibid., 8–9.

17. Ibid., 10.

18. Ibid., 10.

no aversion to reading shall secure them from the incessant battery of words, words, words. They do not know what the words mean; they do not know how to ward them off or blunt their edge or fling them back; they are a prey to words in their emotions instead of being the masters of them in their intellects.[19]

Sayers, at this point in her paper, turns from simply describing the advantages of the medieval approach to education, to do something much more daring. She says, "We cannot go back to the Middle Ages—or can we?"[20] She proceeds to explicate her plan—not a plan for going back in time to reinstate all the features of medieval education, but a plan for "the revision of an error" through the use of the medieval concept of the Trivium. Clearly, we cannot literally go back to the Middle Ages in the sense of the actual fourteenth century, but there is no reason why we should not return to a particular educational technique:

Let us amuse ourselves by imagining that such progressive retrogression is possible. Let us make a clean sweep of all educational authorities, and furnish ourselves with a nice little school of boys and girls whom we may experimentally equip for the intellectual conflict along lines chosen by ourselves. We will endow them with exceptionally docile parents; we will staff our school with teachers who are themselves perfectly familiar with the aims and methods of the Trivium; we will have our buildings and staff large enough to allow our classes to be small enough for adequate handling; and we will postulate a Board of Examiners willing and qualified to test the products we turn out. Thus prepared, we will attempt to sketch out a syllabus—a modern Trivium "with modifications"; and we will see where we get to.[21]

This extreme proposal naturally provokes incredulity, but a surprisingly successful direction in modern education has actually developed in direct response to it. Sayers's idea was more doable than her audience in 1947 could have dreamt, perhaps even more than she herself dreamt, as the American "Logos" schools have proven. Since the first one was founded in 1981 under the leadership of Douglas Wilson, Logos Schools have attempted to follow the classical Trivium model, as described by Sayers. Douglas Wilson's book on this "Classical" Christian School movement, published in 1991, was called *Recovering the Lost Tools of Learning* to

19. Ibid., 12.
20. Ibid., 13.
21. Ibid., 14.

indicate the great debt to Sayers.[22] It produced much interest nationwide in the classical approach to education. The Logos school movement contributed to the formation of the Association of Classical & Christian Schools (ACCS), that continues to offer annual national conferences and practical assistance in the forming and growing of classical Christian schools.

Sayers's paper goes on to develop the details of her proposed syllabus. What she proposes appears initially to have most to do with lower levels of education, and little to do with the issue of *higher* education. However, the whole point of the Trivium-based education in elementary and high schools is that it provides the necessary solid basis for higher education. A brief look at her proposed program will allow us to more fully appreciate the implications it has for higher education.

It is impossible to begin the Trivium *too* early. The earlier one begins to educate children properly, the less they will have to unlearn. Sayers proposes three stages of early childhood development: the *"Poll-parrot"* stage when learning by heart is easy and reasoning difficult; the *"Pert"* stage, characterized by "contradicting, answering-back, liking to 'catch people out' (especially one's elders)" and in the wrestling with conundrums; and the *"Poetic"* stage, (corresponding with puberty), which is characterized by self-centeredness, restlessness, and the yearning to express oneself and exert independence.[23] This last stage has much promise, however, since it is also a time of creativity, "a reaching-out towards a synthesis of what it already knows, and a deliberate eagerness to know and do some one thing in preference to all others."[24]

Sayers applies these three stages to the Trivium, showing how *Grammar* is best learned at the Poll-parrot stage, *Dialectic* at the Pert stage, and *Rhetoric* at the Poetic stage.[25]

Teaching at the *Grammar* level should include not only a foreign language, but also other subjects like literature, history, geography, science, mathematics, and theology. The focus at this stage, however, should be on memorization, recitation, and the acquisition of basic facts about things. Modern education does this to a large extent, but Sayers argues that teachers need to view "all these activities less as 'subjects' in themselves than as a

22. Douglas Wilson, *Recovering the Lost Tools of Learning* (Wheaton, IL: Crossway, 1991).

23. Sayers, *The Lost Tools of Learning*, 15.

24. Ibid., 15.

25. Ibid., 15.

gathering-together of *material* for use in the next part of the Trivium."[26] It is thus understood to be good and necessary to encourage memorization, even of things that the child cannot yet rationally explain or analyze. The key thing about this stage is that material is being collected and stored.

Next, at the Pert stage, the subject is *Dialectic*. The "master-faculty" of this stage is "the Discursive Reason" and the focus of study is formal logic[27]—a subject area popular in the Middle Ages that has since been almost totally lost:

> The disrepute into which Formal Logic has fallen is entirely unjustified; and its neglect is the root cause of nearly all those disquieting symptoms which we have noted in the modern intellectual constitution. Logic has been discredited, partly because we have fallen into a habit of supposing that we are conditioned almost entirely by the intuitive and the unconscious . . . A secondary cause for the disfavour into which Formal Logic has fallen is the belief that it is necessarily based on universal assumptions that are either unprovable or tautological. This is not true. Not all universal propositions are of this kind . . . Logic is the art of arguing correctly . . . Indeed, the practical utility of Formal Logic today lies not so much in the establishment of positive conclusions as in the prompt detection and exposure of invalid inference.[28]

Sayers proceeds to address the way *Dialectic* should be used in a range of subjects, focusing on techniques of argument, debate, criticism, and evaluation. Since children of this age are naturally argumentative, this tendency must be channeled for good use, but teachers must be up to the task of answering their pupils. Toward the end of this stage, students will begin to realize the limitations of their own knowledge and reason, and the faculty of imagination will come into play, leading to the synthesis of elements of the first two stages.

This brings us, of course, to the Poetic stage, in which *Rhetoric* is the focus. During this stage, Sayers proposes, students should be encouraged to specialize in one or two subject areas or interest areas, while not wholly abandoning others. Such specialization in the latter part of high school will allow for the "final synthesis of the Trivium—the presentation of a

---

26. Ibid., 19.
27. Ibid., 20.
28. Ibid., 21.

public defense of the thesis."[29] Sayers believes that this valuable exercise "should be restored in some form; perhaps as a kind of 'leaving examination' during the last term at school."[30]

At the age of sixteen, students are prepared to pursue "subjects" of university study—the higher education that corresponds to the medieval Quadrivium:

> For the tools of learning are the same, in any and every subject; and the person who knows how to use them will, at any age, get the mastery of a new subject in half the time and with a quarter of the effort expended by the person who has not the tools at his command. To learn six subjects without remembering how they were learnt does nothing to ease the approach to a seventh; to have learnt and remembered the art of learning makes the approach to every subject an open door.[31]

Though some of the good things in the medieval system of education have lingered on in the education of the later centuries, they have been steadily fading. By the 1940s most of the men and women who handled public affairs, wrote books and newspapers, participated in research and the arts, and educated young people had "never, even in a lingering traditional memory, undergone the scholastic discipline."[32] Sayers powerfully uses her metaphor of "tools" in the closing paragraph of her paper:

> We have lost the tools of learning—the axe and the wedge, the hammer and the saw, the chisel and the plane—that were so adaptable to all tasks. Instead of them, we have merely a set of complicated jigs, each of which will do but one task and no more, and in using which eye and hand receive no training, so that no man ever sees the work as a whole, or "looks to the end of the work." What use is it to pile task on task and prolong the days of labour, if at the close the chief object is left unobtained? It is not the fault of the teachers—they work only too hard already. The combined folly of a civilization that has forgotten its own roots is forcing them to shore up the tottering weight of an educational structure that is built upon sand. They are doing for their pupils the work which the pupils themselves ought to do. For the sole true end of education is simply this: to teach men

29. Ibid., 26.
30. Ibid.
31. Ibid., 28.
32. Ibid., 30.

how to learn for themselves; and whatever instruction fails to do this is effort spent in vain.[33]

## A UNIVERSITY AS A "HOME OF LOST CAUSES"

We turn now from Sayers's view of the necessary preparation for higher education to her thoughts on the best sort of higher education. For this the model was Oxford.

Oxford University is in many ways the quintessential university. No other institution of higher education has had a greater influence; no other has so represented the ultimate in learning.

Sayers graduated from Oxford in 1915, and because she happened to have been born there (though her parents lived there only briefly) she thought of Oxford—both the city and the University—as doubly hers. In a youthful poem she wrote, "Oxford! . . . / I that am twice thy child, have known thee, worshipped thee, loved thee."[34] By looking closely at what Sayers said about Oxford, including her designation of it as "the home of lost causes," we discover what she believed to be most valuable in higher education.

It was Matthew Arnold who first proposed that Oxford was "the home of lost causes." It is an ambiguous proclamation, but one that has stuck. Taken at face value it may seem to be a condemnation of an Oxford education as something that is ultimately useless, and—by transference— a condemnation of all higher education that is traditionally based in the humanities as Oxford is. But many people have *admiringly* called Oxford "the home of lost causes," and Dorothy L. Sayers was one of them. The expression actually does point to what it was she wanted to affirm about Oxford in particular, and about a certain kind of higher education, generally.

Since the expression may mean different things to different people, let us consider Arnold's "lost causes" comment in its context to try to determine what *he* meant by it:

> Beautiful city! so venerable, so lovely . . . And yet, steeped in sentiment as she lies, spreading her gardens to the moonlight, and whispering from her towers the last enchantments of the Middle Age, who will deny that Oxford, by her ineffable charm, keeps ever calling us nearer to the true goal of all of us, to the

33. Ibid.
34. Dorothy L. Sayers, "Lay," lines 1, 3, in *Op I.* (Oxford: Blackwell, 1916).

ideal, to perfection,—to beauty, in a word, which is only truth
seen from another side? . . . Adorable dreamer, whose heart has
been so romantic! who hast given thyself so prodigally, given
thyself to sides and to heroes not mine, only never to the Philistines! home of lost causes, and forsaken beliefs, and unpopular
names, and impossible loyalties! . . . what is our puny warfare
against the Philistines, compared with the warfare which this
queen of romance has been aging against them for centuries,
and will wage after we are gone?[35]

Many of the words in this passage are very positive. Everyone who
has experienced Oxford, however briefly, recognizes its extreme loveliness
of appearance and atmosphere, and, clearly, Arnold—modern nineteenth
century man though he was—found that beauty intoxicating. Arnold also
praises Oxford for always standing against what he calls the "Philistines,"
by which he meant the lowbrow and uncultured people. What Arnold, on
the other hand, disapproves of about Oxford is significant and at least par-
tially valid. He is accurate in connecting Oxford closely with the Middle
Ages; yet we see that he means this as something undesirable, because he
proceeds to call it a "dreamer" and "romantic" and a "queen of romance,"
and identifies it with things of the past that he viewed as archaic. To Arnold the things that Oxford stood for were largely irrelevant to the modern
world of the late nineteenth century, and he makes it clear that he does not
admire many of the "heroes" with whom Oxford sided. It is these people—
the ultimate scholars—that Arnold sees as having "unpopular names" and
as holding "beliefs" that the world has now "forsaken."

Sayers was just as enthralled by the beauty of Oxford, but she was
quite the opposite of Matthew Arnold in her view of these *seemingly*
"lost causes." Her use of the phrase occurs in a scene in the novel *Gaudy
Night,* during a formal dinner in a women's college. The novel's protago-
nist, Harriet, muses on what is being said about the University's ultimate
significance:

[The speaker] spoke gravely, unrolling the great scroll of history,
pleading for the Humanities, proclaiming the Pax Academica in
a world of terrified unrest. "Oxford has been called the home of
lost causes: if the love of learning for its own sake is a lost cause
everywhere else in the world, let us see to it that here at least,
it finds an abiding home." . . . [Harriet] saw it as a Holy War,
and . . . that even slightly absurd collection of chattering women

35. Matthew Arnold, "Oxford," *Passages from the Prose Writings of Matthew Arnold*
(New York: MacMillan, 1880), 74–75.

fused into a corporate unity with one another, and with every
man and woman to whom integrity of mind meant more than
material gain . . . [O]ne could realize that one was a citizen of no
mean city. It might be an old and an old-fashioned city, with in-
convenient buildings, and narrow streets . . . but her foundations
were set upon the holy hills and her spires touched heaven.[36]

From this passage we see that Sayers understands the "love of learning for
its own sake" and the valuing of "integrity of mind" more than financial
gain to be the things which are highly prized in Oxford, but often de-
spised—indeed considered to be "lost causes"—by the rest of the world.

Many ordinary citizens of Sayers's day expressed such prejudice
against Oxford. There were frequent complaints in the public press about
the money wasted on such an impractical thing as a university education.
Oxford's sort of education was commonly discussed (perhaps by the sort
of people that Arnold would call Philistines), and people would express
their opinions as to "what was wrong with Oxford."

Sayers decided to reply to these ill-founded accusations. Her paper
"What Is Right with Oxford?" appeared in the 1935 Summer issue of a
University publication called *Oxford*. It challenged the view that "the older
universities have 'lost touch with modern conditions' and must either be
'brought in line' or abolished," and took exception to the view that Oxford graduates "carry away nothing but a sense of failure and futility."[37]
What is found at Oxford, Sayers explains, is something "more seemly,
more beautiful, and more valuable than the commodities of the common
market-place."[38] That something can be largely summed up by one word—
*scholarship*. It is a word that is shied away from in newspaper columns,
the kind of word of which, she believes, "agitators are ashamed or afraid,
because it brings time to the bar of eternity."[39]

With this mention of "the bar of eternity" we see a connection with
the *Gaudy Night* passage quoted above, in which Oxford is pictured as
having foundations that are "set upon the holy hills" and spires that touch
heaven. For Sayers, loving learning and loving God are inextricably linked,
and the scholars of the Middle Ages would certainly have made the same

36. Dorothy L. Sayers, *Gaudy Night* (London: Gollancz, 1935), 29–30.

37. Dorothy L. Sayers, "What Is Right with Oxford?" *Oxford* 2.1 (Summer, 1935)
34–35.

38. Ibid., 35.

39. Ibid., 36.

connection. The otherworldliness implied by valuing "integrity of mind" more than "material gain" was a kind spiritually akin to religious faith.[40]

Scholarship was, for Sayers, the validating characteristic of higher education. She continues the argument of "What Is Right with Oxford?" affirming that the fact that a university turns out not just "graduates," but "scholars," is precisely what *does* make it relevant in the modern world:

> Oxford, however strange or repugnant it may appear, was after all founded for scholars, and it is by her scholarship that she must survive if she survives at all. Nor was there perhaps ever a time in the world's history when scholarship was so bitterly needed as it is today . . . [I]t is surely of great use to acquire the scholarly judgment that can settle any doctrine upon the evidence, without haste, without passion, and without self-interest. The integrity of mind that money cannot buy; the humility in the face of the facts that self-esteem cannot corrupt: these are the fruits of scholarship, without which all statement is propaganda and all argument special pleading . . . The most striking characteristic of the man who has been semi-educated in an unscholarly tradition is his pathetic helplessness under the domination of words.[41]

Sayers goes on, in the same paper, to point out that it is a huge mistake "to suppose that the scholarly habit of mind is necessarily unpractical" and to argue that "it is the scholar's great strength that he is, in the last resort, more supple and adaptable than the doctrinaire."[42] For example, an Oxford graduate, hired to work in a bookstore, may initially disappoint his employer by his lack of skill in manual tasks like the tying up of parcels. However, Sayers firmly believes that if that graduate is indeed a *scholar,* such technical incapacities will be more than compensated for by his intrinsic humility and eagerness to learn.

Scholarship is essentially not about what one *does*; it has more to do with what one *is*. It is something that grows with us over a lifetime. "[I]f scholarship and the scholarly outlook are what we really value in Oxford men and women," Sayers points out, "it ought not to surprise us if these qualities are still imperfectly developed at the age of twenty-two."[43] But

40. Sayers, *Gaudy Night,* 37.
41. Sayers, "What Is Right with Oxford?" 36–37.
42. Ibid., 37, 38.
43. Ibid., 3.

when the root of scholarship is there, planted by an institution of higher education, the fruits come slowly but steadily to maturity.

To be such a passionate lover of learning is both exciting and demanding—demanding even for the bystanders, like family and friends:

> Indeed, the insatiable and embarrassing appetite for miscellaneous instruction which all great scholars exhibit is often disconcerting for their friends, and makes their company as exacting and exhausting as that of an intelligent and inquisitive child . . . [The scholar] is apt to puzzle his colleagues by the lightness with which he sits to his task, and by his extraordinary habit of cheerfully discussing all kinds of things which others take for granted; but he is liked for his disinterestedness and generosity of mind.[44]

Schools of higher education must operate on the assumption, and instill the conviction, that learning is not a means to an end, but an end in itself. "It might even be well, at the present day," Sayers says, "to discourage people from coming to the universities unless they are prepared to look on learning as its own reward."[45]

What a person gains from such a college or university education lasts a lifetime. Part of this is, of course, bound up with the mystique of memories. Sayers was nostalgic in looking back on her Oxford days, remembering "moonlight over Radcliffe Square," "bells that ring to evening prayer," "winter nights with lamps agleam," and "worn steps of an ancient stair."[46] But, though precious, such memories are trivial compared to the integral and lasting quality of *mind* (and perhaps even of *soul*) that is developed through this kind of higher education:

> It is a simple fact that the brain (commonly speaking) outlasts both the body and the emotions, so that it is rare indeed for the scholar to outlive his own interests and usefulness . . . [Oxford's sort of education] value is not in the sentimental memories of our youth, but in the unquenchable enthusiasms of our old age. If we alter schools and syllabuses in the name of progress, there is no harm done; but if we alter the spirit in which we undertake them, we shall show ourselves not progressive but afraid; and

44. Ibid., 39–40.
45. Ibid., 40.
46. Sayers, "Lay, IX," lines 135, 137, 141, 145, in *Op I.*

there is fear enough in the world to-day, without our joining in the rout.[47]


## CHRISTIANITY AND EDUCATION

Medieval education was an integral part of medieval Christianity, and universities like Oxford and Cambridge were founded and operated by scholars who were churchmen. It was not that they *happened* to be both academics and clergy; in the Middle Ages to be one was to also be the other. It was precisely because Sayers held a Christian worldview that she so strongly affirmed the best qualities of the medieval educational system and the best qualities of the ancient universities. As late as the middle of the twentieth century, the school system in England was closely connected to the state church—the Church of England. State funded education was, at least nominally, thought of as Christian education.

In 1942 Sayers was asked to write a foreword to a publication called *What Is Christian Education?* It was a report on a study conducted by the Education Committee of the Christian Auxiliary Movement. In this study, and in Sayers's foreword to it, no distinction is made between Christian education and good education of a general sort. It seems that neither the Education Committee nor Sayers felt that such a distinction was necessary. It was the record of a "piece of group thinking" by a group of teachers, clergy, and parents about the system of public education, and it was hoped that the report would "help teachers who are Christians to see the implications of their faith in terms of their professional work."[48]

It is easy to see from Sayers's foreword how closely she identifies ideals of education delineated in "The Lost Tools of Learning" and "What Is Right with Oxford?" with the concept of "Christian Education."

> Christian education is based upon a coherent philosophy interpreting all experience: that is, it educates the child to be (*a*) a man (*b*) among men (*c*) in a universe which makes sense. Purely "technical" education, ignoring man's nature, tends to educate him "to make a living," thus treating him not as a man but as a unit in an economic scheme; purely "humanist" education, lacking any basic assumptions about the universe, tends toward a skeptical lack of purpose—since man, when unexplained by

47. Sayers, "What Is Right with Oxford?" 41.

48. Dorothy L. Sayers, "Foreword," in *What is Christian Education? A Piece of Group Thinking,* Recorded by Reeves and Drewett (New York: MacMillan, 1942), xiii.

any doctrine of sinfulness, offers but a shifting and unsatisfactory exemplar for his own guidance. The opposition and conflict between humanist and technical education occur only in the absence of a religious philosophy which can combine the two within a consistent pattern of man's double relation to God and creation, and so give reality to his relations with his fellow-men.[49]

I should like to lay particular stress upon this synthesis of philosophy and technique, which demands that the young person should learn not only to do his job well, but to do it with an eager understanding of its (and his) value and meaning in the scheme of things as a whole.[50]

In a society which prefers cheap work to good work and deleterious rubbish to beautiful and useful products, it is difficult to persuade the worker to assign eternal values to the results of his labour. It is, as the report makes clear, this confusion of values which has degraded the position of the "humanities" in the eyes of the common man. Academic learning, divorced from technical skill and given an artificial "value" in terms of salary and social status, has become a preserve of privilege. A violent reaction against this unnatural state of things has produced that contempt of learning which characterizes the present age, with the result that the creative imagination and the critical control of the intellect have been driven out of daily life and public affairs. Without these, the mass of the people are left at the mercy of any propaganda that exploits their appetites and emotions.[51]

No one tries to harmonize his life or see it whole. Not only, then, do we need a better understanding of the function of the community and the school in education, but also of the Christian doctrine of the wholeness of personality.[52]

## CONCLUSION

What Dorothy L. Sayers had to say sixty years ago has much relevance today. She expressed her Christian view of higher education in pointing out

49. Ibid., vii–viii.
50. Ibid., viii.
51. Ibid., viii.
52. Ibid., xi–xii.

the need to recover the "lost tools of learning," in connecting a university education with ideals of scholarship that the modern world views as "lost causes," and in identifying holistic education as Christian education.

Sayers was not the only one, or the first one, to say such things. A hundred years earlier John Henry Newman eloquently defended the same educational values in *The Idea of a University*.[53] We have numerous recent examples, like Mark Noll in *The Scandal of the Evangelical Mind* (1995)[54] arguing for the necessity of real scholarship, and Norman Klassen and Jens Zimmermann in *The Passionate Intellect* (2006)[55] promoting "incarnational humanism" as the Christian essence that should be the bedrock of higher education.

The reaffirmation of traditional educational values is an ongoing struggle, but not a futile one. Its nature is expressed most profoundly in the passage from which my opening epigraph was taken—from the fifth movement of T. S. Eliot's "East Coker," one of the *Four Quartets*:

> And what there is to conquer
> By strength and submission, has already been discovered
> Once or twice, or several times, by men whom one cannot hope
> To emulate—but there is no competition—
> There is only the fight to recover what has been lost
> And found and lost again and again: and now, under conditions
> That seem unpropitious. But perhaps neither gain nor loss.
> For us, there is only the trying. The rest is not our business.[56]

Here Eliot is speaking of much more than his own struggle as a Christian poet; it is the struggle of the church militant to affirm Christian values in all aspects of culture. The strong opinions of Dorothy L. Sayers on higher education were not rooted in anything as trivial as personal preference; nor were her ideas simply the product of her position in time and space. Her voice is part of a chorus of voices. The battle for traditional educational values is not a series of individual, unconnected skirmishes over the past hundred fifty years or so. It is part of the church's constant

53. John Henry Newman, *The Idea of a University* (New Haven: Yale University Press, 1996).

54. Mark A. Noll, *The Scandal of the Evangelical Mind* (Grand Rapids: Eerdmans, 1995).

55. Norman Klassen and Jens Zimmermann, *The Passionate Intellect: Incarnational Humanism and the Future of University Education* (Grand Rapids: Baker Academic, 2006).

56. T. S. Eliot, "East Coker," Movement V, in *Four Quartets* (Orlando: Harcourt, 1968).

warfare against spiritual adversaries—a warfare that must be waged in each generation so that people can again perceive what was good in the old ways, and reach back for what has been lost. Though conditions "seem unpropitious," this is the area in which we must go on trying; this is indeed "our business."

# 8

# "What Do They Teach Them in These Schools?"

## C. S. Lewis on Reading, Education, and Psychagogia

### James G. Dixon

IN *THE VOYAGE OF the Dawn Treader*, the third of the children's books he wrote in his series *The Chronicles of Narnia*, C. S. Lewis begins with the following two paragraphs, which give us some idea of his views on education:

> There was a boy called Eustace Clarence Scrubb, and he almost deserved it. His parents called him Eustace Clarence and his schoolmasters called him Scrubb. I can't tell you how his friends spoke to him, for he had none. He didn't call his father and mother "Father" and "Mother," but Harold and Alberta. They were very up-to-date and advanced people. They were vegetarians, nonsmokers and teetotalers and wore a special kind of underclothes. In their house there was very little furniture and very few clothes on the beds and the windows were always open.

> Eustace Clarence liked animals, especially beetles, if they were dead and pinned on a card. He liked books if they were books of information and had pictures of grain elevators or of fat foreign children doing exercises in model schools.[1]

Well, if you know the story, you know that Eustace Clarence Scrubb finds himself on a most unusual adventure for which he is quite unprepared because—and this becomes a recurring refrain in the book—he had read all the wrong books. One of the most significant adventures for Eustace is when he wanders off from the others, gets lost, and sees a strange creature coming out of a cave:

> Something *was* crawling. Worse still, something was coming out. Edmund or Lucy or you would have recognized it at once, but Eustace had read none of the right books. The thing that came out of the cave was something he had never even imagined—a long lead-coloured snout, dull red eyes, no feather or fur, a long lithe body that trailed on the ground, legs whose elbows went up higher than its back like a spider's, cruel claws, bat's wings that made a rasping noise on the stones, yards of tail.[2]

Lewis goes on to say that Eustace had no idea what kind of creature he was seeing. But I trust that you have read the right books and know that of course it was a dragon. So Lewis returns to his refrain:

> . . . as I said before, Eustace had read only the wrong books. They had a lot to say about exports and imports and governments and drains, but they were weak on dragons.[3]

Lewis published this story in 1952, and two years earlier he had published the first of the Narnia books, *The Lion, the Witch and the Wardrobe*, in which the wise old Professor Kirk, in helping the Pevensie children make sense of their first encounter with Narnia, exclaims in recurring frustration, "Bless me, what *do* they teach them in these schools?"[4] This was a question that bothered Lewis himself for many years but finds its fullest explication in the book-length essay he wrote in 1944, *The Abolition of Man*. In this essay, and in other works published throughout his career, Lewis reveals a Classical approach to education, with a particular focus

---

1. C. S. Lewis, *The Voyage of the Dawn Treader* (New York: Macmillan, 1952), 1–2.
2. Ibid., 69.
3. Ibid., 71.
4. Lewis, *The Lion, the Witch and the Wardrobe* (New York: Macmillan, 1950), 186.

on the power of reading to shape character and to effect what the Greeks called *psychagogia,* the leading of the soul to virtue.[5]

Lewis acknowledges that the impetus for writing *The Abolition of Man* came through the mail. One day the publisher of an elementary school textbook on reading sent Lewis a complimentary copy for his perusal and, presumably, some quotable complimentary comments that could help in marketing the text. What resulted was quite the opposite, so Lewis had the courtesy to change the names of the authors to Gaius and Titius and the title of the textbook to *The Green Book,* to protect the guilty. Lewis's main concern with this book was that the authors were seeking to inculcate a cynicism about language—and consequently about truth—by teaching the students to be "knowing" readers who are trained to "see through" what the author of a book they might happen to read is trying to sell them regarding "the nature of things":

> In their second chapter Gaius and Titius quote the well-known story of Coleridge at the waterfall. You remember that there were two tourists present: that one called it "sublime" and the other "pretty": and that Coleridge mentally endorsed the first judgement and rejected the second with disgust. Gaius and Titius comment as follows: "When the man said *That is sublime,* he appeared to be making a remark about the waterfall. . . . Actually . . . he was not making a remark about the waterfall, but a remark about his own feelings. What he was saying was really *I have feelings associated in my mind with the word 'Sublime,'* or shortly, *I have sublime feelings.*" Here are a good many deep questions settled in a pretty summary fashion. But the authors are not yet finished. They add: "This confusion is continually present in language as we use it. We appear to be saying something very important about something: and actually we are only saying something about our own feelings."[6]

Lewis adds that the "boy who thinks he is 'doing' his 'English prep' . . . has no notion that ethics, theology, and politics are all at stake" in the relativism that such a method teaches.[7] As an example of steeling yourself against what an author is trying to sell you, Gaius and Titius "quote a silly advertisement of a pleasure cruise" that promises that those who buy tickets "will go 'across the Western Ocean where Drake of Devon sailed,'

5. Walter Jackson Bate, ed., *Criticism: The Major Texts* (New York: Harcourt Brace Jovanovich, 1952, 1970), 6–7.

6. Lewis, *The Abolition of* Man (New York: Touchstone, 1996), 18.

7. Ibid., 20.

'adventuring after the treasures of the Indies,' and bringing home themselves also a 'treasure' of 'golden hours' and 'glowing colours.'"[8]

Gaius and Titius rightly debunk such emotionally exploitative language, but they fail to put it side by side with literature that more honestly taps into those same emotions, literature that rightly seeks to engender in its readers the wonder of being enlarged by one's travels. Lewis cites a number of authors who do this well: Samuel Johnson, William Wordsworth, Virgil—and we, a few years later, could add his own *Voyage of the Dawn Treader*. For Eustace Clarence Scrubb was just such a student whose worldview had been shaped by the debunking process of Gaius and Titius. As Lewis reports, their student

> is encouraged to reject the lure of the "Western Ocean" on the very dangerous ground that in so doing he will prove himself a knowing fellow who can't be bubbled out of his cash. Gaius and Titius, while teaching him nothing about letters, have cut out of his soul, long before he is old enough to choose, the possibility of having certain experiences which thinkers of more authority than they have held to be generous, fruitful, and humane.[9]

This is what Lewis refers to in his title, *The Abolition of Man*, and it has happened to Eustace. Such a child, and such a cynic. He refuses to be drawn into wonder at the strange things he encounters in Narnia on just such a sea voyage as Gaius and Titius debunk in their textbook. Lewis is careful to provide such wonder through characters we come to admire, such as Reepicheep, the courtly mouse, and young King Caspian. On the threshold of their voyage into unknown waters, they seek as much information as they can find from all the old sea captains,

> and many a tall yarn [they] heard in return. But those who seemed the most truthful could tell of no lands beyond the Lone Islands, and many thought that if you sailed too far east you would come into the surges of a sea without lands that swirled perpetually round the rim of the world . . . The rest had only wild stories of islands inhabited by headless men, floating islands, waterspouts, and a fire that burned along the water. Only one, to Reepicheep's delight, said, "And beyond that, Aslan's country. But that's beyond the end of the world and you can't get

---

8. Ibid.,21.

9. Ibid., 23.

there." But when they questioned him he could only say that he'd heard it from his father.[10]

The difference between this passage and the advertisement that Gaius and Titius debunk is that Reepicheep's longing relates to something real, and the story is a record of his quest to fulfill that longing. At the end, he does achieve Aslan's country, and it is a proper wonder.

Along the way, Eustace's experience with the dragon is enough to correct the gaps and errors of his education and to transform the cynicism isolating him from his fellow travelers into a joy for learning from his travels. When he becomes a dragon himself, he realizes how beastly and isolated he has become, and he discovers that only the sharp claws of the lion Aslan are sufficient for ripping away the dragon skin that had encrusted on his very nature. Eustace recognizes what a monster he has become, and he hates it and seeks desperately to rejoin the human race.

This should be the purpose of education, according to Lewis: to inculcate in our students the knowledge of what it means to be human, and the longing to fulfill that knowledge in themselves. And for Lewis this meant encouraging in them the proper emotions toward genuine realities in relation to the nature of man, God, and the universe. He cites Aristotle, who says that "the aim of education is to make the pupil like and dislike what he ought,"[11] and Plato, who argued that "the little human animal will not at first have the right responses. It must be trained to feel pleasure, liking, disgust, and hatred at those things which really are pleasant, likeable, disgusting, and hateful."[12] The tourist who called the waterfall sublime was acknowledging "that the object was one which *merited* those emotions"[13] and which calls upon the soul to seek beyond itself to be enlarged by that which is larger than the self.

Lewis grants that Gaius and Titius may have been motivated by a genuine desire to protect their students against the emotions that propaganda often exploits,

> and they conclude that the best thing they can do is to fortify the minds of young people against emotion. My own experience as a teacher tells an opposite tale. For every one pupil who needs to be guarded from a weak excess of sensibility there are three who need to be awakened from the slumber of cold vulgarity.

10. Lewis, *The Voyage of the Dawn Treader*, 52.

11. Lewis, *The Abolition of Man*, 29.

12. Ibid.

13. Ibid., 28.

> The task of the modern educator is not to cut down jungles but to irrigate deserts. The right defence against false sentiments is to inculcate just sentiments. By starving the sensibility of our pupils we only make them easier prey to the propagandist when he comes. For famished nature will be avenged and a hard heart is no infallible protection against a soft head.[14]

The irony here is that Lewis's experience as an educator was with university students. The cynicism they had learned in the elementary grades had left them hungry for sentiment of any kind, and that hunger will be satisfied one way or another, unfortunately often in their succumbing to propaganda or advertisements that succeed in commodifying them because they have nowhere experienced the process of *psychagogia* that would lead their souls to a higher and more substantial understanding of their human nature.

This leads us to the thesis of *The Abolition of Man* and the goal of education for Lewis: it is to inculcate in our students what he calls "the doctrine of objective value, the belief that certain attitudes are really true, and others really false, to the kind of thing the universe is and the kind of things we are."[15] Because he believes that such understanding of things is universal, he chooses to use the Chinese word *Tao*, which means "the reality beyond all predicates . . . It is Nature, it is the Way, the Road."[16] (*Tao* is also, though Lewis doesn't mention this, the word for *logos* in the standard Chinese translation of John 1: "In the beginning was the Tao, and the Tao was with God, and the Tao was God.") Lewis demonstrates the universality of the *Tao* by citing many examples of common moral law from different cultures and religions throughout the world and throughout history, such as the prohibitions against murder and theft and the injunctions to observe the golden rule, justice, mercy, and respect for one's parents and elders. The *Tao* is what theologians might call general revelation, the law of God that is written on the hearts of all humans.

Lewis was a professor of medieval and Renaissance literature at Oxford University for most of his career. Certainly he had vested interests in teaching the classics of Western literature and in maintaining their privileged status as seminal in Western civilization. One could argue, I suppose, that all of his arguments toward universal truth and morality are but unexamined ploys to preserve his privileged position and the privileged

14. Ibid., 26–27.
15. Ibid., 31.
16. Ibid., 30.

position of the texts he spent his life teaching. Contemporary criticism might position him as a quintessentially Enlightenment writer, mustering logic and rationality to prove universal truth, which a Foucauldian critic might argue is just another demonstration of the hegemonic discourses by which the British Empire established itself and by which the West still seeks to dominate the world. Such critics would charge that Lewis's appropriation of bits and pieces from the religious and philosophical writings of other cultures does violence to those cultures by subsuming them under a single umbrella of "universal truth."

Lewis certainly was a man of his time. But he was also a man who lived in other times and places through his vast reading. He hated what he called the "chronological snobbery" of those who believed that anything that was old was inferior to anything that was modern.[17] And it was his firm belief that the best way of escaping the limits of the parochialism of one's own little time and place was to travel through reading. In *An Experiment in Criticism* he poses the question, "What then is the good of—what is even the defence for—occupying our hearts with stories of what never happened and entering vicariously into feelings which we should try to avoid having in our own person? Or of fixing our inner eye earnestly on things that can never exist?"[18] And he provides the following answer:

> The nearest I have yet got to an answer is that we seek an enlargement of our being. We want to be more than ourselves. Each of us by nature sees the whole world from one point of view with a perspective and a selectiveness peculiar to himself . . . We want to see with other eyes, to imagine with other imaginations, to feel with other hearts, as well as with our own. We are not content to be Leibnitzian monads. We demand windows. Literature as Logos is a series of windows, even of doors. One of the things we feel after reading a great work is "I have got out." Or from another point of view, "I have got in"; pierced the shell of some other monad and discovered what it is like inside.[19]

Here Lewis voices a belief similar to that of the poet Percy Bysshe Shelley, who wrote in *A Defence of Poetry* that "the great secret of morals is love; or a going out of our own nature," and adds that "the great instrument of moral good is the imagination; and poetry administers to the

17. Lewis, *Surprised by Joy* (New York: Harvest, 1955), 207.

18. Lewis, *An Experiment in Criticism* (New York: Cambridge University Press, 1961), 137.

19. Ibid., 137–38.

effect by acting on the cause."[20] Like Shelley, Lewis compares good reading with love and morality but includes any intellectual activity as well: they all require one to go beyond the self, "to go out of the self, to correct its provincialism and heal its loneliness . . . Obviously this process can be described either as an enlargement or as a temporary annihilation of the self. But that is an old paradox; 'he that loseth his life shall save it.'"[21]

Lewis returns to this theme in the conclusion of *An Experiment in Criticism:*

> The man who is contented to be only himself, and therefore less a self, is in prison. My own eyes are not enough for me, I will see through those of others. Reality, even seen through the eyes of many, is not enough. I will see what others have invented . . . Literary experience heals the wound, without undermining the privilege, of individuality . . . [I]n reading great literature I become a thousand men and yet remain myself . . . Here, as in worship, in love, in moral action, and in knowing, I transcend myself; and am never more myself than when I do.[22]

This is the classical purpose of literature and of education. It involves what Plato and Aristotle understood as *psychagogia,* the leading of the soul beyond itself toward that which is objectively beautiful, true, and good. Walter Jackson Bate summarizes the importance of this quality for the Greeks and for all Western civilization since:

> Hence the confidence of the Greeks in the immense power of art—which they called *psychagogia* (a *leading* or *persuading* of the soul)—as a molding or formative agent in developing human feelings and motivations. Thus the artist's function . . . was given, for the first time, an unparalleled importance and dignity. For with the vision of human perfection before them, the Greeks raised the whole concept of education far above the routine acquirement of simple memory, mechanical skills, and vocational apprenticeship. In an imperishable example to the human race, their desire to *educate*—their wish to mold and shape human character, as they conceived it, and thus to complete human potentiality in the light of the highest standard of excellence or nobility—became the most distinctive and all-important of

20. Percy Bysshe Shelley, "A Defense of Poetry," in *Criticism: Major Statements,* eds. Charles Kaplan and William Davis Anderson, 4th ed. (Boston: Bedford/St. Martin's, 2000), 294.

21. Lewis, *An Experiment in Criticism,* 138.

22. Ibid., 140–41.

> Greek ideals . . . [A]rt is capable of developing [our] capacity to
> react vitally and sympathetically to the truth. It thus assumes
> dignity and genuine value as a nourisher, enlarger, and shaper
> of the mind and heart . . .[23]

But Lewis believed that this could happen in literature only when we
read to *receive* the work, not to *use* it. "When we 'receive' it we exert our
senses and imagination and various other powers according to a pattern
invented by the artist. When we use it we treat it as assistance for our own
activities."[24] Using a work reduces it to one's own already limited range of
thought. Receiving a work allows us to be enlarged by it. And with this
Lewis returns to the question of how best to educate the young in terms
of reading:

> For this reason I am very doubtful whether criticism is a proper
> exercise for boys and girls . . . The necessary condition of all
> good reading is 'to get ourselves out of the way'; we do not help
> the young to do this by forcing them to keep on expressing
> opinions. Especially poisonous is the kind of teaching which en-
> courages them to approach every literary work with suspicion.
> It springs from a very reasonable motive. In a world full of soph-
> istry and propaganda, we want to protect the rising generation
> from being deceived, to forearm them against the invitations to
> false sentiment and muddled thinking which printed words will
> so often offer them. Unfortunately, the very same habit which
> makes them impervious to the bad writing may make them im-
> pervious also to the good . . . No poem will give up its secrets to
> a reader who enters it regarding the poet as a potential deceiver,
> and determined not to be taken in. We must risk being taken in,
> if we are to get anything.[25]

As we saw in our discussion of *The Abolition of Man*, Lewis found
this "poisonous" kind of teaching rampant at the elementary level, and he
designed his character Eustace Clarence Scrubb to illustrate the consequences of that kind of teaching.

But he also found such consequences rampant at the university level,
among his own students. And his complaint here anticipates what philosopher Paul Ricoeur has termed "the hermeneutic of suspicion" in the

23. Bate, *Criticism: The Major Texts*, 6–7.

24. Lewis, *An Experiment in Criticism*, 88.

25. Ibid., 93–94.

literary criticism of the twentieth century.[26] In 1961, when Lewis wrote *An Experiment in Criticism,* he was already lamenting the tendency of his best university students to read literature only through the lenses of the critics. "Less and less," he wrote, "do we meet the individual response. The all-important conjunction (Reader Meets Text) never seems to have been allowed to occur of itself and develop spontaneously. Here, plainly, are young people drenched, dizzied, and bedeviled by criticism to a point at which primary literary experience is no longer possible."[27] He concludes that "such a surfeit of criticism" is actually dangerous to our culture, and so he proposes "a ten or twenty years' abstinence both from the reading and from the writing of evaluative criticism" as a cure.[28]

Ah, but instead of abstinence, the next few decades up to the present have seen a veritable orgy of criticism, beyond what even Lewis could have imagined. From the relatively tame New Criticism that emerged in the mid-twentieth century to help unlock the mysteries of modernist literature, literary criticism has mushroomed into a growth industry beyond anyone's wildest dreams in the early 1960s. We now have deconstruction, Marxist literary criticism, psychoanalytic criticism, reader-response criticism, feminist criticism of all stripes, Foucauldian criticism, Bakhtinian criticism, multicultural criticism, and new historicism, to name a few, all firmly entrenched in the English departments of universities throughout Western civilization. And more and more, these departments are teaching criticism at the lower levels to provide students with the lenses they need in order to make sense of the literature they will encounter in their literature courses. I myself have devised just such a course for our English majors at Grove City College in order to acquaint them with the theories they will encounter if they go on to graduate school. But we begin the course with a half semester's immersion in the theories of the classical tradition, and we conclude by returning to that tradition in Lewis's *Abolition of Man.* And our students cannot take this course until they are juniors or seniors.

Nonetheless, one of my greatest concerns in teaching this course is that I don't want my students to lose that love of reading, of that direct encounter with a text that was genuinely life changing and which no doubt led most of them to become English majors in the first place. Fortunately, the strategy seems to be working. We don't lose any English majors as

26. Raman Selden, ed., *The Cambridge History of Literary Criticism,* vol. 8, *From Formalism to Poststructuralism* (Cambridge: Cambridge University Press, 1995), 280–81.

27. Lewis, *An Experiment in Criticism,* 128–29.

28. Ibid., 129.

a result of their taking this course, and our major remains very strong and one of the largest in the college. But this is not true in many other schools across the country. Bruce Fleming, a professor of literature at the U. S. Naval Academy, addresses this in his essay in *The Chronicle of Higher Education*, "Leaving Literature Behind":

> The major victory of professors of literature in the last half-century—the Great March from the New Criticism through structuralism, deconstruction, Foucauldianism, and multi-culturalism—has been the invention and codification of a professionalized study of literature. We've made ourselves into a priestly caste: To understand literature, we tell students, you have to come to us. Yet professionalization is a pyrrhic victory: We've won the battle but lost the war. We've turned revelation into drudgery, shut ourselves in airless rooms, and covered over the windows.
>
> The good news is that we've created a discipline: literary studies. The bad news is that we've made ourselves rulers of a realm that has separated itself almost completely from the rest of the world. In the process, we've lost many of the students—I'd say, many of them men—and even some of the professors. And yet still we teach literature as if to future versions of ourselves—not that there will be many jobs for them. The vast majority of students don't even want to be professors: They'd like to get something from a book they can use in their lives outside the classroom. What right have we to forget them?
>
> Students get something out of a book by reading it. Love of reading was, after all, what got most of us into this business to begin with. We are killing that experience with the discipline of literary studies, with its network of relations in which an individual work almost becomes incidental. But it's the individual work that changes lives.[29]

Lewis would resonate with Fleming's diagnosis of the current malaise in academic study of literature. But since it is not really feasible to conduct an abstinence-only policy regarding critical theory in our teaching of literature at the college level—nor would it be wise or fair to send our students out into the larger world so ill-prepared to encounter what they will find there—then how might we best teach literature and criticism without squeezing the joy out of reading? Here again Lewis anticipates our

29. Bruce Fleming, "Leaving Literature Behind," *The Chronicle of Higher Education* 55/17 (2008) B14.

current situation and provides some perspective. In *The Abolition of Man* he returns to his thesis:

> This thing which I have called for convenience the *Tao*, and which others may call Natural Law or Traditional Morality or the First Principles of Practical Reason or the First Platitudes, is not one among a series of possible systems of value. It is the sole source of all value judgements. If it is rejected, all value is rejected. If any value is retained, it is retained. The effort to refute it and raise a new system of value in its place is self-contradictory. There never has been, and never will be, a radically new judgement of value in the history of the world. What purport to be new systems or (as they now call them) "ideologies," all consist of fragments from the *Tao* itself, arbitrarily wrenched from their context in the whole and then swollen to madness in their isolation, yet still owing to the *Tao* and to it alone such validity as they possess . . . The rebellion of new ideologies against the *Tao* is a rebellion of the branches against the tree: if the rebels could succeed they would find that they had destroyed themselves. The human mind has no more power of inventing a new value than of imagining a new primary colour, or, indeed, of creating a new sun and a new sky for it to move in.[30]

Such a perspective might help us in the present situation by leading us to two main conclusions. The first is that most ideologies or new schools of critical theory have some validity in the degree to which they reflect some aspect of the *Tao*, or the true nature of things. Deconstruction, for instance, can remind us of the slippery nature of language and of the inability of words to perfectly stand in for that which they seek to represent, encouraging in us a humility in the fragility of our verbal constructions and a joy in the playfulness of language. Feminism reminds us of the patriarchal biases that have too often crept in to our judgments of literature and canon-formation. Marxism likewise can reveal the economic and material foundations of much of culture and literature and even provide necessary critiques of the commodification produced by capitalism.

The second conclusion is that any one of these approaches to literature and culture is insufficient in itself. Too often the proponents of these theories present them as the one and only way of approaching literature, which Lewis argues "arbitrarily wrenches" them from "their context in the whole" and swells them "to madness in their isolation." Deconstruction, pushed too far, results in a debilitating agnosticism and even a Nietzschean

30. Lewis, *The Abolition of Man*, 55–56.

nihilism regarding language. Radical feminism and Marxism can become crusades that seek to destroy or dismiss what their proponents find oppressive. The psychoanalytic critic can end up reducing a work of literature to a complex web of neuroses in the author, the characters, or even the reader. Each of these approaches can result in its own variety of reductionism, of reducing the complex work of literature to nothing but an illustration of what the theory already knew. The work is subordinated to the theory and is thus depleted of its psychagogic power. Samuel Taylor Coleridge railed against the kind of critic who approaches Shakespeare in order to bring him down to size, who "blind and deaf, fills his three-ounce phial at the waters of Niagara; and determines positively the greatness of the cataract to be neither more nor less than his three-ounce phial has been able to receive."[31] Lewis would agree.

Lewis addresses this in a sermon he preached on Whit-Sunday in Mansfield College Chapel, Oxford, May 28, 1944, titled "Transposition," in which he distinguishes between criticism from below and criticism from above:

> I have tried to stress throughout the inevitableness of the error made about every transposition by one who approaches it from the lower medium only. The strength of such a critic lies in the words "merely" or "nothing but." He sees all the facts but not the meaning. Quite truly, therefore, he claims to have seen all the facts. There *is* nothing else there; except the meaning. He is therefore, as regards the matter in hand, in the position of an animal. You will have noticed that most dogs cannot understand *pointing*. You point to a bit of food on the floor: the dog, instead of looking at the floor, sniffs at your finger. A finger is a finger to him, and that is all. His world is all fact and no meaning. . . The critique of every experience from below . . . will always have the same plausibility. There will always be evidence, and every month fresh evidence, to show that religion is only psychological, justice only self-protection, politics only economics, love only lust, and thought itself only cerebral biochemistry.[32]

And so it is with literature. We can examine the thing itself, like dogs sniffing the finger, but we can miss entirely what the thing is pointing to.

---

31. Samuel Taylor Coleridge, "Shakespeare's Judgment Equal to His Genius," in *Criticism: The Major Texts*, ed. Walter Jackson Bate (New York: Harcourt Brace Jovanovich, 1952, 1970), 390.

32. C. S. Lewis, "Transposition," in *The Weight of Glory: And Other Addresses* (Grand Rapids: Eerdmans, 1949), 28–29.

With my students I use the analogy of the six blind men and the elephant: each man approaches the elephant and, touching only one part of it, describes this creature from his own very limited perspective: the one who examines the leg declares, "It is a tree!" The one who examines the trunk declares, "It is a snake!" The one who examines the tail: "It is a rope!" and so on. The error comes if each should then say "It is only a tree!" or "It is nothing but a snake!" So I encourage my students to take each critical perspective for what it has to offer without allowing that perspective to nullify other perspectives. And when we have read them all, we still do not have the thing itself, the work of literature that exists beyond any one perspective of it. In this respect, Derrida and Bakhtin on "unfinalizability" can be quite helpful. Or St. Ephrem the Syrian, whom Charles Williams was quite fond of quoting, on all of our descriptions and metaphors for God: "This also is thou; neither is this thou."[33]

This brings us full circle to the Narnia Chronicles, where we started, with Eustace Clarence Scrubb having read all the wrong books, and Professor Kirk fretting about "What do they teach them in these schools?" For it isn't just *which* books are read, but *how* they are read that matters. As with travel, so with reading. We all know of people who when they travel reduce everything to their own limited experiences and tastes, who prefer McDonalds fast-food to native cuisine, who are glad to get back home where people eat, dress, and think right (like them). So with reading: even reading the "right books" won't help if one persists in the habit of reducing them to one's limited perspective. Even when Eustace began to have the same experiences that led the others to wonder, it wasn't until Aslan helped him get out of his own skin that he could experience the wonder himself and be enlarged by it.

Lewis believed in literature's power of *psychagogia,* of pointing the soul of the individual reader toward the truth of things, toward the *Tao.* And he longed for an approach to education that would assist students to encounter that psychagogic power in literature directly. But for Lewis this was related to more than just literature. Near the end of *The Abolition of Man,* he calls for a new humane science, a worldview even, to correct the reductionism of the age:

> Is it, then, possible to imagine a new Natural Philosophy, continually conscious that the "natural object" produced by analysis

33. Quoted in Kallistos Ware, *The Orthodox Way* (Yonkers, NY: St. Vladimir's Seminary Press, 1979), 121; and Lewis *Letters to Malcolm: Chiefly on Prayer* (New York: Harvest, 1973 [1963]), 74.

> and abstraction is not reality but only a view, and always cor-
> recting the abstraction? . . . The regenerate science which I have
> in mind would not do even to minerals and vegetables what
> modern science threatens to do to man himself. When it ex-
> plained, it would not explain away. When it spoke of the parts it
> would remember the whole . . . Its followers would not be free
> with the words *only* and *merely.*[34]

Lewis calls for resistance to any approach that would "reduce the *Tao* to a mere natural product,"[35] and he warns of the dangers of what Paul Ricouer has since called the "hermeneutic of suspicion" (though with Ricouer, Lewis would allow that such a hermeneutic could be creative and productive if properly employed). At the conclusion of *The Last Battle*, the last of the seven Narnia Chronicles, a group of dwarfs find themselves on the inside of a stable door, which has actually proven to be a portal to Aslan's country. But the dwarfs are a very suspicious lot and have learned from experience to steel themselves against being taken in. "Dwarfs are for the dwarfs," they repeat as a kind of defensive mantra.[36] And so they cannot see the fact that they are in Aslan's country, where the air is clear, and the grass smells as fresh as the day of creation. They persist in see-ing only the inside of a stable at night: dark and dank and smelling of manure. This is similar to the Marxist or multicultural critic who can see Shakespeare's *The Tempest* only as a marker of European colonialism and cultural hegemony and who thereby misses the beauty of the language, the wonder of the magic, reconciliation, and spiritual growth that occur in the characters. Or the Freudian critic who reduces Hamlet's complex emotional and metaphysical journey to the outworkings of an unresolved Oedipal complex and so misses the larger universal questions regarding man's place in the universe and coming to terms with mortality.

Lewis concludes *The Abolition of Man* with a reflection on this men-tality, and it relates to the study of literature, and to modern education, as well as it does to the dwarfs in *The Last Battle:*

> But you cannot go on "explaining away" for ever: you will find
> that you have explained explanation itself away. You cannot go
> on "seeing through" things for ever. The whole point seeing
> through something is to see something through it. It is good
> that the window should be transparent, because the street or

34. Lewis, *The Abolition of Man*, 85.
35. Ibid., 86.
36. C. S. Lewis, *The Last Battle* (New York: Macmillan, 1956), 148.

garden beyond it is opaque. How if you saw through the garden too? It is no use trying to "see through" first principles. If you see through everything, then everything is transparent. But a wholly transparent world is an invisible world. To "see through" all things is the same as not to see.[37]

The goal of reading, and of all education, is to equip ourselves to see the truth, goodness, and beauty that exist in the nature of things and to have our souls shaped by that reality.

In contrast to the dwarfs at the end of *The Last Battle*, the children who enter Aslan's country discover that what they had experienced before was, as Professor Kirk explains, "only a shadow or a copy of the real Narnia . . . All of the old Narnia that mattered, all the dear creatures, have been drawn into the real Narnia through the Door. And of course it is different; as different as a real thing is from a shadow or as waking life is from a dream." Because they had opened themselves earlier to experiences that drew their souls to wonder at realities larger than themselves, they were able to see the truth beyond the shadows. And then Professor Kirk mutters under his breath one last time, "It's all in Plato, all in Plato: bless me, what *do* they teach them at these schools!"[38]

37. Lewis, *The Abolition of Man*, 86–87.
38. Lewis, *The Last Battle*, 169–70.

# 9

# Curriculum and Culture according to Wendell Berry

## Andrew J. Harvey

LIBRARIANS AT MAJOR UNIVERSITIES live for the acquisition of special collections devoted to famous writers, especially if an author has a personal connection to their school. I recall the buzz on campus in the 1990s when the University of North Carolina received the personal library and notebooks of alumnus Walker Percy. Such a collection becomes the focal point for future research by literary, historical, and cultural scholars, leverages the preeminence of the school as a research institution, and attracts patronage from donors and alumni. It is perfectly natural then that Wendell Berry, the most famous and important living writer from Kentucky, had donated over the years much of his personal papers to his alma mater and former employer, the University of Kentucky. Correspondingly the university had begun to let their librarians do what such librarians do—acquire rare first editions, correspondence, and everything else useful for rounding out a special collection. But just this summer Wendell Berry thoughtfully, conscientiously, shockingly did what no other writer of his stature has ever done: he reneged and demanded all his personal papers back. There will no longer be any Wendell Berry Special Holdings in Lexington. To the University of Kentucky's library this is nothing less than a tragedy, but for Berry it is a triumph of sorts. His rationale for taking this bold stance and the university's response to his wishes demonstrate in microcosm the complex criticism of higher education that Berry has articulated for years in his fiction, poetry, and essays.

Berry's vision and his values, of course, begin with the land, and no discussion of Berry's life and work can go far without acknowledging his agrarian first principles. "What I stand for is what I stand on" has been his battle cry now for almost fifty years of publishing fiction, poetry, and nonfiction. This commitment to the land makes Berry staunchly against strip mining or mountaintop removal in particular and against the entire coal industry in general. Berry pulled his papers from the University of Kentucky primarily because of its recent gifts from the coal industry. As Berry explained further, "that—added to the 'Top 20' project and the president's exclusive 'focus' on science, technology, engineering, and mathematics—puts an end to my willingness to be associated in any way officially with the University."[1] So Berry's motives were primarily a sense of justice but also curricular and philosophical. But not without regret; Berry expressed his deep obligation to the school where he earned bachelor's and master's degrees as well as served two stints as a faculty member. On the other hand, the official university response ironically yet predictably demonstrated the very mindset that appalls Berry: the university was "disappointed by Berry's decision . . . particularly because UK has purchased a significant portion of his works, which are in the UK libraries archives' permanent collection."[2] Pragmatic, monetary concerns and petulance over a now incomplete archive perfectly reflect the cold, corporate mindset of the modern research university that Berry has railed against in his essays and speeches. In sum, they failed to appreciate his argument against institutional hypocrisy and corruption and instead dismissed it as merely an anticoal political stunt. In so doing the university revealed its heart of hearts (or lack of heart)—it would rather sever ties built over a lifetime with its most famous and revered literary son than risk losing access to the deep pockets of big coal.

As one might expect, many bloggers assumed Berry to be a man of the Left, politically, but those who are familiar with Berry or his writings know that he is no such ideologue and cannot be so easily stereotyped. Indeed, in many ways his conservationism resembles conservatism. Berry,

1. Cheryl Truman, "Wendell Berry Pulling His Personal Papers from UK: Writer Protesting Coal's Influence," *Lexington Herald-Leader,* Wednesday, June 23, 2010, Online: http://www.kentucky.com/2010/06/23/1319383/wendell-berry-pulling-his-personal.html.

2. Ibid.

for instance, unabashedly calls himself a Christian. He is an ardent champion of "the permanent things" as arch-conservative Russell Kirk would say, and advocates a sense of natural moral order in the face of cultural chaos with clarity and precision. No doubt this was why the Intercollegiate Studies Institute recently devoted an entire conference to "The Humane Vision of Wendell Berry." But while Wendell Berry embraces his friends from the Right, the Left also often considers him one of theirs, especially because of his pacifism and his critique of global corporations such as big coal. So, he remains (and perhaps he himself relishes this fact) a difficult man to classify on the political spectrum. Indeed, Berry's religious views and political stances have at times confused some Christian readers and frequently vex his otherwise appreciative readers on the political Right.

My goal in this essay is threefold: first, to dispel the vexations and confusions Berry has stirred up among his fellow Christians; second, to do likewise with the controversies his thinking rouses among the political Right. In the sort of homiletic tradition that Berry has satirized and mocked on multiple occasions, I could reduce the three points of my discussion to: 1) the Christianity of Wendell Berry, 2) the Conservatism of Wendell Berry, and 3) the Curriculum of Wendell Berry. But I will not do so out of respect to Wendell Berry, who teaches us, if nothing else, to always resist reductionism.

I should point out the genuine trepidation I feel in embarking on such an essay on Berry, who at the beginning of his great novel *Jayber Crow* banishes to a desert island all "persons attempting to explain, interpret, explicate, analyze, deconstruct, or otherwise 'understand' it."[3] I will not be offering, therefore, an explanation, an interpretation, an explication, or even an analysis. Instead consider me a sort of forest ranger: we are touring the woods and landscapes Berry has presented us. Chiefly we will be going through his more recent fiction and essays where I will simply be pointing out some interesting features for our mutual admiration, perhaps admonishment, and hopefully edification.

For those not familiar with Berry's work, he has produced a steady stream of fiction, lyric poetry, and essays since his 1959 novel *Nathan Coulter*. All the novels and short fiction cohere as the history of several generations in and around the fictional community or "membership" of Port William, Kentucky. The short stories have all been recently published in a single collection—*That Distant Land*—which in addition to the novels

---

3. "Notice," posted as part of the front matter of his novel *Jayber Crow* (Washington, DC: Counterpoint, 2000).

totals around a dozen volumes. He has produced a similar amount of poetry and an even greater amount of essays. His matter is invariably love and death and farming; his style is elegantly plain with flashes of humor and bile. The lucidity of his argument and the winsomeness of his storytelling has proved irresistible to a remarkable range of readers—urban and rural, conservative and liberal, old and young, secular and Christian—despite his eschewal early on of big-time publishers. In short, he is a force.

## THE CHRISTIANITY OF WENDELL BERRY

But the earth speaks to us of Heaven.[4]

I feel more religious, in fact, here beside this corrupt and holy stream. I am not sectarian or evangelical. I don't want to argue with anybody about religion . . . I'm a literal reader of the Scriptures, and so I see the difficulties . . . I am maybe, the ultimate Protestant, the man at the end of the Protestant road, for as I have read the Gospels over the years, the belief has grown in me that Christ did not come to found an organized religion but came to found an unorganized one. He seems to have come to carry religion out of the temples into the fields and sheep pastures, onto the roadsides and the banks of rivers, into the houses of sinners and publicans, into the town and the wilderness, toward the membership of all that is here.[5]

The above quotations are not exactly Wendell Berry's words; they are sentiments Berry expresses through the voice of Jayber Crow, town barber of Port William and the narrator of the novel of the same name. But they clearly echo Berry's own theology and practice. His emphasis on God's immanent presence in his creation (as opposed to the doctrine of God's transcendence) and his profound diffidence about the church as an institution lead some Christian readers to distrust Berry's orthodoxy and even his Christianity altogether. The suspicions arise from the theological language with which he trumpets his agrarian virtues. The first quotation, for instance, merely echoes the Psalmist's observation that the whole creation declares the glory of God, but to some it can sound like pantheism—God is everywhere and in everything. Combined with the notion of "ultimate Protestantism" expressed in the second quotation, it seems as if Berry is saying the land itself, through a person's healthy relationship with

4. Berry, *Jayber Crow* (Washington, DC: Counterpoint, 2000), 354.
5. Ibid., 321.

it, conveys grace and does so perhaps even more reliably than the church itself. There are two points at issue here: first, how does the land convey grace; and second, what exactly is Berry's criticism of the church?

In Berry's fiction one is hard pressed to find a good farmer who is a bad person or, vice versa, a bad person who manages to be a good farmer. I should emphasize at the outset that Berry's imagined world of Port William never has a villain: one encounters sinners who are more or less lost, certainly, but no personal villains. Villainy is invariably impersonal—either technological or institutional. The challenge for the reader and for Berry's characters is to learn how even those who are most lost must still be loved. A man of nonviolence, Berry is extending the ethical injunction of the Gospels—love thine enemies—to include his fictional characters as well. He never allows the sympathetic reader of a short story or of a novel to hate a character, even one who does despicable things, e.g., deforestation, murder, or adultery. Berry's other characters in his tragic stories are correspondingly drawn along a spectrum according to their capacity for mercy and forgiveness.

For Berry's literary characters the qualities of mercy and forgiveness tend to arise out of, and express themselves through, the proper love and care of the land. This proper love, as well as faith itself, is born from the humility and patience that stem from one's submission to one's Creator and the natural order of things. The agrarian lifestyle, therefore, because of its intimate interdependent connection between person and place manages "to preserve in memory and even in practice the ancient human gifts of reverence, fidelity, neighborliness, and stewardship."[6] A proper relationship with the land, therefore, can be beneficent and tends to make a man more virtuous. Berry certainly dramatizes this efficacious principle in the imagined lives of many of his characters. But by making a man a better neighbor or a better steward of God's creation, is the earth saving that man's soul in the Christian sense? Does it actually convey grace or in some way mediate God's presence?

The answer is yes, and this is the major source of vexation for some of Berry's Christian readers who are unaccustomed to assigning such efficacy to the land. To understand Berry's radical affirmation of the grace found in the earth, we need to notice two essential concepts: that salvation is a dynamic process and not a static condition, and that God—the Word-made-flesh—is always present in his creation. Theologian and literary scholar Ralph Wood, who calls himself "Baptist-Orthodox," correctly recognizes

---

6. Berry, *Life Is a Miracle* (Washington, DC: Counterpoint, 2000), 132.

this fundamental crux in Berry's thought. According to Wood, Berry's essays, fiction, and poetry exhibit "the Christian insistence that holy things will always come to us in communal and mediated form."[7] Wood, however, then misinterprets Berry's emphasis on God's immanence as reflecting not a sacramental view of creation but a Stoic view of nature. "Berry's view of nature is Stoic rather than Christian—'everything fulfills its function by its *physis*, the principal of growth intrinsic to it.' Berry misses the 'otherness of God' and settles for a deeply natural theology in which God's transcendence is absent."[8] What Wood fails to recognize is that Berry is not "settling" for such a natural theology and neglecting the doctrine of God's transcendence.

Berry, rather, is asserting such a natural theology and emphasizing God's immanence quite deliberately to counterbalance what he sees as a deleterious preoccupation with God's transcendence. Consider Jayber Crow's critique of the young seminarian preachers that pass through Port William:

> They learned to have a very high opinion of God and a very low opinion of His works—although they could tell you that this world had been made by God Himself. What they didn't see was that it is beautiful, and that some of the greatest beauties are the briefest. They had imagined the church, which is an organization, but not the world, which is an order and a mystery. To them, the church did not exist in the world where people earn their living and have their being, but rather in the world where they fear death and Hell, which is not much of a world. To them, the soul was something dark and musty, stuck away for later. In their brief passage through or over it, most of the young preachers knew Port William only as it theoretically was ("lost") and as it theoretically might be ("saved"). And they wanted us all to do our part to spread this bad news to others who had not heard it—the Catholics, the Hindus, the Muslims, the Buddhists, and the others—or else they (and maybe we) would go to Hell. I did not believe it.[9]

7. Ralph Wood, quoted in Ragan Sutterfield, "Imagining a Different Way to Live," *Christianity Today*, Nov 2006, 63.

8. Sutterfied paraphrasing and quoting Wood in "Imagining a Different Way to Live."

9. Berry, *Jayber Crow*, 160–61.

For Berry a so-called gospel that explicitly or implicitly denies God's presence in his creation and that denies that salvation is a process is no gospel at all but "bad news" that he will have no part in spreading.

The Gospel according to Berry starts from an insistence on God's immanence and prefers a circuitous pilgrimage as its prevailing metaphor for salvation. First, let me explain the metaphor of circuitous pilgrimage. *Jayber Crow* as a novel alludes thematically and structurally to Dante's *Divine Comedy*. Jayber himself alludes to Dante's magnum opus of a spiritual pilgrimage several times. Here is the most telling of these allusions: "it would be a good idea to live your life in a straight line—starting, say, in the Dark Wood of Error, and proceeding by logical steps through Hell and Purgatory and into Heaven . . . but my pilgrimage has been wandering and unmarked . . . I have known something of Hell, Purgatory, and Heaven, but not always in that order."[10] Salvation in Jayber Crow's experience has been a dynamic process and not a straight line or a discrete conversion from "lost" to "saved." Perhaps *organic* would be more appropriate to describe this concept of salvation: the deliberate cultivation of a spirit of compassion and of a habit of charity.

I previously described Berry's view of nature as potentially "sacramental" and the quality of sacramentalism in this sense would best be understood as the opposite of materialism. A materialist worldview asserts that everything, all of reality, is simply some phase of matter-in-motion that operates along mechanistic principles, and asserts further that there is no other reality. A sacramentalist, on the other hand, sees the cosmos as the visible, physical expression of an invisible, spiritual reality. To the sacramentalist that tree over there in the midst of the garden might not be just a tree, it could be the tree of the knowledge of good and evil. Our daily bread and our wine could also be our Savior's body and blood. It may be irrational, beyond perception by the senses, mythic, or mystical, but sacramental reality is no less real. In fact, it is more real since it establishes the true significance of things.

Berry's articulation of a sacramental worldview grows over the span of his writing career and finds its fullest expression in his later works after his long and fruitful friendship with the Orthodox philosopher and theologian from Oxford, Philip Sherrard. On the manifest reality of God's immanence in creation Sherrard is elegantly blunt: "If God is not present in a grain of sand then He is not present in Heaven either."[11] For Sherrard

10. Ibid., 133.

11. Philip Sherrard, *The Rape of Man and Nature: An Enquiry into the Origins and*

the dichotomy of God's transcendence and his immanence is false and disastrous in its evacuation of God's sacred presence from the natural world. This false dichotomy between transcendence and immanence, therefore, is the first step toward what Sherrard calls "the desacralization of nature" and opens the way for its exploitation as raw materials or "natural resources" to fuel the engine of industrialization. Berry's thinking follows Sherrard closely on these points, which is why he is so keen on emphasizing divine immanence.

Sherrard himself affirms the centrality of the doctrine of God's presence in his creation to a sacramental view of nature: "The sacramental understanding of nature depends, as we have seen, upon the recognition of the actual immanence of nature in the divine, the sense that the creative energies of God did not merely produce the created world from without like a builder or an engineer, but are the ever-present, indwelling and spontaneous causes of every manifestation of life within it, whatever form this may take."[12] Notice that Sherrard goes so far as to invert the conventional expression and to say "the actual immanence of nature in the divine." Is the divine in nature or nature in the divine? Sherrard would answer yes. And the habit of thinking in binary, either/or terms is the sort of misunderstanding that Sherrard and Berry both attempt to rectify. So there is a reciprocity or coinherence between God and his creation by means of his "creative energies." Clearly this natural theology is foreign to Protestant discourse, but neither is it Stoic, as Ralph Wood suggests. Sherrard is articulating the sacramental worldview found in the Greek Church fathers, which he thinks is the best antidote for the excesses of Western secularization and industrialization.

Sherrard, therefore, accounts for how a farmer at "the end of the Protestant road" can express a sacramental view of nature. It is entirely possible that a farmer such as Berry could have intuited his sacramentalism from his work with the land, but Sherrard at least supplies the theological heavy-lifting that enables Berry to focus on his more pragmatic concerns and enables his reader to rest assured that Berry's natural theology is avowedly Christian. Remember, it was Ralph Wood, of all people, who suspected Stoicism behind Berry's theology of nature. The irony here is that I can think of no other scholar whose theological tradition and experience is more similar to Berry's own.

*Consequences of Modern Science* (Ipswich, UK: Golgonooza, 1987), 113.

    12. Ibid., 111.

Both were bred as Baptists who through intellectual curiosity and charity have embraced "mere Christian" kindred spirits from a range of Christian stripes. Both possess a familiarity with Orthodox Christianity, so Wood's conclusion about Berry's Stoic view of nature is particularly surprising. The explanation, I suppose, is that Wood—who may not have read Sherrard but is deeply familiar with the theology of the Eastern Church—has no reason to suspect Berry's relationship with Sherrard. Indeed, Wood is quite justified: Sherrard's works are all out of print and were always obscure, and Berry only quotes Sherrard once and hardly mentions him anywhere else.[13] The only reason I was able to connect the two was by asking Wendell Berry himself.[14] I had noticed his allusion to Sherrard, whom I had read closely in my own journey to the Orthodox Church, and wondered why Berry would have read, much less quoted from, Sherrard. Though, upon reflection, it is remarkable how two men of letters could come to such similar conclusions about the world and about God from such different paths. Berry agreed and recalled the long relationship they shared and the intense time he devoted to understanding Sherrard's arguments throughout the 1980s and early 1990s.[15]

Berry's orthodoxy, therefore, is in fact surprisingly and authentically Orthodox. And in this regard his idiosyncratic amalgam of theological traditions is neither unlike C. S. Lewis's mere Christianity nor T. S. Eliot's own conflation of things Puritan, Protestant, and Roman Catholic. Indeed, Russell Kirk suggests that such a spiritual hybrid is what it takes to defend the norms of culture and civil order in an age seemingly bent towards nihilism. Kirk puts Eliot in a line with Virgil and Dante as prophetic voices of principle that "showed the way back to the permanent things."[16] Berry, who calls himself an amateur poet, would no doubt balk at the company, but he also knows that he has put his hand to the same plow. The permanent things, therefore, are the best place to start a discussion of Wendell Berry's conservatism.

13. Berry uses a quotation from Sherrard as an opening epigram to his short essay "Is Life a Miracle?" (*The Citizenship Papers* [Washington, DC: Shoemaker & Hoard, 2003], 181). Berry also dedicates one sabbath poem from 1993 to "Philip," who most certainly is Philip Sherrard (*A Timbered Choir*, 1995, v, 171)

14. This personal conversation occurred during the Intercollegiate Studies Institute's regional conference, "The Humane Vision of Wendell Berry," Lexington, KY, October 20, 2007.

15. See especially Sherrard's *The Rape of Man and Nature* and *Christianity and Eros* (London: SPCK, 1976).

16. Russell Kirk, *The Conservative Mind: From Burke to Eliot* (Washington, DC: Regnery, 1985), 495.

## THE CONSERVATISM AND CONSERVATIONISM OF WENDELL BERRY

My colleague, New Testament scholar, T. David Gordon, relishes the time when an exasperated friend declared, "you are simultaneously the most conservative and the most liberal man I've ever met." But the more I read Wendell Berry, the more I realize that Berry is simultaneously more conservative and more liberal than perhaps any of us. Who of us, driven by his conservative or liberal principles, has concluded never to use, much less own, a personal computer? And who of us likens the Buddhist vow to save all sentient beings to Christ's parable of the lost sheep in order to assert pacifism? These both are universals to Berry: he has no use for war or computers anywhere, any time. You can see how Berry can baffle his political bedfellows and be a burr under the saddle of both Left and Right. Berry himself finds his appeal to both ends of the spectrum curious, and when asked about this phenomenon he wryly noted that while the Left say nice things about him, the Right come and visit him.[17] In some ways he is a conservative's conservative, who never saw a government program or a political movement he liked or at least was not deeply suspicious of; on the other hand, he was a tree hugger, a pacifist, and an antiglobalist before any of these became trendy or cool among Democrats. A laundry list of issues and Berry's stances on them, then, is not the right way to begin. If we start, however, with "the permanent things," Berry emerges as another conservative poetic voice defending against the dehumanizing and secular forces of the age.

Berry, much more so than even Eliot, has directly taken on the political arena, especially in his essays and in particular in those published after September 11, 2001, in a volume called *Citizenship Papers.* So Berry provides us much more confession than Eliot did about his political convictions. But Russell Kirk's starting place in understanding Eliot's "conservative mind" would serve us as well: "frequently in his deeper assumptions concerning the soul, justice, and order, a poet reveals the political background of his vision."[18] The vision of the poet is beyond fads or factions, Kirk explains, and seeks to preserve the ancient paths and to rail against "the follies of the time." To such a visionary, "every age is out of joint, in the sense that man and society never are what they ought to be; and the poet senses that he is born to set the time right—not, however, by leading a

17. ISI Conference, question-and-answer session, 2007.
18. Kirk, *The Conservative Mind,* 497.

march to some New Jerusalem, but by rallying in his art to the permanent things."[19] And it is precisely the permanent things that animate Berry's art: in one of his most widely cited "Sabbath poems" Berry muses that he would not have been "a writer at all except /. . .words have come to me / Out of their deep caves / Needing to be remembered."[20]

Kirk suggested that a poet's attitude toward the soul, justice, and order reveals his political vision. And in this poem Berry identifies his muses as love, fear, and the past; his art must do justice to the past as if one's soul depended on it. The fear that the future inspires, of which Berry speaks here, is primarily the fear that we do not possess the virtues our forebears did, the virtues that life will require of us.

The first principles of his art, therefore, are inherently conservative, and this is borne out consistently in his skepticism of progress. There is no technology, science, or political agenda that will rescue us from our own age's nihilistic tendencies to destroy our environment, our culture, and ourselves. "The idea that science and industry and government can discover for the rest of us the ultimate truths of nature and human nature, which then can be infallibly used to regulate our life, is wrong. The true work of the sciences and the arts is to keep all of us moving, in our own lives in our own places, between the cultural landscapes and the actual landscapes, making the always necessary and the forever unfinished corrections."[21] This is a complex passage: I would like to get into what Berry means by "the true work of the sciences and the arts" in my next section, and here to merely emphasize his point about the fallacy of big government. Government, as George Washington noted, is force, and so are science, technology, industry. Therefore, they cannot, be said to possess personal virtues such as compassion or trustworthiness. By nature they are impersonal and dehumanizing and can only be administered according to mechanistic bureaucracies that reduce people and places to measurable units. By definition, the timeless things—home and hearth, beauty, holiness—are not even under consideration. The paradigm of government-technology-industry, rather than saving us from, can only perpetuate our culture of death.

Culture of death—that evocative phrase of Pope John Paul II—provides a lot of fodder for discussion of Berry's art. First the death part. One of the difficulties in politically pigeonholing Berry is that he is consistently

19. Ibid.

20. Berry, *A Timbered Choir*, 1994. "VII," lines 8, 10–12, p. 182

21. Berry, *Citizenship Papers*, 95.

nonviolent: anti-abortion, anti-euthanasia, anti-capital punishment, and anti-war. On that score he never has a party on the ticket. But *culture* is more interesting because it shares roots etymologically with *agriculture*, *cultivate*, and *cult*. The earth we cultivate in order to live is inextricably bound up with what we venerate and worship and what we value enough to cultivate in the lives of our young. And so this one word *culture* points to the nexus that yokes farm to church to school.

## THE CURRICULUM OF WENDELL BERRY

The idea of school as what we cultivate within the minds of our young, what we want them to remember and to perpetuate, brings us back to Berry's concern with higher education and the "true work of the sciences and arts." First, some preliminary background: it is often overlooked that Berry himself is an academic. Berry has indeed continuously farmed his land in Port Royal, Kentucky, since the 1960s, but for many of those years he also taught at a major research university—the University of Kentucky. So Berry knows of what he speaks when he avers, as he did at the 2008 commencement address at Bellarmine University in Louisville, that small Christian liberal arts schools offer the best hope of an education. They can do so because they have the potential to address in an interdisciplinary way the needs and values of the local community; they best can carry on a dialogue between what Berry calls "the Two Minds" of the arts and sciences, and they uniquely can cultivate the Christian virtues in defiance of the spirit of the age.

As Berry lays out in his extended essay *Life Is a Miracle,* the single most important ethical question to ask about anything is, what will this do to our community, or what are the needs of our community? In a college, all the disciplines and administrative divisions can address this question fruitfully. It opens a whole network of issues before one even gets to the curricular concerns: town-gown relations; energy; food and water supply; the aesthetics of campus; the fauna and flora of campus; college history and traditions; alumni relations, and so forth. Community, Berry insists, should be defined as broadly as possible to include not only students, faculty, and staff, but our neighbors, our alumni living and dead, the plant and animal life on campus and nearby, as well as the land itself. This requires a college community to ask, where are we?—and to do so as locally as possible. For instance, Grove City College is entailed certain obligations merely by being in Pennsylvania, in Mercer County, and along

160

the banks of Wolf Creek. And we suffer the consequences if we fail these obligations. Once these broad questions have been asked, one can then start addressing more practical matters of a college: what can we do here, what are our abilities, and what are our responsibilities? Certainly, a broad array of bright minds from every academic department could have something to contribute in assessing these abilities and obligations. Berry offers a checklist of these basic questions in *Life Is a Miracle: An Essay against Modern Superstition.*[22]

Having mentioned this book and its subtitle, it is only fair to mention that the "modern superstition" Berry has in mind is the myth of scientism—the belief that science can solve every problem, and that every unknown is merely a thing yet to be known. Berry holds in particular derision the dreaded S-T-E-M—the Science-Technology-Engineering-Mathematics juggernaut that has taken over many campuses. Berry to his credit manages never to refer to this as the Four Horsemen of the Apocalypse, but the charity ends there. STEM is the bureaucratic manifestation of the "Rational Mind," which is "objective, analytical, and empirical," as well as the mind we all are supposed to have, the mind the powerful think they have, and the one our schools educate us to have.[23] In sum, the Rational Mind is "the official mind of science, industry, and government."[24] Furthermore, by limiting itself to a strictly empirical methodology, the Rational Mind has cut itself off "from all of human life that involves feeling, affection, familiarity, reverence, faith, and loyalty."[25] This "Rational Mind" is the spirit of our age and is at once antisacramental in Sherrard's reckoning, inhumane, and dehumanizing. Genuine intellectual enterprise can also be further compromised by federal or corporate grants that subsidize most research in the sciences and social sciences. As Berry puts it elsewhere, "the sciences are sectioned like a stockyard the better to serve the corporations."[26] One can see more clearly how the University of Kentucky is merely a handy example of a ubiquitous phenomenon in Berry's estimation.

Though himself a man in the humanities, Berry is no less brutal in his diagnosis of what ails most colleges of arts and letters: "the so-called humanities, which might have supplied at least a corrective or chastening remembrance of the good that humans have sometimes accomplished,

---

22. Berry, *Life Is a Miracle* 14.
23. Berry, *Citizenship Papers*, 88.
24. Ibid.
25. Ibid.
26. Berry, *Life Is a Miracle*, 123.

have been dismembered into utter fecklessness, turning out 'communicators' who have nothing to say and 'educators' who have nothing to teach."[27] Berry's hyperbole and perhaps oversimplification here should not dull his larger point. This kind of humane letters is not human at all; it has yielded not only to the imperialism of the Rational Mind but to the current trends of compartmentalization and professionalization. This is also why on almost every campus the individual tends to be reduced to membership in groups organized along race, class, and gender. Whereas the humanities should be the citadel of the "Sympathetic Mind," they have abdicated their responsibility of providing any notion of propriety or an ethical voice other than the crude form of class warfare known as political correctness.[28] Berry does not flinch from criticizing the dangerous folly at work on either side of campus.

Nor does he hold back from suggesting a positive alternative, though this is more vague and inherently interdisciplinary. The arts are for learning both how to appreciate beautiful things and how to make them. These things not only include the fine arts but should also include stories, histories, marriages, families, and relationships. The arts in this sense would include much of the social sciences. The sciences, properly subordinated to the Sympathetic Mind, would rightly help understand the natural order of things and how man can live healthily in local places. Berry is quite adamant that the arts and sciences are not really at odds—they are simply ways of "doing" and ways of "knowing." As tools their proper function is to "build and maintain our dwelling here on earth."[29] "Our dwelling" is Berry's way of emphasizing the necessity of smallness of scale in order to properly respect local communities, which are and stand for civilization as a whole. In this regard Berry's "dwelling" is analogous to Plato's "polis" and to Kirk's "civilization," all of which oppose "The Waste Land" of modernity that Eliot describes so well.

Berry's censure of and recommendations for academe provide a challenge to any campus. Few campuses in fact could measure up completely to his ideals. For instance, to achieve the relative purity of the sciences that

27. Ibid.

28. Berry's critique is certainly not unique on these points, nor is he particularly "conservative" in doing so. See Stanley Fish, *Save the World on Your Own Time* (New York: Oxford University Press, 2008). on the impropriety and narrowness of contemporary political correctness on campus. Fish is excerpted and rejoined from various points of view in Elizabeth Kiss and J. Peter Euben, eds., *Debating Moral Education: Rethinking the Role of the Modern University* (Durham: Duke University Press, 2009).

29. Berry, *Life Is a Miracle*, 122.

Berry recommends, a school would have to refuse federal funding. But to do that, as the Supreme Court has spelled out through various decisions, would prevent a college from even allowing its students to receive federal student aid. Only two schools—Grove City College and Hillsdale College—have gone to this extreme. Grove City College goes one step further by severely restricting corporate-sponsored monies, which Berry would undoubtedly applaud. Berry, however, would not stop with the funding of research. His rules for local economy require a school to analyze line by line its entire financial structure. He simply asks to follow the money: after determining where does it come from and where does it go, the goal is to keep it as local as possible. Such an approach would completely transform the way many colleges and universities do their budgets and do business. It is doubtful if *any* school has actually gone so far, but in the areas where they do adopt Berry's ethical concerns, they tend to advertise it well. Thus, one often hears of various "green" initiatives on campuses all over the country: "zero landfill" programs, watershed cleanup days, recycling, campus vegetable gardens, etc. Such efforts in every case are well intentioned and commendable by Berry's standards insofar as they are meaningful acts we can do. But Berry challenges schools to think out how they relate to and train students for being out of school.

Berry painfully identifies the deepest prejudices of academia: every institution implicitly reaffirms that science/technology has the answers for society's problems, and tacitly promises that there is a job out there for every graduate and it will not be on a farm or in a factory. Berry's critique of the Rational Mind calls for a wholly different kind of intellectual diversity than either the Left or the Right have imagined. To combat the "superstition," as Berry calls it, that science can solve virtually every problem of our day, Berry insists that a campus should have a healthy mixture of humane scientists and rational humanists to balance what he terms the Rational and Sympathetic Minds. The fundamental question these minds should dutifully apply their intellects, their sense of mystery and wonder, and their reverent ignorance to is "How should we live in this place?" This question honestly and rigorously asked across the disciplines over four years would profoundly impact students in a myriad of ways, and it could offer an equally profound preparation for graduates.

Almost every institution of higher learning, to provide one last salient example of how radically Berry's ideas could affect a campus, has committed itself to technology. Most schools have a technological competency requirement and require students to use a computer; some schools include a laptop with tuition, all schools provide access to the Internet twenty-four hours a day. One simple thing Berry suggests with respect to technology is simple subtraction: count up what we have gained by the technology, look at the cost of implementation and maintenance, and reckon the value of the technology. The very students today who learned first in "wired" classrooms then in "wireless" spaces are increasingly being forbidden to use their laptops in law-school classrooms. Berry revels in such examples because they reveal the backwardness of "forward" thinking: no one thought to ask, before installing all the cable and transponders and servers, "What will this do to our learning community?"

The word *community* offers a convenient coda here because ultimately living in a place, for Berry, comes down to an authentic sense of community. One popular trend on campuses is community- or service-learning initiatives. This is a broad term for a range of curricular activities, but anything that engages more students in the community as part of their coursework—Berry calls this "learning out of school"—is good. With all three of these initiatives—technology, sustainability, and community learning—a comparison with peer institutions would be enlightening to any campus.

One of Berry's most perspicacious observations is that our age has dislocated the actual landscape from its cultural landscape. The actual landscape is the actual terrain our food comes from—the one we have inherited, and the one, if we are meek enough, we shall inherit. Our cultural landscape is the sum of what we think and feel—what we were taught, and what we value enough to teach the next generations. Cultural conservatism, therefore, is meaningless in Berry's reckoning if it is not also conservationist. "A vital, functioning intellectual community *could* not sponsor patterns of land use that are increasingly toxic, violent, and destructive of rural communities."[30] Berry's charge to any college is that every academic department can look for ways to connect the two landscapes. Berry suspects that small liberal arts colleges, where individual people share a place for four years, become members of a shared body, and thus participate in and build a history together, are the most likely to offer such an education. To offer, that is, what a true "alma mater" should provide.

30. Ibid.,129.

## 10

# Great Books, Students' Souls, and Political Freedom

*Reflections on Allan Bloom's*
The Closing of the American Mind

---

## Michael Coulter

MANY BOOKS HAVE BEEN and continue to be important in American higher education, but there are few important books *about* American higher education. If such a list were compiled, some of the books on that list would be important for historical reasons, and those books would be little read today. An example of such a book would be William Buckley's *God and Man at Yale*. That book provides an important critique of trends in American higher education at the time it was published, but it is important because it comes from Buckley and is also important as an artifact of the then-emerging conservative movement. More recently, Stanley Fish's *Save the World on Your Own Time* has attracted significant interest. One book that would likely make many lists of important books about American higher education and perhaps be at the top of those lists would be *The Closing of the American Mind* by Allan Bloom (1930–1992). Despite the idiosyncrasies of both the author and the book, Bloom's meditation on the mode, means, and purpose of higher education in America is still relevant, even if his examples and his Tocqueville-like description of student habits may no longer be so, because he instructs us that higher education is about more than technical proficiency or cultural literacy, both of which are laudable but not the highest or most important end of education. Bloom makes the case that higher education should be oriented toward enriching the rational souls of students and that this task has an essential role in preserving democratic order.

## AN UNUSUAL BEST SELLER

*Closing* was published in 1987 and immediately gained fanfare and was a best seller. At the time that it was published Bloom was a little-known academic. He was then a part of the prestigious Committee on Social Thought at the University of Chicago, and he had previously taught at Yale, Cornell, and the University of Toronto. He authored, edited, or translated eight books during his career, but prior to *Closing* was best known for translations of Plato's *Republic* (1968) and Rousseau's *Emile* (1979). Bloom's academic life started at the University of Chicago at the age of sixteen where he earned his BA in 1949 and his PhD from the Committee on Social Thought in 1955. He died in 1992 because of liver failure.[1]

*Closing* is likely one of few books in the history of the *New York Times* best-seller list that include extended discussions of Aristophanes, Friedrich Nietzsche, and Martin Heidegger. The volume of sales of the book was a complete surprise. Simon & Schuster published the book with some hesitation. Bloom received a small advance and initially only ten thousand copies were printed. The publisher arranged for Bloom's colleague and friend, Saul Bellow, a much better-known author and Nobel laureate, to write a foreword for the book in order to help with sales. The book immediately caught the attention of an interested public and editors and news producers. The book was reviewed in hundreds of publications, including newspapers, magazines, and academic journals. In an era with limited television programming featuring author interviews, Bloom made many appearances on television. In the end, the book sold nearly a million copies and stayed near the top of the best-seller list for roughly thirty weeks.

---

1. *New York Times,* October 8, 1992 (national edition), 1.

The themes of the book can be seen in essays that Bloom wrote much earlier in his life, but the book itself grew out of an article that Bloom wrote for the *National Review* in 1982.[2] The *National Review* essay was a relatively brief critique of the intellectual life found in American higher education. Bellow encouraged Bloom to expand the essay into a book.

## A BOOK ON THE AMERICAN SOUL

The book is not solely about higher education. In many ways it is an erudite reflection on American intellectual life. Bloom says that it is "a meditation on the state of our souls, particularly those of the young, and their education."[3] This is important because modern nations "have founded themselves on reason in its various uses more than did any nations in the past" and therefore "crisis in the university, the home of reason, is perhaps the profoundest crisis they face."[4] The work is divided into three parts. The first part, which examines students, is the section that was most likely read by most people. The second part is called "Nihilism, American Style," and it examines the intellectual influences that led to relativism. In the final part, Bloom critiques higher education and the state of contemporary intellectual life as well as offering a defense of an education centered on the careful study of great texts.

Before Part 1, there is a lengthy introduction bearing the title, "Our Virtue." It is not simply "Virtue"; when he speaks of our virtue, he is referring to a particular "excellence" of Americans. Our current virtue is our "openness" to any idea, or, conversely, our being closed to any claim of truth. Bloom's opening line makes this point bluntly: "There is one thing a professor can be absolutely certain of: almost every student entering the university believes, or says that he believes, that truth is relative."[5] Students, Bloom says, regard this as essentially a self-evident truth. Related

2. Bloom wrote several essays about higher education and the study of texts, including "The Crisis of Liberal Education," which appeared in *Higher Education and Modern Democracy*, ed. Robert Goldwin (Chicago: Rand McNally, 1967), and "The Democratization of the University," which appeared in *How Democratic Is America?*, ed. Robert Goldwin (Chicago: Rand McNally, 1967). Another Bloom essay prefiguring the arguments in *Closing* is "The Study of Texts," which appeared in *Political Theory and Political Education*, ed. M. Richter (Princeton: Princeton University Press, 1980).

3. Alan Bloom, *The Closing of the American Mind* (New York: Simon & Schuster, 1987), 19

4. Ibid., 22.

5. Ibid., 25.

to relativism is "their allegiance to equality."[6] Believing in relativism and equality are not the products of long philosophical reflection on the part of students, but are "moral postulates" upon which they believe a free society is based. Related to this view of relativism is the idea that believing in moral absolutes is harmful for political society and is the cause of war and oppression. It might be asserted that Bloom's view of students was shaped by his experience at elite universities and that most students could not be characterized as relativists. Yet polling data seems to confirm Bloom's view of widespread moral relativism.[7] This openness is not only the openness to values, but also openness to the claim that any culture is superior to another.

The educational "openness" that Bloom describes is presented as an alternative mode of defending democratic order and making democratic citizens. Education for Bloom is always closely related to politics because all education has a moral intention, and an important moral intention is the right forming of the thoughts and practices of citizens.

American education once supported an earlier idea of democratic order and citizens. Bloom says that "we began with the model of the rational and industrious man," which is a direct reference to John Locke's political teaching. That man "was honest, respected the laws, and was dedicated to the family" and "above all he was to know the rights doctrine, the Constitution, which embodied it; and American history."[8] In this old form of education, the Declaration of Independence's claim that it was self-evident that individuals possessed rights was believed to be true. Thus, the equality of natural rights became the basis of American equality. Part of the belief in natural rights was a belief in the capacity of human rationality to understand these concepts. Rights were not merely the product of a pre-rational religious teaching or an assertion of the will. Immigrants to America could then readily adopt this viewpoint and become American.

Bloom then argues that "openness . . . eventually won out over natural rights."[9] The liberalism of the twentieth century as seen in the utilitarian defender of democracy John Dewey or the Kantian John Rawls was

---

6. Ibid.

7. According to a 2005 survey by the Barna Group, 35 percent believed in moral absolutes; most of those who affirmed this view identified as evangelical. See "Most Adults Feel Accepted by God, But Lack a Biblical Worldview," Barna Group; online: http://www.barna.org/barna-update/article/5-barna-update/174-most-adults-feel-accepted-by-god-but-lack-a-biblical-worldview.

8. Bloom, *Closing*, 27

9. Ibid., 29.

liberalism without natural rights. Rights language might exist and be used, but those rights were not rationally discoverable and proven. Rights, if they existed at all, were to be assumed and were at best an unstable ground for democratic politics. This shift in the self-understanding of liberalism brought with it a support for cultural relativism. Under the old understanding of liberalism, a belief in natural rights would lead to the view that individuals should receive the benefit of equal protection of the laws. Equal protection did not mean being free from contempt or prejudice. Bloom says that in the new defense of liberal politics that "openness was designed to wrest respect from those who were not disposed to give it— and to weaken the sense of superiority of the dominant majority."[10] Ultimately, the "teachers of openness had either no interest in or were actively hostile to the Declaration of Independence and the Constitution."[11] The consequence of this new emphasis on "openness" in both academia and the culture at large is that we are closed to the possibility of a universal claim of natural rights. Bloom asserts that "cultural relativism succeeds in destroying the West's universal or intellectually imperialistic claims, leaving it to be just another culture."[12] Bloom then illustrates this "closedness" to the claims of truth by recounting a conversation with the psychology professor who saw his job as a teacher as having the responsibility to destroy the beliefs of students by getting them to believe that they were only prejudices.

## ON THE SOULS OF STUDENTS

The first major section of *Closing* is the one most likely read by those who purchased the book. It contains his analysis of contemporary students. Bloom's style is reminiscent of Tocqueville's analysis of the United States. There are many striking comments about students but little discussion of the observations on which they are based. These observations of contemporary students, however, are not unrelated to the analyses of American intellectual life in Part Two or the contemporary university in Part Three. Bloom does not directly state this point, but it seems that Bloom believes that students are what they are because of the state of American intellectual culture and the institutions of higher learning.

10. Ibid., 31.
11. Ibid., 33.
12. Ibid., 39.

Bloom begins with a discussion of what he calls the "The Clean Slate." He is not talking of Locke's *tabula rasa*, but of the contemporary student who enters higher education without having been formed in a serious intellectual environment. He compares American students with those French students he knew during his time in Paris who were influenced by one of the two great intellectual currents in France—that of either Pascal or Descartes. He says that "openness has driven out the local deities, leaving only the speechless, meaningless country."[13] He adds that "students now arrive at the university ignorant and cynical about our political heritage, lacking the wherewithal to be either inspired by it or seriously critical of it."[14]

In addition to the absence of political knowledge, students lack religious knowledge, and here Bloom blames families who "have nothing to give their children in the way of a vision of the world."[15] Parents do not seriously pass on tradition with its related rituals and ceremonies, nor do families make serious use of books. In part, parents do not pass on a tradition because they largely lack it themselves.

Students have little connection to books and this is a cause for great concern for Bloom, who advocates an education in which the careful reading of great texts is primary. He says that this attention to books cannot be acquired late in life. Bloom says that he has "begun to wonder whether the experience of the greatest texts from early childhood is not a prerequisite for a concern throughout life for them."[16] Bloom describes his experience asking students about the books that have been important for them. Few students list any books, and those that do somewhat perfunctorily cite the Bible and a few others list a book that they read in high school. The student who does not have a serious interest in books is like a young person wandering through the great museums in Europe with no knowledge of what he sees. It is all "colors and forms."[17] Students are disconnected from the entire literary and historical tradition, and this cuts students off from being

13. Ibid., 56.

14. Ibid. Confirming Bloom's assertion that students know little about history, a 2006 study by the Intercollegiate Studies Institute found that students could only answer half of the questions on a sixty question test on American history and politics. See "The Coming Crisis in Citizenship; Unprecedented Study Exposes Higher Education's Failure to Teach America's History and Essential Institutions," Intercollegiate Studies Institute, http://www.americancivicliteracy.org/resources/content/civlit_9-26-06.pdf.

15. Ibid., 57.

16. Ibid., 61.

17. Ibid., 63.

itself. Bloom does not believe that the serious texts can be introduced to every student, but they can be an important part of some serious students' education. In addition to difficulty of reading serious books, the study of texts is challenged by modern ideologies that see all old texts as racist and sexist, although Bloom is particularly concerned about the latter.

Bloom also examines the relationship between students and their music. During his early years as a teacher in the 1950s, popular music was an interest to a small portion of students and classical music was of interest to some brighter students. Bloom says that his students in the 1980s had popular music as an integral part of their lives, and classical music as only a specialized taste for a rare few. Bloom cites the arguments in Plato and Aristotle that music inflames the passions at the expense of reason. He says that modern-day rationalists, such as economists, ignore rock music while the "irrationalists are all for it."[18] Bloom claims that "rock music has one appeal only, a barbaric appeal, to sexual desire—not love, not eros, but sexual desire undeveloped and untutored."[19] He observes that contemporary music also has themes of "hate [and] a smarmy, hypocritical version of brotherly love."[20] Bloom offers some criticism of parents, but he is also critical of the rock business, which he says has all the "moral dignity of drug trafficking."[21] The Left, says Bloom, is willing to criticize capitalism, but is unwilling to challenge rock music—in part because it is working towards the same goal of personal liberation as the trendiest elements of contemporary thought. He concludes the section by saying that his primary concern is not with the moral consequences of lyrics, but says that "the issue here is its effect on education, and I believe that it ruins the imagination of young people and makes it very difficult for them" to experience serious liberal education.

Bloom further explores the students' relationships with others and considers self-centeredness, equality, race, sex, separateness, divorce, love, and eros. With respect to self-centeredness, he says that students are "nice," but not particularly "moral or noble."[22] Students have few, if any, attachments. They are separate from their family, community, and tradition. Regarding equality, Bloom asserts that any remaining elements of aristocracy have been washed away. He writes that "no longer do universities

18. Ibid., 72.
19. Ibid., 73.
20. Ibid., 74.
21. Ibid., 74.
22. Ibid., 82.

have the vocation of producing gentlemen as well as scholars."[23] In a later section on connectedness, Bloom believes that students have no conception of real connections with others. It is as if individualism has obliterated any conception of human community. The racial relationships among students, Bloom claims, is not what one would expect. Blacks and whites have not become friends and this is partly due to self-segregation among blacks and also probably largely due to the unintended consequences of affirmative action that have created suspicions among students.

Bloom devotes considerable attention to the relationship between the sexes. He has observed significant changes regarding sexual activity that have been the consequences of the sexual revolution and feminism. Bloom argues that cultures have for millennia sought to restrict and control sexual relations and, now that those restrictions have been lifted, there is now a passionlessness to sexual activity that "makes the younger generation more or less incomprehensible to older folks."[24] The culture of "hooking up," described in several recent exposés, would seem to confirm Bloom's observations. Bloom partly blames the evisceration of religion for the new attitudes towards sexual relations, but he also blames feminism, which has advocated the "suppression of modesty."[25] Also regarding male-female relationships, Bloom comments on divorce and says that "the decomposition of this bond is surely America's most urgent social problem." Children coming from these homes often have a "slight deformity of the spirit."[26] Because of the freewheeling nature of sex and relationships, love is damaged. Bloom says that "'relationships' not love affairs, are what they have." In Bloom's final book, *Love and Friendship*, he asserts that Shakespeare's characters loved one another and were not "in relationships." Bloom makes clear that family arrangements in the past were not always perfect, but also that the current attempts to strip human beings from their natural orientations and from the institutions that have supported marriage and family life are fraught with difficulty. The state of relationships may seem far afield from higher education, but for Bloom higher education must work with the students that come to it, and the individualism and lack of tradition in modernity has harmed the souls of today's students and has made the task of education ever more difficult.

23. Ibid., 89.
24. Ibid., 99.
25. Ibid., 101.
26. Ibid., 120.

## THE DEFORMING OF THE AMERICAN MIND

If Part 1 is the section that was most often read, Part 2, titled "Nihilism, American Style," is probably the section that was least read. Yet this section is vitally important to Bloom's project because therein he attempts to explain how American intellectual life has come to accept the relativism so characteristic of modernity. The general argument is that elements of German philosophy—the products of Nietzsche, Freud, and Weber—have infiltrated the American academy and then American culture. Bloom asserts that ideas of value relativism have been uncritically adopted by Americans, and now Americans speak the language of these thinkers without fully understanding what they are saying. Bloom cites Louis Armstrong's singing "Mack the Knife," which is a translation of a song from Bertolt Brecht and Kurt Weill's *Threepenny Opera* as emblematic of what happened. Bloom contends that "our stars are singing a song they do not understand, translated from a German original and having a huge popular success with unknown but wide-ranging consequences."[27]

Bloom argues that American political and intellectual culture was largely the product of Lockean political philosophy with its emphasis on the need for careful work to overcome nature and the need for stable political institutions to protect property. Bloom clearly notes that Locke is not purely good. The other tradition affecting Americans is that which comes from Jean-Jacques Rousseau. Rousseau presents a different account of man's origin and development. According to Bloom, "the opposition between nature and society is Rousseau's interpretation of the cause of the dividedness of man."[28] The conflict between these two views of the state of nature and understanding of human beings and their relation to society takes place in twentieth-century America. For Bloom, the descendants of Rousseau have vaulted to the forefront in American life.

*Closing* includes an extended treatment of the origin and use of the term *values*. Values, according to Bloom, is a term that comes from Nietzsche but was mediated through the far more acceptable Max Weber. Nietzsche argues that there is no longer good and evil; instead, there are the value-creating acts of individuals, such as Moses, Homer, and Jesus. According to Bloom, "it is not the truth of their thought that distinguished them, but its capacity to generate culture."[29] Values are significant

27. Ibid., 152.
28. Ibid., 169.
29. Ibid., 201.

Is Nietzsche wrong? certainly, but Values can be embodied by myths — affirming one is not denying the other.

to Nietzsche because they are "life-preserving and life-enhancing." They are not grounded in rationality because rationality "cannot make them believed."[30] The great change can be seen in this, says Bloom: "Not love of truth but intellectual honesty characterizes the proper state of mind."[31] Following from this view of values, Nietzsche is a cultural relativist. He is also a nihilist, but Americans do not adopt Nietzschean nihilism. Weber becomes the important figure in translating Nietzsche. It is Weber who speaks of worldviews and values as guiding cultures. Weber examines the charisma of leaders, rather than their rational guidance. Weber speaks of "'worldviews' or 'world-interpretations' with no foundation other than the selves of the Protestants."[32] In a brief period of time, the Weberian terminology took hold. Bloom observes that "whatever the merit of Weber's analysis and categories, they became holy writ for hosts of intellectuals."[33] If culture then guides politics, and culture is without a rational foundation, politics then cannot be expected to have a rational orientation. Thus cultural analysis becomes an integral part of "academic psychology, sociology, comparative literature, and anthropology" and from these disciplines has a great effect on the political Left in the United States.[34]

## THE ANARCHY OF THE AMERICAN UNIVERSITY

In the final part of *Closing*, Bloom examines the modern university and provides some prescriptions towards a correction. The section begins not with an account of what universities are doing, but with an analysis of Tocqueville's account of intellectual life that appeared in *Democracy in America*, which Bloom says "gave voice to my inchoate sentiments."[35] Bloom describes Tocqueville as concerned about intellectual conformity and the failure to use reason independently in a democratic age. Public opinion can be an all-powerful force in a democracy. The university then has a special role in a democratic order: it is to preserve reason. Bloom says that "the most important function of the university in an age of reason is to protect reason from itself, by being the model of true openness."[36] He

30. Ibid., 201.
31. Ibid., 202.
32. Ibid., 209.
33. Ibid., 213.
34. Ibid., 226.
35. Ibid., 246.
36. Ibid., 253.

wants to defend reason by allowing the possibility that reason can defend claims of truth. This is particularly needed in a democracy in an age of reason where reason is seen as a prejudice. The university, Bloom claims, must work against the prejudices common in a democracy.

*Closing* concludes with an intellectual history of the university quickly traversing from the medieval era to the twentieth century. Bloom asserts that the modern university as we know it is a product of the Enlightenment. In this modern university, the Socratic claim on the importance of self-knowledge was practiced, or at least functioned as an ideal. Bloom then examines Rousseau's critique of the Enlightenment and how it affected the university. "The fringe bohemian, the sentimentalist, the artist became at least much the teacher and the model as the scientist," writes Bloom.[37] Bloom then argues that these new teachers in the French and German universities ignore or, at best, marginalize the claims of classical philosophy. In a sense, this culminates in the Nietzschean claim that intellectual life erred with Socrates and there was a need to go to pre-Socratic thinkers for an alternative to rationalism. Martin Heidegger, according to Bloom, becomes the epitome of the influence of Nietzsche. Heidegger clearly appreciated classical philosophy, but like Nietzsche he was drawn to pre-Socratics. Bloom examines Heidegger's famous statement about university life, which in English is titled, "The Self-Assertion of the German University," that he delivered when he became rector of the University of Freiburg on May 1, 1933. Bloom reasons that Heidegger, who officially joined the Nazi Party, "put philosophy at the service of the German culture."[38] Heidegger does not directly praise Hitler or the Nazi Party, but he does speak of the "spiritual mission" of the Germans and speaks of the power of "willing" throughout the address.

Bloom argues that intellectual change led to underlying weakness in American universities. These intellectually limited institutions could not withstand the challenge that came from the radicals in the 1960s. To demonstrate the change that came in the 1960s, Bloom recounts his own experience at Cornell during those turbulent days. At Cornell, students took over the administration building, and in the end the administration capitulated to their demands and many changes in the both the social and intellectual life of universities ensued. Bloom asserts that "so far as the universities are concerned, I know of nothing positive coming from that

37. Ibid., 299.
38. Ibid., 311.

period; it was an unmitigated disaster for them."[39] Bloom describes the evisceration of core requirements, the trivialization of the curriculum, and the abandonment of *in loco parentis*. Bloom does not describe this in *Closing*, but he was so dispirited by what happened at Cornell that he left that institution and spent the next decade at the University of Toronto.[40]

In the final section, Bloom examines the state of liberal arts education, provides an analysis of contemporary academic disciplines, and offers some suggestions of what might revive the intellectual life for some students and faculty. The university, writes Bloom, "offers no distinctive visage to the young person."[41] Bloom claims there is a "democracy of the disciplines" which in reality is "anarchy" and leads to "dispiritedness."[42] There are many departments and many majors, but there is no agreement about what a student should study. Bloom laments the lack of any agreement about what an educated human being should read or consider. Instead of core courses, there are no requirements at all, or there are long lists of courses in many departments that can satisfy institutional requirements and that the "student must navigate among a collection of carnival barkers, each trying to lure him into a particular sideshow."[43]

Bloom alludes to the solution for which this book is best known—a Great Books Program, which "means reading certain generally recognized classic texts, just reading them, letting them dictate what the questions are and the method of approaching them."[44] He argues that where this approach has been taken the students have been "excited and satisfied."[45] Through these books, students can consider the important questions and models of how those questions can be addressed. The problem is that only a small number in a modern university have an interest or appreciation of the study of Great Books. Contemporary social scientists, says Bloom, are often hostile to Great Books because they reject the normative aspects of the works and instead favor an approach that is only empirical and makes no claims about what is good for human beings. Even the humanities are

39. Ibid., 320.

40. Werner Dannhauser, "Allan Bloom: A Reminiscence," in *Political Philosophy and the Human Soul: Essays in Memory of Allan Bloom*, ed. Michael Palmer and Thomas L. Pangle (Lanham, MD: Rowman & Littlefield, 1995), 11–12.

41. Bloom, *Closing*, 337.

42. Ibid.

43. Ibid., 339.

44. Ibid., 344.

45. Ibid.

not interested in Great Books education as they have been overly specialized and are interested only in problems within narrow subdisciplines.

There follows a more lengthy "tour" through those many disciplines
and departments vying for the attention of students. Bloom asserts that
there exists no community of scholars; there is only a collection of academics in the same place with greatly different approaches and goals.
Natural science has largely avoided the conflict over the mission of the
university. Natural scientists work on their own projects and only engage
others in the university when it comes to fights over the distribution of
resources. In the humanities, however, one finds "hysterical supporters of
the revolution."[46] Some elements of social science—such as economics and
quantitative political science—were attacked by the radicals in the 1960s,
but offered no vision for the intellectual life, and instead only sought to defend their use of instrumental reason. Overall, Bloom presents academia
as divided about what is good for human beings. We can know much
about man, but we have cut ourselves off from the possibility of knowing
what is the enduring good for man.

Bloom includes a few notes of optimism, but a reader who is persuaded by Bloom's overarching argument would generally despair of the
current state and likely future of American higher education. Bloom does
not indicate that the intellectual trends that he has described are revers-
ible. In fact, it could be argued that implied within Bloom's argument is
that the decline was inevitable because of the excessive individualism
within the natural-rights tradition. Here I believe that Bloom had misread
the American founders (in fact, he seems to have not read them at all as
they are not referred to in any significant manner), who sought to mitigate
the individualism of Locke with elements of classical Republicanism and
Christianity.[47] Thus Bloom's analysis of the problem may be, at least in
part, misguided.

Bloom's defense of Great Books programs and call for a revivified
core drew the attention of many people after the publication of *Closing*.
There were some corrections against the gutting of core curricula that
had occurred during the tumultuous 1960s and thereafter. But Bloom's
jeremiad led to no vast changes in American higher education. In fact, it

46. Ibid., 351.

47. See Thomas G. West, "Allan Bloom and America," The Claremont Institute,
Online: http://www.claremont.org/publications/pubid.664/pub_detail.asp/ for an exploration of Bloom's neglect of the founding as a corrective to excessive individualism.

appears that the momentum created by Bloom and other proponents of a strengthened core seems to have dissipated.[48]

Nevertheless, for anyone concerned about the mission of higher education and its relationship to American political and social life, Bloom's work remains a challenge. We are challenged by the argument that the American political order was founded upon a claim that natural rights  were self-evident—which means discoverable through reason—and that when that claim becomes unintelligible through an attack upon the capacity and significance of reason, the American order itself is challenged. We are also challenged by Bloom to never forget the larger meaning of higher education in our own lives. It is all too easy to be concerned about the distribution of resources and our own disciplinary concerns. Bloom challenges his readers to see that the university plays an important role in helping students consider the important questions of our humanity. We are to consider the claims of religion, the meaning of our freedom, and the significance of virtue, especially in our democratic regime where there is, as Tocqueville tells, a great power in the thought of the majority. As his subtitle to the work so starkly put it, we cannot let higher education fail democracy or impoverish the souls of our students.

48. See Alex Beam's *A Great Idea at the Time: The Rise, Fall, and Curious Afterlife of the Great Books* (New York: Public Affairs, 2008).

**11**

# How to Keep a Christian College Christian

## William P. Anderson

JOHN HENRY NEWMAN DESCRIBES the institutional Church in a way that also captures the essence of a Christian college and the challenges of keeping it so. He writes:

> It is a vast assemblage of human beings with willful intellects and wild passions, brought together into one by the beauty and the Majesty of a Superhuman Power . . . brought together as if into some moral factory, for the melting, refining, and molding, by an incessant and noisy process, of the raw material of human nature, so excellent, so dangerous, so capable of divine purposes.[1]

"Willful intellects and wild passions brought together into one . . . so excellent, so dangerous, so capable of divine purposes." Isn't that *exciting*? For *divine* purposes! Not ours, but Christ's . . . It is hard to imagine a more exciting calling today than to be in Christian higher education. Here are some reasons why:

First, a Christian college builds a faculty who are experts in their disciplines yet whose hearts are touched by the burning coal of God's

---

1. John Henry Newman, *Apologia Pro Vita Sua* (London: Longmans, Green, 1865), 253.

grace—a grace unveiling our Lord's role in the advance of knowledge and how it is shared and learned—a sense of calling, so to speak.

Second, a Christian college seeks and attracts students committed to stretching themselves intellectually, to understand knowledge in new and challenging ways, and to enjoy and grow in their faith and learning.

Third, a Christian college crafts a curriculum that speaks coherently to the times without surrendering its heritage and past, a curriculum unafraid to engage the world that surrounds us and unafraid to speak of Christ and His position at the apex of knowledge and learning. In fact, unafraid to assert his claim over all learning and all culture, showing what He extends to a broken and heartsick world hungry for Him.

However, late modernity creates challenges for Christian higher education.[2] Our lives are increasingly lived in an era of discontinuity—of social and cultural fragmentation—which works against transcendent narratives to explain our world and to secure us a place within it. Jobs and careers are rarely for a lifetime; indeed a lifetime's work means nine to ten jobs and four to five different careers—so much for trying to major in one field. Politics disappoints us, and we vote new candidates into office during every election cycle. Families are spread across the country as we move into new houses, neighborhoods, cities, and states. Life is disconnected from what we once could depend upon, and our worlds seem uncertain and fluid.

Frankly, it's dizzying, almost as if one were in a state of vertigo. But there is a way to recover our balance: As Cornelius Van Til teaches us, only Christianity, the Faith, suffices as a transcendent narrative, for it brings unity and coherence to our stories, learning, and understanding. Most important of all, it brings truth. Only when we implicate our seemingly fragmented worlds into Christ do they reveal a common truth and unity missing from our eyes.[3] A Christian education teaches the essential truth that all facts, all things, all creation, are part of God; in other words, it unifies learning and knowledge rather than splintering it. Christian institutions are needed more than ever to prepare graduates with the unifying Christian perspective to engage public issues critically at their source and in their personal, political, and economic manifestations—for issues whose roots are religious and moral split our culture. That same culture, on the other hand, rejects absolutist positions and thereby denies the capability

2. Jock Young, *The Vertigo of Late Modernity* (Los Angeles: Sage, 2007).

3. Greg Bahnsen, *Van Til's Apologetic* (Phillipsburg, NJ: P&R, 1998), 169. See also John Frame, *Cornelius Van Til: An Analysis of His Thought* (Phillipsburg, NJ: P&R, 1995), 90–93.

of transcendent moral and religious values to offer solutions. Dominated by bureaucratic tendencies in all institutional spheres—from government to corporations to mammoth universities and even to megachurches—our society sifts and smooths these political, moral, and religious issues into administrative problems and processes.[4] But we Christians know that not all problems can be concealed behind procedure or policy. Regardless of how adroitly they are recategorized, the values underlying them as issues continue. Indeed, it only is in thinking God's thoughts after him that our knowledge and our lives can have coherence. A Christian education purposely connecting all learning to Christ Jesus is the only way. We will have graduates able to bring the coherence of Christianity to bear upon today's issues, men and women able to discern them and join together in their resolution.

Sadly at the very moment when the clarity of a Christian education is most needed, the coherency a Christian education provides is even more up for grabs than before. Higher education is as multisectored as our culture (a mixture of vocational and liberal arts, public and private, for-profit and not-for-profit, adult and traditional-age, and in-person or online) and overwhelmingly indifferent to faith-based colleges if not outright hostile to them.

Christian colleges already educate from a weak position in late modernity. C. Wright Mills observes that religion today is no longer among the central institutions in society but is pushed to the periphery—partly by choice, partly not. Subordinate to the major institutions of politics and economics, religion—and by extension much of Christianity—has redefined its mission away from the prophetic to the therapeutic. Mills writes, "[Today, the church] does not originate; it reacts. It does not denounce; it adapts. It does not set forth new models of conduct and sensibility; it imitates . . . It has become less a revitalization of the spirit in permanent tension with the world than a respectable distraction from the sourness of life."[5] Because of the importance of the credential of a college degree, recovering an education blending *both* faith and learning is even more important. Restoring the Christian college will demand that we cease being cultural mirrors or second-class citizens. We must recapture, through our

---

4. Karl Mannheim, *Ideology and Utopia,* trans. Louis Wirth and Edward A. Shils (New York: Harvest, 1936), 118.

5. C. Wright Mills, "A Pagan Sermon to the Christian Clergy," in *The Politics of Truth: Selected Writings of C. Wright Mills.* ed. John H. Summers (New York: Oxford University Press, 2008), 166.

curriculum and faculty, our prophetic call during times seemingly deaf to our voice.

Drifting into a secondary role, many Christian institutions recognize their waning influence. They often panic and are tempted to respond in two ways. They desperately scramble for relevance and market share as they face cultural, financial, and enrollment pressures, which can and do alter their missions. The temptation is to become chameleon-like, to copy our rivals in higher education but baptize our programming with the label *Christian* and nothing more—more vocational majors, watered-down core curricula, blurred religious missions: in other words, abandoning our distinctives for the sake of acceptability and learning. Here even the label *Christian* itself becomes a commodity for consumption, a catchphrase intended to trigger interest and spending from a particular niche of families who ascribe to it whatever meaning they wish. Such is the economic necessity in these times, and such is the reason why the Christian logo must reflect the reality within the institution, not be the empty words of a marketing sales pitch. On the other hand, some Christian colleges flee to their own style of identity politics, a kind of "Gotcha Christianity." Here, we fall back upon a narcissitic essentialism about who we are and who others are not.[6] In other words, compromising learning for the mantle of unacceptability and asserted purity. Either response continues the exile of Christianity from late modernity; the first wishes away any gap between ourselves and our culture; the second imposes too great a one. A truly Christian education requires embedding in our culture, serving students and parents, and engaging the culture while nonetheless remaining faithful to a college's Christian mission so as to restore balance to the cultural vertigo of our times. But it is not getting any easier.

We experience enormous cultural pressures to compromise our moral stances and institutional missions. In 2005, Pope Benedict XVI warned that contemporary culture pushes a "dictatorship of relativism." Only the individual's self and his or her own selfish desires are definitive. Consequently, institutions committed to firm moral standards are reinterpreted as threats and are smeared with perhaps the two worst labels one can paste to others today: *fundamentalist* and *intolerant*. Translating that out of late-modernity-speak, that is to say, "You have standards and you stick to them; shame on you!"

Once abandoned, a college's Christian identity is hard to restore. Every college lost from the Faith means the loss of countless future graduates

---

6. Young, *Vertigo*, 5–7.

capable of articulating a Christian vision for society, and no less worse, not equipped with the love of neighbor and devotion to family, community, and church that heals and restores our country. Every college lost from the Faith leaves the public square less accountable, more fragmented, subject to childish quarreling, and increasingly the politics of personal destruction—all stealing the intellectual defense our churches, families, and communities are so much in need of today. Gone are the charity, wisdom, love, and mercy Christians bring to public debate.

Is it any wonder that the clarity and unity of a Christian vision for higher education is necessary now more than ever? Is it any wonder that protecting that vision is so crucial in our day? Moreover, how do we bring the Old Faith—the Faith of our fathers—to a New World of instant gratification, hyperconsumerism, texting, biotechnology, celebrity, and increasingly asymmetrical violence?

So, just how does a Christian college remain Christian when many see its education as irrelevant or a prejudiced copy of what non-Christian institutions provide? How can we mold those "willful intellects and wild passions" into one body eager to contribute to a society indifferent, even passive, toward them? Our answer must go beyond the pietistic language that so easily flows from our lips. A college is kept Christian when it steps forward confident in its identity, when as a community it testifies to a unifying Christian ethos that begins within itself as a learning community, then reaches out to the world. That ethos must transcend "Christian-speak" and be found in our daily actions toward one another. A Christian ethos, remember, is most deeply etched in what we do, especially in the smallest acts. The acts of love and forgiveness, spoken and shown by faculty toward their students, students toward each other, and among all the members of the community illustrate, indeed promote, faithfulness to that call. But they must occur within the context of something larger: an intentionally *Christian* faculty, *Christian* curriculum, and *Christian* student life that go beyond words and pietistic catchphrases to deeper significance in our actions. This paper focuses upon two important academic parts of that community: faculty and curriculum.


## THE FACULTY

In 1853 University of South Carolina president and Southern Presbyterian divine James Henley Thornwell put the matter of a Christian faculty succinctly: "Have godly teachers, and you will have comparatively a godly college."[7] Thornwell's position is clear and correct: with Christian faculty, one may rightly claim a Christian college; without them, one cannot. In the same letter to Governor Manning, he further lays out how Christianity unites a curriculum: "A godless education is worse than none . . . Man is essentially a religious being and to make no provision for this noblest element of his nature, to ignore and preclude it from any distinct consideration, is to leave him but half-educated . . . Science languishes, letters pine and refinement is lost, wherever and whenever the genius of religion is excluded."[8]

What faculty teach (combined with the way in which they do so and how they present themselves) is formative to a student's education and preparation for life. So, what kind of faculty member keeps a Christian college Christian? Here are some observations about what they should be, drawn from my own twenty-five years in Christian higher education and eleven years as an academic vice president:

*First, they should be professing Christians.* For a Christian college, different from a *sectarian or confessional* institution, faculty should be able to subscribe to the basic tenets of the historic creeds of the Faith in having a personal faith in Jesus Christ and the promise to follow him as their Lord and Savior. In addition, they should have a high view of the Holy Scriptures—as at least inspired by the breath of God.

*Second, be Christian intellectuals—not having sectarian or ideological agendas in the classroom.* While it certainly is appropriate for Christian colleges to be an extension of their denominational affiliation where applicable, Christian colleges can easily misunderstand themselves to be churches. But a college is not a church, and our responsibilities under our Lord are quite different. Again, Cardinal Newman writes:

> If then a University is a direct preparation for this world, let it be what it professes. It is not a Convent, it is not a Seminary; it is a place to fit men of the world for the world. We cannot possibly keep them from plunging into the world (with all its ways and principles and maxims) when their time comes; but

7. James Henley Thornwell, *Letter to His Excellency Governor Manning on Public Instruction in South Carolina* (Columbia, SC: R. W. Gibbs, 1853), 23.

8. Ibid., 29. Thornwell later emphasizes that much confusion arises from "confounding the dogmatic peculiarities of sects with the spirit of religion." The former acts more to nudge religion out of public institutions than to promote it. He then adds, "What is wanted [in a college] is the pervading influence of religion as a life, the habitual sense of responsibility to God and the true worth and destiny of the soul, which shall give tone to the character and regulate all the pursuits of the place" (ibid., 30).

we can prepare them against what is inevitable; and it is not the way to learn how to swim in troubled waters never to have gone into them.[9]

Because a Christian college's faculty are foremost intellectuals and scholars, they are responsible for teaching divergent points of view without losing their Christian perspective or attempting to build a cult of admirers around themselves. Young and eager minds can be too easily swayed by the personal charisma of their professors. How easy it is for we faculty to leverage our personalities and learning, even the power of a gradebook, to cultivate disciples to our personal ideological or sectarian battles. Such agendas are always tempting to us. But, such is not teaching, nor is it education. As the German sociologist Max Weber wrote, "The prophet and the demagogue do not belong on the academic platform . . . After all, it is somewhat too convenient to demonstrate one's courage in taking a stand where the audience and possible opponents are condemned to silence."[10]

The professoriate is no substitute for the pastorate. Just as a college is not a church, professors are not called to be clergy. Their responsibilities are broader and more inclusive, especially to show intellectual patience, guidance, and a willingness to dialogue, not indoctrination or closed-mindedness when it comes to the intellectual and spiritual development of students or trends of the day. Faculty should show an affirming tone and, when needed, be gentle shepherds as they guide students to the correct answers. That is what it means to be committed to objective truth.

*Third, be subject-matter specialists.* Christian colleges have no license to compromise the academic quality of their faculty just because they are Christians. Too often Christian colleges are accused of this; too often we stand guilty as charged. Again, it is important to remember that a Christian college is not a church, its classrooms not Sunday schools. The faith commitment of a faculty is essential but is only one part of the qualifications. Without a faith commitment, faculty should not be hired; however, possessing such a commitment should not guarantee being hired.

*Fourth, be committed to the integration of faith and learning.* This area is perhaps the most challenging for assembling a faculty. Graduate education does not encourage it and the profession does not reward it. Few

9. John Henry Newman, *The Idea of a University: Defined and Illustrated* (1858; reprint, London: Longmans, Green, and Company, 1907), 232.

10. Max Weber, "Science as a Vocation," in *From Max Weber: Essays in Sociology,* ed. and trans. Hans Gerth and C. Wright Mills (New York: Oxford University Press, 1946), 146, 150.

graduate students have opportunity to prepare themselves for serving in a Christian college—or, upon realizing that it is a lifelong process, to stick with it.

*Fifth, faculty in a Christian college must be open to collegiality and personal and spiritual growth in themselves and their students.* One of the deepest rewards of being a professor comes from how the Lord develops each of us intellectually and spiritually as we advance in our careers. Serving as members of a community of Christian scholars of diverse backgrounds can be the positive catalyst for such development—for students too, as they watch their professors grow. Faculty should love their students and love teaching their students.

At a Christian college the faculty bear the responsibility to develop and educate their students in several ways. They are to teach them the rudiments of their subjects of course—be they sociology or engineering or philosophy or music theory. Yet that is not all. A college wishing to remain Christian should challenge its students beyond academic rigor. First, students need to be challenged to think empathetically about others and other ideas—and to do so with respect and civility. The faculty should be accepting of their students' viewpoints, holding back from immediate condemnation or correction especially when they differ from their own, modeling an irenic spirit of give-and-take irresistible to a student's mind and heart. Second, students should be challenged to be independent thinkers beyond what they are taught. The greatest compliment students extend to faculty is not when they parrot our thoughts back to us or form a cult around us, but when they develop their own ideas from what they have learned from us. Not recklessly, of course; the fallen mind certainly needs the limits and guidance of a well-grounded faith and education. This is a diverse world hungry for Christians who can articulate the reason why we believe as we do but can do so in a winsome and loving way. The faculty in a Christian college are best prepared to teach this, recognizing the importance of working through these issues because they know how the voice of faith informed where they are today and how they got there. It is this shared sense of gratitude within a Christian learning community that leaves a legacy for the next generation. Unless we Christian educators give a reason for the faith that is in us and do so toward our students and to each other, we cannot expect to graduate students able to carry the same spirit into the world.

So, how do you keep a Christian college Christian? First, build a Christian faculty.

## THE CURRICULUM

Recognizing that no major can prepare students for a lifetime that will include at least five career changes, we should highlight the skills that can and do. The liberal arts cultivate those skills through their emphasis upon writing, speaking, quantitative reasoning, and content-area grounding. They prepare graduates for any job, any career, because they hone lifelong skills easily transferable across diverse jobs and spanning different careers. Next, that curriculum should be woven together by unifying Christian principles while insisting upon openness to questions life asks us and the answers the Faith affirms. Then, the curriculum approaches what it should be—a lifelong foundation for Christian living. There are plenty of influences to deter a Christian college from crafting a cohesive curriculum—especially in a consumption-driven culture like ours. Today, too many Christian students and parents expect the same sovereign consumer experience they claim entitlement to when shopping at their nearby mall—a sparkling retail mix of majors with flattering tuition discounts, course options galore, ready customization of programs, an excellent return on their investment in a job or prestigious graduate-school placement, and a recognizable athletic logo to go with it. But a Christian college is no more an outlet mall than it is a church, and faculty should not be pressured to perfectly satisfy customers any more than they should be expected to be clergy. No education caving into the consumerist ethos can still deliver an education worth its name, especially not a Christian one.

We must begin by combating the ongoing fragmentation of knowledge. Fields of study, especially general education, are being transformed into discrete curricular units out of touch with one another, indeed so distant as sometimes not to recognize their own discord. This is most frequently found in general education curricula. Reflecting the same consumerism it tries to educate against, many Christian colleges offer core curricula packed with distribution requirements peddling large numbers of courses from which students may pick and choose how to meet an educational objective. They lack a commonality of educational purpose, a unity of content and perspective. Absent the unifying principle and spirit of the Faith, an education dissolves into topics apathetic to one another—not even connected enough to be adversarial. Soon, a college degree is reduced to a checklist of general education courses safely cordoned off so students can take the highly specialized courses for a single career they may never possess in their lives, given today's economy. Not surprisingly, Faith then is compartmentalized in a college education as it is in our culture—hidden from public view and appropriate only to certain majors and courses.

Students next should be touched by the richness of Christian learning across the curriculum, thereby strengthening the transformation of their lives. Doing so, we must find creative ways to offset the pressures to increase the number of courses required by majors. Such "credit creep" is subtle. Its roots are twofold. First, outside disciplinary (not regional) accrediting bodies demand more specialization of undergraduates than ever before. For them, the unifying foundation of faith and learning is secondary. Be it in the fine arts, teacher preparation, business, or science and engineering, these accreditations require adding even more courses to majors already crammed to their limits. Christian college programs need these accreditations, unfortunately, and must comply if they wish to have the quality and market value of accreditation. Yet they come at the price of sacrificing much.

Credit creep also comes from misunderstanding the purposes of the core general education curriculum and free electives. For some, general education is considered to carry the bulk of liberal learning for everyone, and electives are luxuries. General education is thought of as supplementary to vocational preparation within the major, and available credits and hours should be shifted to the major. This approach sacrifices free electives and breadth of learning. It promotes the pigeonholing, then calcification, of the Christian mind.

Either attitude toward curriculum eats away at the ideal of liberal learning and the liberally educated graduate. Elective courses are downgraded to insignificance or an extravagance. Students' opportunities to take elective hours are reduced; in some disciplines only one or two free electives are available to students graduating in four years. How can our graduates ever enjoy the delight of discovering new subjects that excite them or broaden their minds and hearts without having some options outside of their major or general education requirements?

In other words, free electives in a Christian college are no luxury; they are a necessity. In broadening us, they protect us from being beleaguered by the world we confront. Along with a strong core curriculum, they are the solid ground on which graduates can engage the onrush of life and events because a broad Christian liberal education inculcates clarity of vision and unity of purpose across all fields. Free electives, indeed, open students to see beyond their majors and into a better comprehension of who they are in that world. Electives set into place opportunities to engage our culture and times through a humane vision that allows for some narrowness and specialty without losing a sense of the whole.

Electives are especially needed to balance overspecialization in technical subjects with a strong emphasis upon method. Beautiful in its own right, the technical mind naturally seeks mastery over its subject—be that ways to teach, ways to engineer, ways to study Scripture grammatically, ways to study people, or whatever. But technique is limited in its understanding, often missing the mystery of things by reducing them to "facts" methodically extracted from the dynamic web of their contextual relationships. The technical mind's danger is when it exceeds the boundaries of its charge. Driven by the necessitarianism of its formal rationality, it invades areas beyond its competency, then delimits and tries to resolve all problems as technical ones easily subject to instrumental reason—i.e., just a tweak here and there to create the optimal solution. Sadly, our culture leans toward the sterile and thereby reductionistic nature of technique. It gives us a way to escape speaking to our common humanity in the midst of our diversity, our values, and the dignity of all peoples. The result is anesthetic—because it ignores the person, "the problems of the human heart [ever] in conflict with itself."[11]

The technical mind left to its own devices threatens all of us, perhaps most of all itself. It can only be guided and channeled to the good things, the permanent things if it is referenced and augmented by the benefits of a broad Christian education. We need scientists with Christian educations to guide us in emerging biotechnology fields, and well-rounded Christian educators to lead us in educational reform. But if we fail to keep our Christian colleges Christian, where can these people be found? How can they be witnesses to our age, prophets to our time, if their educations lack the faith and broad learning upon which to draw?

Our third challenge is restoring the rightful place of theology and Christian philosophy to the curriculum. Religion today increasingly is perceived in one of two ways—as too divisive and thus excluded through bureaucratic policies and processes, or as too private and beyond the reach of science.[12] In these views, faith is disruptive or, worse, immeasurable and unverifiable in many respects; so it is reduced to a personal opinion without truth claims superior to any other and deserving no legitimate part in a college education. Such prejudice is anti-intellectual. John Henry

11. William Faulkner, "Upon Receiving the Nobel Prize for Literature, 1950," in *Essays, Speeches, and Public Letters*. ed. James B. Meriwether (New York: Modern Library, 2004), 119.

12. Newman, *Idea*, 387–89.

Newman writes in *The Idea of a University* that each academic discipline has its distinct sphere. Exclude one, and the quality of the whole education is compromised. Other fields exceed their bounds when they rush into the vacuum to take Christianity's place in higher learning. Newman speaks even more strongly than this: "[these other disciplines] intrude where they have no right." Thus to lose theology from the curriculum is to pervert the other disciplines because they exclude the facts and interpretations only it can reach and contribute.[13] The curriculum of a college that wishes to remain Christian, then, cannot exclude theology or the study of the Holy Scriptures from its education. They are its foundation and contribute important and unique ideas to the other disciplines, as Cardinal Newman notes.

From here, let us cover two areas: academic majors and general education.

Within the academic major, the subject matter should be taught with reference to its Christian foundations. Courses within a major should be open to and inclusive of the Christian presuppositions underlying the truths of their disciplines. That does not mean that the Scriptures are to be treated as a textbook in all subjects. Nor does it mean that theology need be forced where it may not be readily apparent. Yet the reference point of a discipline's knowledge should be our Christian tradition and heritage, a promoter of humane learning and serious scientific exploration of the beauty of God's creation. How that is worked out is unique to each field, easier in some than in others. But the result should be the same: graduating students able to think Christianly about their lives and their professions.

What about general education or the core curriculum? For a Christian college to remain Christian, the center of its general education curriculum should be a healthy Christian humanism committed to the nurture of wisdom and virtue and to the love of beauty.  God created us in his image, and though fallen, we are given grace to stand and accomplish wonderful things for "divine purposes." Indeed, his very Son became incarnate in human flesh, not by converting his Godhead into our flesh but instead by taking our flesh onto him. Thus, though fallen and prone to sin, people possess a certain dignity as part of God's creation and through the iconography of Christ in our flesh. This is very important to keep in mind when constructing a curriculum, particularly a general education

13. Newman, *Idea*; see especially Part I: Discourse IV "The Bearing of Other Parts of Knowledge on Theology," 71–98.

curriculum; it ensures that our curriculum will be integrated so all courses speak to one another. It sensitizes us to all God's creation, the development of knowledge he bequeaths to us, and a deeper appreciation of him and our fellow men and women. A healthy Christian humanism protects our graduates from seeing their education self-centeredly or instrumentally—i.e., as what their degree does *for them* materially and vocationally, keeping them ever comfortable with the status quo of our time because they would fit so neatly into it. Instead, they hopefully come to appreciate their education Christianly—i.e., how it privileges them to serve others and to bring the faith to bear on issues public and private.

Today, then, the curriculum of a college that wishes to remain Christian will inevitably be a counterpoise to the spirit of the age because it will be *coherent,* implicating all subjects and topics into God. And so, with such a coherency, it will raise questions about existing social forms—mass urbanization, government and politics, private and public education, consumerism, family, free market vs. command economies, the privileged position claimed of science in our public ethos, questions of justice and fairness and equity and, of course, freedom. The general education curriculum will confront the mores of our age, asking our culture with the Psalmist's words in Psalm 8:4, "What is man, that thou art mindful of him?" And it will bring to those topics the respect for life and for God's call to us to engage the world. As Hilaire Belloc once said, "That same force which ignores human dignity also ignores human suffering."[14]

Perhaps most important, the general education of a college that wants to remain Christian should emphasize the consilience of all disciplines, their consummation being in God. Therefore it must include several specific subjects from science to literature to art to history and mathematics, along with the civic foundation in history and politics to prepare graduates to contribute to their communities and to the nation.

*First, the curriculum must provide strong foundation in the Scriptures and the Christian tradition that has produced them.* How can we expect to graduate students prepared to articulate their faith if they have an insufficient grasp of its major source documents?

*Second, the curriculum must provide an understanding of how Christian ethics apply to their daily lives.* The Faith is more than doctrines and concepts, fun as those may be to extract and debate. Christ asks that we apply His teachings, regardless of our academic major and faith tradition. Learning these applications can be included in the general education

14. Hilaire Belloc, *The Great Heresies* (Radford, VA: Wilder, 2008), 125.

curriculum and also introduced in specific disciplines and courses through opportunities for civic engagement.

*Third, the curriculum must provide an appreciation for the beautiful.* God created us to recognize beauty—to love it and re-create it. It is hard to remember, given the ugliness of our culture today, that there are indeed Christian understandings of the beautiful and good. We should not surrender the arts to the crudeness of late modernity. Without teaching literature, art, and aesthetics from a Christian worldview, our graduates will have deformed moral imaginations unable to recognize what is beautiful, what can be beautiful, and, by extension, the beauty of God and his creation. Lacking such a Christian aesthetic sense, they cannot reproduce the beautiful in their own lives or be enriched by its presence in the lives of others.

*Fourth, the curriculum must provide a critical perspective on the popular media and pop culture.* This area is one too long ignored by Christian colleges. We do so at our peril. Movies, music, and the Internet are becoming the virtual reference points for values, ethics, even heroes and models as the celebrity images fold back upon our reality and become our common narrative. A college that wishes to remain Christian must take this area of late-modern life seriously and prepare its students to be discerning of what they see, hear, and read.

*Fifth, the curriculum must provide an understanding of how we got here and the interconnectedness of today's world.* By this, I mean a strong foundation in world history capped by a deeper appreciation of all cultures and traditions and religions along with the interplay of those factors and geopolitics. Obviously, concentrated study in modern languages is important. Remember, we "People of the Cross" are a people of history and a people of many nations. We look back, we look forward, and we look across to other cultures and peoples.

*Sixth, the curriculum must provide a critical understanding of disciplines that have rushed to fill the vacuum left by the exclusion of theology from the modern college and university curriculum.* Typically, these have been the social sciences, but some of the natural sciences have also strayed into imposing substitute meanings on subjects outside their competency. Consequently, courses that critically examine the presuppositions of various disciplines—particularly their views of human nature and society and ethics—should be offered.

*Seventh, the curriculum must provide science and mathematical education.* To counter the materialist understandings of our day, our students should learn to hear in nature's broken accents the voice of God.[15] Yes, students must be conversant in the latest findings in science and mathematics. Biology, chemistry, physics, indeed the material world around us, is not all there is, however. God can be detected behind all of them. Thus instruction in these areas or even specialized instruction purposely team-teaching from the humanities and scientific programs of a college is essential.

*Eighth, the curriculum must teach the unity of body and spirit.* Too many institutions have dropped courses in physical education today. But we are given our bodies, too, to be in service to God. Physical health enhances intellectual and social health. Physical education develops those habits essential to ongoing success in life, especially lifelong fitness and nutrition. It teaches us one of the great lessons of life: we have strengths and weaknesses, but with patience and hard work we can persevere; in other words, it teaches us how to handle success and overcome failure. It cultivates leadership gifts and teamwork abilities, both essential to our families and communities.

How else do you keep a Christian college Christian? Provide a curriculum that is intentionally grounded in the Faith, unified from humanities to sciences to mathematics to physical fitness. Only Christian education, informing and uniting all disciplines, is comprehensive enough to suffice to educate today's students. Then, with the integration of faith and learning, those graduates enter their adult lives capable of reasserting the relevance and importance of Christianity to our culture and society.

## IN CONCLUSION

Keeping a Christian college Christian is as essential today as ever before. Many potential threats face Christian colleges. These are simply possible threats, though. None is predestined. All will force us to choose the future of Christian higher education. Whether we realize it or not, these challenges are calls to Christian higher education to remain distinctively Christian. They point toward our opportunity to influence our students and the world in which we are embedded by teaching how all true knowledge and learning is God's Truth. As John Henry Newman writes in the "Tamworth Reading Room,"

15. John Henry Newman, "The Influence of Natural and Revealed Religion Respectively," in *Fifty Sermons Preached before the Oxford University* (London: Longmans, Green, 1909), 31.

Christianity, and nothing short of it, must be made the element and principle of all education. Where it has been laid as the first stone, and acknowledged as the governing spirit, it will take up into itself, assimilate, and give a character to literature and science. Where Revealed Truth has given the aim and direction to Knowledge, Knowledge of all kinds will minister to Revealed Truth.[16]

16. John Henry Newman, "The Tamworth Reading Room," in *Discussions and Arguments* (London: Longmans, Green, 1907), 274.

# Contributors

**William P. Anderson** is Provost and Vice President for Academic Affairs at Grove City College, in which capacity he has served since 2001. At Grove City College he also has served as Dean for the Calderwood School of Arts and Letters, Assistant Dean, and Chair of the Department of Sociology. He has published articles in *Social Psychology Quarterly* and *Vitae Scholasticae*, contributed a chapter to *A Meere Scholler: Cross-Cultural Perspectives on our Educational Heritage* (Leadership and Educational Policy Studies Press, 1996), and has been book-review editor for *The Christian Sociologist*.

**Janice Brown** is a Canadian and was educated at Memorial University of Newfoundland, from which she received a BA, BEd., MA, and PhD. Her PhD dissertation was on Dorothy L. Sayers. Since 1994 she has taught British literature at Grove City College. Her book *The Seven Deadly Sins in the Work of Dorothy L. Sayers* was published by Kent State University Press in 1998 and it was a finalist for an Edgar Allan Poe award.

**Michael Coulter** is Professor of Political Science and Humanities at Grove City College. He is the coeditor of the *Encyclopedia of Catholic Social Thought, Social Science and Social Policy*, Volumes 1 and 2 (Scarecrow Press, 2007) and Volume 3 (Scarecrow Press, 2012). He has contributed chapters to *Church-State Issues in America Today* (Praeger, 2008) and *Catholic Social Thought: American Reflections on the Compendium* (Lexington Press, 2009).

**James G. Dixon** is Chair of the Department of English and Professor of English and Theatre at Grove City College, where he has been teaching since 1976. His subjects include Shakespeare, Classical literature, literary criticism and theory, and fantasy literature. He has directed over forty main stage productions of a wide range of plays, from *Waiting for Godot* to *Murder in the Cathedral* to *The Brothers Karamazov* and several Shakespearean dramas. He has also published numerous articles on the Inklings, dramatic literature, and Shakespeare.

**Mark W. Graham** is Associate Professor in the Department of History at Grove City College. A specialist in Late Antiquity with broad teaching interests in the ancient and medieval worlds, Graham has graduate degrees from Michigan State University (PhD) and the University of South Carolina (MA). He is the author of *News and Frontier Consciousness in the Late Roman Empire* (University of Michigan Press, 2006) and coauthor (with Eric H. Cline) of *Ancient Empires: From Mesopotamia to the Rise of Islam* (Cambridge University Press, 2011) as well as a contributor to *The Encyclopedia of Greece and the Hellenic Tradition* and *Encyclopedia of the Empires of the World*.

**D. G. Hart** is visiting professor of history at Hillsdale College. He is the author of several books on the history of Christianity in the United States, including *The University Gets Religion: Religious Studies and American Higher Education* (Johns Hopkins University Press, 1999) and *From Billy Graham to Sarah Palin: Evangelicals and the Betrayal of American Conservatism* (Eerdmans, 2011). He is currently completing a global history of Calvinism for Yale University Press.

**Andrew J. Harvey**, Associate Professor of English, teaches at Grove City College. A scholar of Renaissance and medieval British literature who has published essays on George Herbert, John Donne, Shakespeare, and sacramental language, he is a convert to the Orthodox Church and contributes frequently on matters of culture and true conservatism on the frontporchrepublic.com/.

**P. C. Kemeny** is Professor of Religion and Humanities at Grove City College. He has degrees from Wake Forest University, Westminster Seminary, Duke University, and Princeton Seminary. He is the author of *Princeton in the Nation's Service: Religious Ideals and Educational Practice, 1868–1928* (Oxford University Press, 1998). He has coedited with Henry Warner Bowden *American Church History: A Reader* (Abingdon, 1998), and also edited *Church, State, and Public Justice: Five Views* (InterVarsity Press,

2006). He has received research grants from the American Academy of Religion, the American Philosophical Society, the Massachusetts Historical Society, and the American Historical Association.

**George M. Marsden** is the Francis A. McAnaney Professor of History Emeritus, University of Notre Dame. His many books include *Jonathan Edwards: A Life*, *The Soul of the American University*, *The Outrageous Idea of Christian Scholarship*, and *Fundamentalism and American Culture*. He has taught history at Calvin College and Duke University Divinity School, as well as at Notre Dame.

**George H. Nash** is a historian, lecturer, and author of seven books, including *The Conservative Intellectual Movement in America Since 1945* and *Reappraising the Right: The Past and Future of American Conservatism*. He has written four volumes about the life of Herbert Hoover and recently edited *Freedom Betrayed: Herbert Hoover's Secret History of the Second World War and Its Aftermath*. A graduate of Amherst College and holder of a PhD in History from Harvard University, he was the 2008 recipient of the Richard M. Weaver Prize for Scholarly Letters. He lives in South Hadley, Massachusetts.

**Gary Scott Smith** chairs the History Department and coordinates the Humanities Core at Grove City College. Smith is the author or editor of nine books, including and *Faith and the Presidency: From George Washington to George W. Bush* (Oxford University Press, 2006) and *Heaven in the American Imagination* (Oxford University Press, 2011).